CONFUSION
TO OUR
ENEMIES

CONFUSION TO OUR ENEMIES

SELECTED JOURNALISM OF ARNOLD KEMP (1939-2002)

EDITED BY JACKIE KEMP

FOREWORD BY PROFESSOR TOM DEVINE

Neil Wilson Publishing • Glasgow

Neil Wilson Publishing
www.nwp.co.uk

© Jackie Kemp and the estate of Arnold Kemp, 2012

The author has established her moral right to be
identified as the Author of this work.

A catalogue record for this book is available
from the British Library.

ISBN: 978-1-906000-19-6
Ebook ISBN: 978-1-906000-20-2

Printed and bound in the EU

Contents

Ackowledgements vi

Foreword vii

Introduction 1

PART I: THEMES

1   Beginnings 11

2   Newspapers 28

3.1 Europe: The East 58

3.2 Europe: The Union 73

PART II: SCOTTISH IDENTITY

4   Religion and the appearance of the secular society 85

5   Scottish nationalism 98

6   Devolution road 120

7   Towards a Scottish Parliament 142

PART III: CULTURE

8   Literature and language 167

9   Food – Scotland's changing tastes 178

10   Sport 189

11   Places 200

12   Music 220

     Afterword 232

Acknowledgements

MANY PEOPLE HAVE HELPED AND supported me in the enjoyable undertaking of putting together a selection of my father's writing.

First, I would like to thank Arnold's long-term partner Anne Simpson for her invaluable help and support thoughout the project, including editing part of this book.

I would also thank contributing editor Anna Burnside; Arnold Kemp's many friends and colleagues who have supported this project including his brother David Kemp, Tom Devine, Magnus Linklater, Harry Reid, Robin McKie, Neal Ascherson and Kenneth Roy and the staff of the *Scottish Review*, who established the Arnold Kemp award for young Scots; *The Herald, The Scotsman* and *The Observer* for allowing me to reprint material; editorial assistant Anne-Marie Hollywood; Christine McGilly et al of *The Herald* Archive at the Mitchell Library, Glasgow and Sally Harrower of the National Library of Scotland (which now has my father's papers); the Scottish Poetry Library; Mary-Jane Bennett for proof-reading the manuscript; Maggie Vaughan, Sarah McKie and Carrie Gracie for reading and making suggestions. Verses from Robert Garioch's *Embro to the Ploy* from *Collected Poems* are reproduced by permission of Polygon, an imprint of Birlinn Ltd.

I would like to thank my mother Sandra Kemp and my sister Susan. Lastly, I would like to thank my husband Rob Bruce for his almost unfailing generosity and support throughout this project.

Jackie Kemp

Foreword

ARNOLD KEMP, ONE OF THE greatest of Scottish journalists and editors of the 20th century, died prematurely at the age of 63 in 2002. He edited *The Herald* with memorable élan and panache between 1981 and 1994 and his prolific writings also regularly graced the pages of *The Scotsman*, *The Guardian* and *The Observer* in a career which spanned more than four decades from the year he began his first job in journalism in 1959.

Arnold left behind him a rich personal but uncatalogued archive of newspaper articles, chapters in books and opinion pieces. These have now been expertly harvested and selected by his daughter Jackie Kemp. Reading them, one is not only reminded again of the salient fact that Kemp was a master of his trade, but also that his published work provides a perceptive and illuminating guide to the key historical events of his lifetime in Scotland.

The period from the early 1960s was indeed momentous for the nation. It encompassed the early rise of nationalism, the traumatic de-industrialisation and then transformation of the economy in the 1980s, the impact of the Thatcher governments on Scotland, the halting progress towards devolution and then the successful establishment of the Scottish Parliament in the last decade of the century. These events and others are all recorded here, not in the arid descriptive prose of the chronicler, but with the eloquence, punch and insight for which Arnold was noted. As a result the recent Scottish past is brought alive in an engaging and highly readable fashion.

Indeed, I was so absorbed by the draft text that I read it from cover to cover in little more than a day. This was not simply because as a professional historian I learnt much that was new to me about these remarkable decades in the history of the nation. It was also because of the immediacy of the reportage, the sense of a writer who because of his journalistic and editorial eminence knew all the principal actors involved and was close to the unfolding of great events. But the collection has other merits. The sense of Arnold as the elegant wordsmith is conveyed on every page. Also, although a passionate Scot to his very bones, he was never afraid to spot and scorn mediocrity, incompetence, humbug and hypocrisy in the political and cultural life of the nation.

Several of the excerpts speak also of fair and balanced judgements, perhaps most notably in the evaluation of the impact of Margaret Thatcher on Scotland. There is a liveliness and breadth in the writing, redolent of Arnold's own personal wide international horizons, his travels in America and Europe, love of conviviality and the craic. The passion for life shines through.

This is an important text for anyone wishing to come to a fuller understanding of how Scotland developed from the dark days of the Second World War to the current debates over independence in the new millennium. It is also a hugely enjoyable read which many will savour with interest and delight for its own sake.

Tom Devine, 2012
Personal Senior Research Professor in History
University of Edinburgh

Introduction

THE TITLE OF THIS COLLECTION was suggested by Robin McKie, who worked with Arnold at *The Observer* and who explains here that this was a toast Arnold used in their visits to the Coach and Horses after work. It appears to have a naval origin; it also appears in *Swallows and Amazons* in the voice of Nancy Blackett. Of course, it was a jovial exclamation which Arnold used simply to mean, 'What a great team we are.'

Some who pick up this book will have come across Arnold Kemp as a writer, editor or public figure. But others will not – for them, and for those who wish to refresh their memories, below are some short biographical sketches by colleagues.

Harry Reid, friend and colleague at *The Scotsman* and *The Herald*:

> For Arnold Kemp getting a paper out each night was not a job; it was an adventure.
>
> Before he was 30 he was appointed production editor of *The Scotsman*, which meant that he was in charge of all the subeditors. The department was full of solemn, erudite men – no women – who worked, rather grimly, in a large room without windows, deep in the interior of that venerable old building on North Bridge, Edinburgh. There was a pervasive dourness. The one bright spark was Arnold, the boss; he welcomed me with real warmth on my first day in 1969, for he was always kind and encouraging to tyro journalists. He did not just have a way with words; he had a way with people, too.
>
> After we had completed work on the first edition it was a thrill – for me, the novice, a very real thrill – to sense the little tremor that gently shook the building as the great presses started rolling several floors beneath us in the vast machine room. Then, a second or so later, we'd hear the rumble as the mighty machines gained full speed. We had a paper. This was a tiny epiphany each night, round about 10.30.
>
> Years later, I heard Kemp describing the excitement he always felt at that moment. We were talking with a senior, hard-bitten Scottish businessman who was unimpressed. Indeed he responded by saying: 'Why were you still around? If the presses were rolling, your job had surely been done?'
>
> Kemp patiently explained that there was always so much more

work to do. Changes for the later editions, pages to be redrawn, general tidying up, mistakes (always quite a few of these) to be remedied, sometimes major new stories to be inserted.

This was the kind of work Kemp relished. He could edit with flair, precision and speed, not only fighting the clock but attending to several different stories at the same time. He was a highly skilled production journalist; but despite his competence and thoroughness he was also well aware of the ludic romance of newspapers, something he cherished.

To return to that little moment of magic that occurred as the old Scotsman presses started rolling: I trust it is not fanciful to suggest that somehow that moment each night at North Bridge was a metaphor for where the Scottish press is today. The hard work has been done, over many generations, but there is still so much to do; and in the time left, the pressures are ever greater.

Arnold was an original thinker, not a man for hackneyed notions, but I did occasionally hear him evoking that old summation of the true purpose of the best journalism: presenting truth to power. He certainly believed, with the authentic newspaperman's fervour, in that necessary process. When it came to the purpose and, as he saw it, the duty of the press, he was tough and uncompromising. As an editor he stoutly resisted commercial or political interference; he fought off anything and everything that in any way threatened his sense of his paper's integrity. That mattered more to him than anything.

And now, as Scotland slowly but surely contends for its independence, there will be a greater need than ever before for truth to be held to power within our country. More than ever do we need a strong, rigorous and confident national press. Such a press should surely be the legacy of Kemp's very distinguished life and work.

His own sense of the ongoing mission of the Scottish press somehow managed to be impish, intuitive and deeply purposeful, all at the same time.

Neal Ascherson recalled in Arnold's obituary in *The Observer* the time they worked as colleagues in the late 1970s at *The Scotsman*:

> Arnold achieved great things, transforming dull pages and papers into theatres of pleasure and surprise; who would have thought in, say, 1970 that a time would soon come when missing a day's

Scotsman would leave a twinge of deprivation? That was Arnold's achievement. Yet he never received the backing, the imaginative investment in success, which would have fulfilled him and pulled the paper over the hill into a new quality altogether.

The old *Scotsman* had been boring and respectable, leavened with *belles-lettres* fine writing for the Edinburgh literati. Now it became a strong but not uncritical supporter of Scottish devolution, craftily steered by editor Eric Mackay against the deep suspicions of the England-based management, while Arnold made it into an arena for talented, lively feature writing and reviewing.

At lunchtime he would lead his writers in a session of impassioned intellectual argument in the Halfway House, followed by a heavy lunch at the Doric Tavern ending, dangerously, in several rounds of Calvados. Scotland, past and future, was always the topic. I see his eyes sparkling as he bent his beefy shoulders forward to ram home a point, and hear his loud, barking laughter. He loved his difficult little country, and like all the best journalists, he was a man for flinging open windows. Scotland must join the world, he felt; he was at home anywhere in Europe.

But he was a vulnerable man; high spirits could suddenly be replaced by black, silent gloom. The failure of the 1979 referendum on devolution shattered him. So did the terrible industrial and staffing disputes that overwhelmed *The Scotsman*. Like many of us, he had fancied the paper was within sight of becoming a great European daily, with the stature of, say, the *Süddeutsche Zeitung*. Now, in a time of dissolving hopes, he left to become editor of *The Glasgow Herald*.

Magnus Linklater, former editor of *The Scotsman*:

Arnold threw himself into the task of reinvigorating *The Glasgow Herald*, re-establishing its credentials as a serious publication, while at the same time encouraging witty reporting and sharp commentary. He believed in the primacy of good writing, and took a personal interest in fostering the careers of young and promising journalists. As a result he engendered a strong sense of solidarity on the paper.

Arnold's period of editorship was rarely dull. Argumentative, occasionally 'thrawn' in his opinions, fiercely loyal to friends and heroes, he would stick with a point long after others might have let it be. In compensation, his belief that most arguments could be sorted out over lunch or in the pub, his disarming wit, and his affable manner, meant that few people fell out with him for long. In the office he would sometimes address his staff standing on his desk with a cloth cap on his head, announcing a 'word of the week' — 'imbroglio' was one - which he wanted to see appearing somewhere in the paper.

In 1983 *The Glasgow Herald* celebrated its 200th anniversary as an independent newspaper - the oldest national English-language daily in the world - and could boast a steadily rising circulation, which peaked in 1991 at 127,000. By the time Arnold stood down, in 1994, it was selling just under 120,000 copies, some 30,000 more than its principal rival. It had also established a reputation for outspoken journalism, which meant that Arnold found himself from time to time on the receiving end of writs under Scotland's strict rules of contempt. He would often repeat the observation that it was the journalist's job 'to reveal to the powerless that which the powerful would rather keep secret.'

My first meeting with Arnold Kemp was inauspicious. We had both been summoned to the New Club in Edinburgh, as editors, respectively of *The Scotsman* and *The Glasgow Herald*. The occasion was the launch of a document which was to become pretty important over the next few years - *A Claim of Right*, which set out the framework of a new constitutional plan for Scotland. There was a problem, however. Neither of us knew how to find the New Club, whose front door entrance on Princes Street is notoriously anonymous. Arnold met me overshooting it in one direction. I met him backtracking in another. Finally, we fumbled our way to the right door. 'I find that encouraging,' said Arnold. 'Neither the editor of the Scotsman nor the Herald knows how to get into the New Club. It shows we're outwith the Scottish establishment - which is exactly how it should be.'

That meeting was the first of many - most of them of the liquid variety, all of them enjoyable. We were both members of the editors' committee of the Scottish Daily Newspaper Society, which involved meetings in one or other of our cities. There were always matters to be pursued afterwards, many of them requiring long lunches, either in the Café Royal in Edinburgh or the Ubiquitous Chip in Glasgow. My secretary became accustomed to these intensive discussions, and to the telephone calls which followed, explaining that my intended return time to the office had had to be postponed, due, of course, to the intensity of the discussion.

For 11 of Arnold's 14 years at *The Herald*, the paper had been owned by the Lonrho multinational company, but in 1992 there was a management buyout and Arnold was co-opted onto the board. The move took place against a background of increasing competition from English papers, anxious to build up their sales in Scotland. For the first time, Arnold had to confront the harsh realities of cost-cutting. It was not a process he enjoyed. Finally, in 1994, he was fired, leaving the paper in an atmosphere of great bitterness. He felt, in his own words, that 'he had been robbed of the thing that defined' him. But in truth, after 14 years at the helm, he could summon no enthusiasm for the dramatic changes that were then transforming the newspaper industry, and found many of the commercial requirements simply unacceptable.

In 1993 Kemp published *The Hollow Drum*, which, for students of Scottish politics, is an indispensable companion. Purportedly an account of Scotland's post-war political history, based on lengthy interviews with many of the principal participants, it became something of a personal testament, concluding that, if the divisive influence of nationalism was to be countered, a new form of political union must begin to emerge. Six years later, the creation of a new Scottish parliament helped to realise that dream.

For a time after leaving *The Herald*, Arnold took no part in active journalism, although among other things he chaired a commission on the future of the voluntary sector in Scotland. Then in 1996 he was invited to work for *The Observer* in London as foreign news editor, while at the same time contributing a weekly column on Scottish affairs. Arnold himself described this period as the Indian summer of his career.

Robin McKie, *The Observer*:

Arnold Kemp arrived at *The Observer* in 1996 as the paper was going through one of its regular bouts of chaos brought about by a change in editor. In the succeeding months and years, he played a critical role in our revitalisation, partly through the awesome journalistic example he set us but also in the way he demonstrated how our craft could be enjoyed. Above all, newspapers should be fun, he decreed.

One of his first, inspired acts was to launch a Roving Briefs award ceremony for those reporters who had submitted the most outrageous, silly stories for the paper's News in Brief columns. Winners received a bottle of champagne draped with an item of underwear. Then there was the letter from the *Camel Racing Post* in Jeddah which convinced one hapless reporter into thinking his 'exposé' of the sport was going to earn him a typical, fat Middle Eastern reprint fee – of a flock of sheep.

But best of all, perhaps, was the task he set himself every Saturday when writing his column for the Scottish edition of *The Observer*. Apart from producing a perfectly honed 700-word feature on the topic of the day, Arnold added an extra condition just to bring frisson to the task – by including a phrase or saying that was to be proposed by the comment department's subeditors, John Barton and Jonathan Bouquet. Their first diktat was straightforward: make sure you include the words 'the revocation of the Edict of Nantes' in your column. Given that Arnold was writing about Scottish tourism that week, this was not an enviable assignment. As you will see from the resulting column, included in this collection, he passed the test with ease.

Other teasers set by Barton and Bouquet included the phrase of Levi Eshkol that if you 'put three Zionists in a room, they will form four parties'; Khrushchev's warning that 'if you start throwing hedge-hogs under me, I shall throw a couple of porcupines under you'; and the apparently legendary story of the one-legged duck of Loch Lomond. Like an international batsman striking every ball through cover, Arnold triumphantly swatted away each of these attempts to bamboozle him and slotted them into his copy as if they were the most natural of phrases that could have been used under the circumstances.

I recall him being perplexed on only one occasion. 'What does the phrase "do androids dream of electric sheep?" mean?', he asked me surreptitiously. (These were pre-Google days.) I explained that it was a reference to a science fiction novel about a dystopian, robot-run future. Arnold smiled. Next day I read his column. It began: 'As every schoolchild knows, *Do Androids Dream of Electric Sheep?* is a science fiction novel about a dystopian, robot-run future.' Then he segued effortlessly into an analysis of the woes then afflicting the Labour party in Scotland. Arnold was a class act and no mistake.

After completing these tests, it was time to head for the pub where Arnold would lead glorious conversations that could go anywhere, from the erratic use of the suspended fifth chord in rock music to the value of personal worth in the novels of Jane Austen. Drinks and colleagues would continue to roll in and the tempo, but not the emotion, would heat up. It was glorious, chaotic, exhilarating mayhem, that ended inevitably with his favourite, stalwart Shakespearian toast, 'Confusion to our enemies'.

Eventually we gave a name to this wonderful state of affairs. We called it Kempistan. Arnold was its life-long president, and the rest of us vied for senior posts: head of secret police, treasurer, or foreign secretary. As science editor I was appointed chief scientist and head of Kempistan's fledgling nuclear programme. Those missing from *The Observer* office for a couple of hours were simply said to be on study leave in Kempistan, a fact that was usually confirmed when he or she staggered back knock-kneed and glassy-eyed from the pub – having been 'Kemped' as it was also known. It was, quite simply, a glorious time to work at *The Observer*.

Arnold Kemp was a newspaperman to his bones. 'It's given me forty great years,' he would say, 'I'm a lucky man.' But really, it was simply fair trade – for he gave journalism four decades of genius and graft.

PART I
THEMES

1

Beginnings

*'What drove me? I think most creative people want to express apprecia-
tion for being able to take advantage of the work that's been done before
... Everything I do depends on other members of our species and the
shoulders that we stand on ... We try to use the talents we do have to
express our deep feelings, to show our appreciation of all the contributions
that came before us and to add something to that flow.'*

Steve Jobs quoted in Walter Isaacson's biography of him.

A DECADE HAS PASSED SINCE my father Arnold Kemp's death. The
elapsed time has allowed a more considered look at the work he left behind.
There was a lot of work to read through – perhaps somewhere in the region
of a million words. While much of it was, in the way of newspapers, ephemer-
al, there is a great deal that merits reading today. Journalism, it is sometimes
said, is history shot on the wing and Arnold's writing downed some significant moments. It also demonstrates the importance and influence of quality
journalism in public life in the post-Second World War period.

This book is not a biography, but an opportunity to read or to re-read
some of Arnold's best writing. The result provides the reader with the pleasure
of a few hours in Arnold's company, enjoying his wide-ranging conversation.

The first part of the book is entitled Themes. Throughout his life and
work, Arnold returned to some themes and interests which were rooted in his
early life, in the shadow of the Second World War. The first chapter therefore
explores these childhood influences, with the help of some contributions
from Arnold's father and grandfather.

Chapter 2 looks at his experience of the newspaper industry. This
demonstrates that through the late 20th century, newspapers rode huge waves
of change – social, technological, political. Communication can take many
forms; it is the content of the communication that matters.

The middle section of the book is on the Scottish identity – Arnold had
an unusual depth of knowledge and understanding of his country's history,
politics and changing culture which is apparent here. This section also covers
politics in the three decades from the first appearance of the SNP as an electoral force in 1967 until the inauguration of the Scottish Parliament – years
when Arnold was a strong and influential advocate of devolution.

The last part of the book, Culture, is a lighter and more eclectic selection of columns Arnold wrote on music, books, food, sport and places that he loved.

Jackie Kemp, 2012

ARNOLD KEMP WAS BORN ON 15 February 1939, into a London on the brink of war. His father, journalist Robert Kemp, was soon to become part of the BBC's war reporting effort. His mother Meta Strachan was a teacher.

His father recorded Arnold's arrival in his diary:

Feb 27 1939 Register Arnold
March 7 1939 Register Arnold 1/- fine.

Robert's writing career began at *The Manchester Guardian* in 1929; he was the last journalist hired by the legendary CP Scott who edited the paper for 57 years. He never tired of the story of the nonconformist parson who often began a prayer: 'O Lord, as doubtless you have seen in yesterday's Manchester Guardian ... '

During his eight-year stint at *The Guardian* he married his student sweetheart and set up home in Lancashire. Robert's journalistic duties included theatre reviewing and he met several people who influenced and inspired him including the German expressionist dramatist Ernst Toller. A German Jew who had been traumatised by the First World War, Toller hanged himself in 1939 in New York after his family had been rounded up and sent to concentration camps. His influence was visible in one of Robert's first radio plays, a Nazi satire, *The Country Mouse Goes to Town*, broadcast in 1937.

Around this time innovative features' director Laurence Gilliam recruited Robert for the BBC. His first programme, a documentary about refugee children arriving in Harwich in the snow, was broadcast in 1938. Robert later recalled that this programme 'had the honour of being attacked by Goebbels in Der Angriff.'

When Arnold was a baby Robert was dispatched to Paris and Holland to cover the 'phoney war', the run-up to the battle of France. Robert's diaries from that time record how he watched waiters prepare crêpes suzette at Quasimodo's and saw the moon rise over Notre Dame in the blacked-out city. But for the most part Robert and Meta's war years were 'miserable days of bombs and reverses, when one year seemed to drag into another without summer or winter and life held small delight for anyone. Of course there was much of interest – meeting with Poles, Free French, London firemen in the Blitz.

Finally [*Robert wrote*] I was summoned to take a hand in the launching of War Report which began on D-Day. We were all prepared for that mighty campaign and yet all was in doubt till the last moment. We knew that it would mean last-minute work of the most hectic kind, but would the correspondents who had set off with the great armada get back their stuff in time? That they did is now a matter of history.

The most wonderful thing of all was I think the arrival of two records from a correspondent, Guy Byam, later killed, who had been dropped by parachute, carrying recording gear. How those records got to London I doubt if anyone ever knew. But they suddenly appeared in the arms of a messenger and were duly broadcast.

One of my greatest pleasures was to hear the voice of my old friend Robert Dunnett, a son of the manse, coming in on a transmitter set up in Normandy after the American landings. I used to feel a sort of reflected glory in the unvarying high quality of his messages.

Robert did not see active service. When he was called up, his medical revealed he had TB. He went home to his minister father's parish of Birse, Aberdeenshire, where eggs and cream were widely available and his mother could nurse him back to health.

Arnold and his older bother David spent a good part of the war at the manse. Their grandfather Arnold Low Kemp, who had the limping gait of childhood rickets, was a contemplator rather than a doer. He spent long hours in his study, the largest and most comfortable room in the manse, reading and writing sermons.

Arnold Low's wife Robina, a vigorous, energetic woman, was a skilled needlewoman who played the piano and organ, raised her family, entertained, visited parishioners with food and advice, wrote several unpublished works of romantic fiction and, through the war years and beyond, fed her household from a large, walled kitchen-garden. Her small grandsons were often sent out to fill a pail of tatties for tea.

For the young Arnold, these were happy days. He wrote later:

I have a particularly vivid recollection of Granny throwing the meal on to the ground for the hens she kept in the yard at the back of the manse and then with a swift twist of her powerful wrists breaking the neck of one for the pot as it happily fed. The fowl suffered no foreknowledge of its fate. Later I watched her clean and pluck it at the kitchen table, she breathed noisily through her nose as she did so.

In the garden of Birse we grandchildren found much happiness. At the front of the manse was a lawn on which we picnicked and beyond was what had been grass tennis courts by then overgrown. To a child the manse, with its long corridors, seemed huge. In the kitchen Grandpa played patience – a variety called Demon 13 – or showed us how to turn old paper into hats, boats or puzzles as Granny prepared the supper. We would wake in the morning to the sound of wind in the pines and the croon of wood pigeons. We would pile into the Baby Austin and drive to Aboyne for the shopping. Naturally Granny was the driver while Grandpa offered advice, philosophy and anecdote.

A few of Arnold Low's wartime sermons survive in the National Library of Scotland. In 1934 he condemned the treatment of Jews in Germany from the pulpit, asking people to take an interest in matters that may have seemed far away: 'There are people who cannot see beyond themselves, or their kin, or their own country ... we share in the amazement at so-called Christian Germany's treatment of Jews.'

Just days before Germany invaded Poland, on 20 August 1939, he gave a sermon on Psalm 57, verse 7, 'My heart is fixed, O God, my heart is fixed: I will sing and give praise'. He compared David and his followers' flight from the persecution of Saul the King, sheltering in the caves at Engedi, to the situation on the German border.

> There is the tension of the times, in the insane and bitter hostility of Saul, the King against his fellow countrymen, represented in David and his followers. There is the cave in which the latter found shelter representing their awareness of the peril in which they lived ... There is undoubted tension over, more or less, the whole inhabited world. We are getting used to the phrase we come upon in the public press, the war of nerves ...
>
> As things are we know not from week to week to what peril from the sudden ravage of war we would stand exposed. We rearm, we dig shelters, we are provided with masks, and disks for the purposes of identification are to be issued to us. Every possible provision is made for the evacuation of women and children from the great centres of population in the event of hostilities. Our cave of Engedi is a vast one and manned against the pitiless eventualities which may befall.

A few weeks after the disaster of Dunkirk, France fell on Saturday, 22 May

1940. The next day Arnold Low preached on 'And I will give thee the treasures of darkness' from Isaiah.

> I met a lady the other day and conversation as so many conversations in these days turned on the war. I was struck with a remark she made in the most casual way. She said, it must be hard for ministers at this time to find words of help and encouragement for their congregations. It struck me as an odd thought ...
>
> Things look black ... But there can be no turning back. There can be no accommodation with the wild doctrines that set Thor and Woden above Jesus; the doctrines of brute force above those of the spirit of power and of love and of a sound mind that is in Christ.
>
> In the faith once delivered to the saints in the days of trial, the dark days of trial are disclosing themselves as rich in the treasure which speaks hope and liberty and lasting peace in the time to come.

On 10 June 1940, the day that Neville Chamberlain resigned to be replaced by Churchill, Jews were being deported across Europe. The sermon was on Genesis, 22, verse 14: 'In the Mount of the Lord it shall be Seen'.

> I suppose there have been no people on earth so beset with searching and bitter criticism as the Jews. The accusations, the insults that are meted out to them in many lands are almost past comprehension; they are regarded as the off-scouring of the earth. There are good, bad and indifferent among all kinds of people ... Do not let any red herring of Jew belittling be drawn across our path to make us forget the undeniable greatness of their witness of old to the power of God and to the love of God.

Arnold Low retired in 1948, moved to Edinburgh but died a year later, aged 80. The manse was an abiding influence in both Robert and Arnold's work. Robert wrote about how the manse had influenced him as a playwright:

> When I was a boy the ministers were expected to be not only solid preachers and good pastors but accomplished public entertainers. The result was that many ministers developed the art of telling a story and holding an audience which would have licked some of the artists at a Royal Command Variety Performance. They could draw roars of laughter from an audience which had nothing to put them in a risible mood beyond a cup of tea and a bag of buns.

The characters of the manse stayed with him.

> I remember the advice of the old beadle to the nervous candidate about to leave the vestry to preach to a strange congregation. 'That's a'richt sir,' he observed. 'Just ca' awa and dinnae care a docken for ony o' them.'
>
> And when I go to the theatre to observe the public response to some artistic venture particularly dear to my heart, I am afraid I often recall the same beadle, who being asked what sort of attendance there was going to be at the evening service, looked through the window for a minute or two and then reported, 'There's twa-three auld wifies just pourin' in.'

At the greater distance of a generation, Arnold recalled:

> I remember the beadle ringing the bell with a chain attached to his foot and summoning the congregation to the simple little church. I can recall my grandfather's teaching but not the content of his sermons beyond the fact that they were faithful expositions of the text which had been read as the lessons.
>
> He had a stock of anecdotes which he repeated as if they were hallowed ritual. When chicken was on the table he would invariably say, 'this bird has not lived in vain', a family incantation which I honour to this day.
>
> Grandpa was not at all a stern moralist of the old Presbyterian variety, but he was prepared to insist on the peace and sanctity of the Sabbath if his grandchildren were making too much noise.
>
> Grandpa let the glebe and when he was required by his wife to work in the large, walled kitchen-garden and could think of no spiritual or pastoral duty that must claim his attention instead, he would amuse himself with a bonfire. Once he contrived a fire which consumed the blackberry bushes, thus avoiding the tiresome task of picking the fruit.
>
> My grandmother's industrious horticulture and my grandfather's pleasure in bonfires passed to my father. From her he acquired conscientious habits and from him a certain dreaminess. Every spring as he surveyed the long and narrow garden of his house in Edinburgh my father would long for a bigger plot.

Arnold thought he saw his grandparents represented in one of Robert's plays, *A Nest of Singers*.

The play is full of personal themes. It is a rejection of the grim Calvinism of the extreme reformed position. In Professor Meldrum and his wife there are echoes of my father's parents, of his mother's struggles to improve the music in the kirks where they laboured and of his father's aspirational dreaming and homely humour. He puts into the professor's mouth the family mantra, 'This bird did not live in vain'.

It seems inconceivable that the question of church music could have caused riots in the streets, yet the play is based on an incident recorded in the annals of Aberdeen. In its light-hearted way, it deals with the enduring mystery at the heart of the Scottish experience, the Reformation and the passions it aroused, the distortions which grew from it like ugly weeds. In the play he honours his parents' life-long assertions that music and laughter are not incompatible with the worship of God.

Towards the end of the war, Robert and his growing family moved to Edinburgh. He was still working for the BBC but noted in his diary: 'The time has come when I need to work all the time if I am to get all my plays down – and must try not to work at anything else.' Encouraged by his role in the first Edinburgh International Festival, in 1948 Robert left the BBC to write full-time.

Many years later, he wrote that the Festival was 'part of the effort which mankind made to throw off the inertia that followed upon the war. There were those who remembered the glories of the opera house, the concert hall and the theatre from the 1930s and were determined to restore them – not in the struggling way in which the arts had preserved their continuity for five years, but sumptuously, with an expenditure of money which would have been unthinkable when guns not butter, much less Mozart, were the priority.'

He heard Artur Schnabel, whom he had met as a young reporter, play Beethoven and saw the French actor Louis Jouvet. He enjoyed one of Jouvet's pieces, Moliere's *L'Ecole des Femmes*, so much that he immediately began work on a Scots translation. *Let Wives Tak Tent* was performed at the Gateway Theatre the following year.

When committee member James Bridie decreed there should be a Scottish input to the second Edinburgh Festival, it fell to Robert to adapt Sir David Lyndsay's 16th-century morality play *Ane Pleasant Satyre of the Thrie Estaitis*. After a long, well-refreshed day spent inspecting every available venue Robert suggested the Assembly Hall on the Mound, home to the Church of Scotland's General Assembly. He recalled:

As soon as he saw it, Tyrone [*Guthrie, the director*] knew it was the place. It gave him the first major opportunity to put into practice ideas of stagecraft which had immense effect.

To everyone engaged in the venture it seemed a huge adventure although up to the opening night the rest of the world seemed indifferent. It was the first time the 'Scottish theatre' had ever worked as a single body and the experience gave a sense of identity which those who took part have never lost.

In an article in the *Scottish Field* for the 21st Edinburgh Festival, in 1967, in the teeth of the Arab-Israeli war. Robert wrote:

Twice before in my life I have seen Europe go dark and watched the doves of peace having their necks wrung. I must still have faith that mankind has not gone entirely mad and that somehow a general war will be averted. If that is so, we shall have our 21st festival. The old city will be floodlit, in her streets strange tongues will be heard. Great artists will weave their spells, and we shall gladly submit to their enchantment. We will be able to share again, in some of the most glorious creations of the human spirit.

Arnold absorbed his father's love of theatre and culture generally. He recalled his father and a group of friends taking over the disused cinema at the top of Leith Walk which became the Gateway Theatre. Later the company, under actor director Tom Fleming, mutated into the Lyceum. Arnold wrote:

Duncan Macrae was released by the Citizens to take the lead in *Let Wives Tak Tent* at the Gateway in 1947. This wonderful actor personified and perhaps inspired the theories my father was building about a Scottish theatre. His flowing movements, his sudden shifts from melancholy to low cunning, the ragged glamour of his costume, the fantastical atmosphere he so quickly created, the richly relished language – all these qualities tallied exactly with the theoretical specification. I have never seen the like of Macrae on stage: he was a genius.

Arnold remembered the furore caused by *The Three Estates*. He wrote:

The play was a sensation. The London critics were dazzled by the colour and energy of the spectacle, its rich language, its broad comedy, the force of the satire, the stunning moment when the clergy remove their dark robes to reveal their scarlet undergarments. Guthrie had restored the apron stage to the theatre. The actors processed or bounded in along the aisles, and this brought cast and audience into an intimacy of a kind long lost in conventional theatre with its lighted tableau.

The experience of *The Three Estates* demonstrated another truth about theatre which, my father believed, was not always grasped by intellectual commentators – that it was not simply text-driven, though textual richness was indispensable, but was organic, arising from the interaction of all the elements in it.

When that amazing opening night took place, I was nine. I have a clear but incomplete memory of it. Just before the lights dimmed, I looked round and caught a glimpse of my father at the back. His face had lost its mask of relaxed good humour and I realised suddenly how enormously nervous he must be. Duncan Macrae, too, I remember, in his comic glory, costumed like a gorgeous bird.

For my father *The Three Estates* was what the physicists would call a point of singularity, a point at which forces come together and then spread out afterwards, as when a rock is thrown into a pool. He found himself with a higher profile; in the Hollywood jargon of our own day, he was 'hot', a condition that comes to most artists maybe only once in their lives. It is a moment that has to be grasped before times change and memory fades. In 1948 my father left the BBC to pursue his own career full-time as a writer. In a small country where a professional writer could only aspire to relatively meagre rewards, it was a brave step, infused by a patriotic determination to put his own people on the stage, to let them speak there on their own terms and in their own words.

This was to be the most fruitful period of Robert's life. Together with actress Lennox Milne and actor-director Tom Fleming he formed The Edinburgh Gateway Company. Friends and acquaintances rattled up £1000, the Scottish Arts Council matched it and they performed 12 seasons between 1953 and 1965.

Not every production was a triumph, however. For Arnold:

Repertory has its limitations. Shakespeare is best done by English actors, O'Casey and Synge by Irish and productions elsewhere must always have the quality of a shadow or pale copy. Yet I look back on these years, when I was a frequent attender of first nights, with great gratitude, for I had a theatrical education of some width. I have always particularly enjoyed theatre in Dublin which has retained much of the warmth that I remember from the Gateway days.

The early years of the Gateway were a period of considerable fecundity for my father. In the first 10 years he wrote 10 original plays. Then the pace began to drop and the ice of an artistic winter began to form over him. When the theatre was municipalized in 1966, and Tom Fleming became the first director of the Lyceum Company, Dad found himself increasingly out of sympathy with theatrical trends, and he fell out with his old friend.

Fleming's highbrow approach, in Robert's phrase, 'emptied the pews'. He wrote instead for TV and radio. There were five novels; Arnold considered *The Malacca Cane*, a comedy set in Edinburgh, the best. Most of the others are reworkings of his plays. 'He *[Robert]* supplemented his income with journalism in *The Glasgow Herald*. Much of polite Edinburgh treated him with indifference. He began to suffer intermittently from depression.'

Arnold recalled his parents as 'religious, but not officiously so'. They went to church – St Stephen's in Stockbridge – but not before devouring 'Oor Wullie' and 'The Broons' in *The Sunday Post*.

Sunday school was followed by an eagerly awaited lunch. 'My mother would have put the roast in the oven before we left and its delicious smells assailed us the moment we came through the door. There was an agonising wait until the vegetables were done, and then we fell upon it.'

Money troubles were a constant and Robert recorded every outgoing from the purchase of a newspaper to the £5 he gave his elderly mother when she went on a trip to London. Arnold recalls his own thrifty mother's 'series of culinary stratagems to make the joint "do another day". First there was broth, and after the bread and gravy. I smack my chops at the memory.

'Plain white slice bread is reviled by faddists today and I suppose it doesn't have much to recommend it – except as a sponge for gravy. Drink was rarely on the table and then only when there were visitors. Sherry might be produced before Christmas lunch or on some other special day.'

Family holidays might be taken, by ferry, to Orkney or Islay. A favourite day trip was to South Queensferry to shuttle across the firth and watch the trains rattling overhead. School fees were an ongoing worry. Arnold recalled: 'On my first day at the Edinburgh Academy I turned back and followed my mother home. My parents had hoped to send us to state school but David had been bullied so much at Wardie, towards the sea at Granton, that they changed their minds.'

Robert's diaries from the period reveal professional and financial pessimism (as well as happier events such as David's decision to take dancing classes, parties and weddings.)

> Nov 25, 1953: This is a black period from the point of view of payments.
>
> Dec 8: I felt a lifting of the load today because I have paid the boys' fees. I have never been so late as this before. Of course the car, the painting of the hall, the holiday will set me back during the summer. I am resolved never again to tax my financial reserves as I have just done. To pay my debts, among which I reckon my overdraft, and be free is my modest ambition. Yet it is tempting. The house needs a new stove to save Meta work, we need to repair the painting and buy a new carpet, the workshop needs to made into a room for Arnold. Perhaps the work will come in. Thank goodness it has been milder. To work in cold weather is beyond me.

Arnold described the Edinburgh Academy as having 'a split personality', with an ethos borrowed from Dr Arnold and English public schools 'ephors' for prefects and games of hailes, played with a flat bat and ball. The ephors once applied the hailes bat to his bum as a punishment, from which he dated his distrust of authority. The preponderance of day boys over boarders, however, saved it from being a cloistered public school and Arnold remained grateful to his teachers – although one who, when teaching French, admitted it was a case of 'the blind leading the blind' caused Robert, when Arnold recounted this at home, 'no little fury'.

Although the academy advocated rugby, and Robert took his sons to all the international games at Murrayfield, Arnold's passion was football. 'We played bounce games in the school yard and the park outside the house. On a Saturday afternoon the roar of the crowd was carried on the wind from Easter Road where Hibs' "Famous Five" beguiled a generation with their brilliant forward play.' Arnold became a supporter in the late 1940s as the team began their dominance of the Scottish game. 'I recite their names – Smith, Johnstone, Reilly, Turnbull and Ormond – as readily as I can remember my mother's old Co-Op number.

'If there were any religious or ethnic undertones to the question of which club to follow in Edinburgh, then I was happily unaware of them. Most of the small boys who kicked a ball around in the local park wanted to be Gordon Smith.'

The Edinburgh of Arnold's youth popped up throughout his writing life. In 1969, in *The Scotsman* reliving a debate about the city's merits, against an Englishman who had 'spent a couple of years here: had found it cold and unfriendly; had despised the hypocrisy of a city which combined a dignified manner with appalling public drunkenness; had detected an inbred philistinism in the inhabitants which made a mockery of the festival; and had contrasted the architectural splendours with the squalor of some of the housing', he wrote: 'I have reached the conclusion that Edinburgh's inbuilt contradictions and hypocrisies are the very things that make her the oddest and most lovable town'.

Of his adored Café Royal he said: 'If one approached it through Saint Andrew Square, passing the sober facades of the great banks, it was positively startling to come suddenly upon this opulent Epicurean temple. The contrast was equally impressive if one came via Woolworth's and the little shops in whose windows we as schoolboys pondered with furtive awe the advertisements for contraceptives and books on sexual technique.'

He continued: 'It is characteristic that in the days before Mr Butler's [*Rab Butler, Home Secretary 1957-62*] act street-walkers promenaded through the dim but expensive byways of the New Town or that the most distinguished New Town houses should be within shouting distance of some of the shabbiest apartments ... Edinburgh is a human, errant place and therein lies its charm. Without its failings, it would be as ghastly as Cumbernauld.'

In his last year at school, Arnold and some friends went youth-hostelling in Paris dressed in their kilts and he recalled later how they took to their heels and fled after a voluptuous black prostitute surrounded by giggling colleagues asked the traditional question about what they wore underneath their 'jupes écossaises'.

Having passed five Highers, Arnold went, without giving it much thought, to Edinburgh University. Later describing himself as 'an unremarkable student', he failed honours in French and German but passed at ordinary level, finally completing his MA by taking a course in geology.

Like most students of his generation, he lived at home. 'As I left the house in the morning I would ponder the profoundly important questions: should I spend my half-crown [*12.5p*] on a frugal lunch or on 10 cigarettes and a game of billiards? The second option usually won. I could always nip home for lunch. I would come running down the basement steps as my father – my mother was by now teaching – prepared the meal, perhaps a succulent Arbroath smokie slowly poached and served with butter and boiled potatoes, or herring in oatmeal.'

He supplemented his income one year by working as an extra in the second film version of John Buchan's *The Thirty Nine Steps*. Arnold was one of the policemen. He is visible for 'about two seconds being vigilant in Waverley Station – it's easy to miss unless you watch very carefully ... My elder brother and I each got £5 a day, sat around doing nothing for most of the time and, returning home still in police uniform, were not required by the tram conductor to pay the fare. It was fortunate, I later reflected, that no criminal outrage or public emergency required our intervention.'

By 1957, as Kemp *[from here on, Kemp will be used rather than Arnold]* wrote years later in *The Hollow Drum*, Edinburgh University was in a period of transition. In earlier days, the lecturers had been paid by the students and they consequently developed techniques of showmanship, which inspired the creation of the character of Sherlock Holmes, and which also made some of them rich. Students showed appreciation by the stamping of feet at the start and end of lectures.

By the late 1950s, this like other customs was dying out. Kemp wrote:

> The rectorial and other campaigns had reached unacceptable levels of violence and the authorities had begun to feel very uneasy about them. My brother David was slightly injured in the Suez riots in the Old Quad in 1956. The most notorious rectorial of the period, in fact, was in Glasgow in 1958, when the installation of Lord Butler as rector was reduced to chaos. The platform party was drenched with flour thrown by the disrespectful student audience. John Mackay, the *Glasgow Herald*'s photographer, was knocked out by a flying cabbage. The authorities had had enough, disciplinary reprisals followed, and rectorial campaigns, with their flour fights among rival factions and a generalised air of anarchy, lost their political innocence and their quality of spontaneous and joyous exuberance.

Kemp's interest in his father's sometime profession began during his student days and Robert recorded proudly in his diary on Thursday 16 July 1959: 'Arnold began work on the Scotsman.' On 1 December he noted: 'Arnold on holiday – it is splendid to see how he has tackled his work and seems so happy in it.'

In 1961, when Kemp had moved to London to work as a sub-editor at *The Guardian*, he penned gossipy letters home, full of reassuring domestic details and breaking political scandals – most revolving around spy scandals. In those days at the height of the Cold War reds appeared to be in many powerful people's beds, as well as lurking under others.

Dear Mum and Dad [*goes the first missive*], I am writing this in the kitchen of the flat, which Bert [*a friend from* The Scotsman *then working at the Press Association*] and I moved into yesterday. I have just come back from work. I washed the dishes (laugh that one off!). [*Kemp's ability to avoid kitchen sink duties was a running family joke.*] It has two rooms - one a bedroom, the other a sitting room with a divan in a kitchen and a bathroom just along the corridor. Bert has just come in from work and we've had a meal of scrambled eggs cooked by me.

In 1962 he reports a week of 'what Mr Maudling [*Reg, then Chancellor of the Exchequer*] would call retrenchment after that expensive weekend in Cardiff.' He and Bert had to hide from the milkman and avoided the newsagent until pay day. Kemp brings in 1963 at a party in Woking that continues until 5am.

All the Scots in London seem to have congregated on this house and a good time was had by all. The highlight of the evening was undoubtedly a snow fight we had in the garden, the French windows were open and several snowballs came whistling into the room and struck guests as they supped their drinks. The few English guests observed the proceedings with mild alarm. They seemed to enjoy it all and as a concession we consented to join them in singing Any Old Iron.

Later that year, he asks the folks back home: 'Have you heard about Profumo, the War Secretary? Apparently he was mixed up with this missing model Christine Keeler, who should have given evidence at the trial of a West Indian accused of attempting to murder her. When she didn't appear, and when the authorities seemed to be making no attempt to find her, it was suggested that it was being hushed up. She's said to be in Paris: it's also said that Paris Match has bought her story and is publishing it next week. If it does come out it won't do the government much good. Their moral tone is pretty low as it is ... Well that's the gossip for the week, cheerio the noo.'

Kemp returned to Edinburgh in 1965, to become production editor at *The Scotsman*. His father continued to struggle, as his diary reveals.

Feb 12, 1967. I loathe television but must keep it up for the money. What am I doing with my life? Nothing.

September 6. Well if it weren't for Meta I think I should be starving this month.

November 7. Had a warning of heart trouble. Chalmers gave me a cardiogram and it seems I do have some slight defect.

This did not stop him working. Robert's last diary entry was made the next day: 'Finished Ben Line' (a promotional film for a shipping company). He died soon after, aged 59.

Kemp was aware of his father's unhappiness in his final years.

He found critics uncomprehending and patronising. Worse, he became aware of their provincialism and deference to London judgements. If there was anything worse than Anglophobia, he wrote, it was Anglophilia of this provincial kind where nothing was accepted in Scotland unless it had the imprimatur of a London critic. He became saddened that he was remembered as the adapter of Lindsay; for subsequent festivals he had adapted Ramsay's The Gentle Shepherd and Joseph Mitchell's Highland Fair. Now he said: 'I have finished with adaptations'. His own plays have considerable merit, particularly the comedies of his best years, like The Penny Wedding, The Scientific Singers, Henrietta MD, and The Other Dear Charmer.

The people in his plays are drawn from life but they are not kitchen comedies; they deal with the great Scottish themes but with a light touch. His greatest gift to the theatre, apart from his sense of comedy and character and his understanding of Scottish theatre, was his easy use of Scots.

This is not the ersatz Scots of the Scots renaissance, whose contortions are sometimes grotesque and risible, but is the spoken Scots of the people among whom he grew up and lived, and whom he loved. The only other contemporary artist, I think, who used Scots with anything like this ease and authority was the poet Robert Garioch.

Above all, as he recognised in a sad speech given towards the end of his life, the forces of centralisation were destroying the Scots which he sought to dignify, the grammatically correct Scots of the old middle classes and the country places.

Looking back on his father in The Scottish Review, Kemp wrote in 2000:

Many years ago Sir Alec Guinness appeared in the West End production of John Mortimer's play A Journey Round My Father. As I recall, the father was a blind barrister and his son's portrait was ambiguous and impressionistic. Indeed the message was that the father, like all fathers, would inevitably remain mysterious to his son. And although my father was as kind, gentle and loving a parent as anyone could wish, I became aware that beyond the attentive domestic figure there was another, subtly different personality that moved about in public, had friends who were talented and raffish, engaged in the politics of the theatre though rarely in the politics of parties and parliaments, loved his Saturday lunchtimes and occasional evenings at the Scottish Arts Club and relished his hour in the Northern Bar on Saturday nights with 'the pink' [the Saturday late edition of The Edinburgh Evening News which contained all the football scores] and a small gathering of friends.

I suspected, too, that in his youth there had been riotous patches. Indeed, my mother once disclosed that he and a friend had been thrown out of a music hall in Manchester. Later I sometimes came upon his spoor, at the Café Royal or the Abbotsford, where those who had known him in the old days spoke of his conviviality. There were occasions, of course, when we glimpsed it at home, when he had visitors, and certainly our household was rarely too far away from laughter. But I suppose he felt he had to set us all an example of restraint, and like all parents, perhaps, kept part of himself hidden.

He tried to inculcate the conventional values of honesty, integrity, sobriety, restraint, good manners and respect for others. But there was talk, too, especially as we grew older, about ideas, history and cultures. And it was through his often complex attitudes that he most truly moulded me. He was the son of the manse and entertained a most lively dislike of science which, I suspect, came down from the days of the old Darwinian controversies. He wanted us to excel in the arts and humanities, though I fear we often disappointed him. He tried to communicate his own love of Scottish traditions, and would offer us a pound if we learned by heart 'The Ballad of Sir Patrick Spens' or 'Tam O'Shanter'. If the school report spoke ill of our attainments in Latin, French or English, his brows would beetle in disapproval. But once I failed a science O-level spectacularly, walking out before the end and scoring three per cent. He was delighted, and congratulated me as if on a notable achievement.

His plays are peopled by the characters who came to the manse which, as he later observed, stood as a panoramic social observation point with an eye on both the gentry and the common folk.

My father was carried away by a stroke which, I suspect, was brought on by medical treatment he was receiving at the time for an ulcer. Scarcely a day goes past when I do not think of him. It is a sad truth that you remember your parents in their declining years more vividly than in their prime. Towards the end of his life he suffered sometimes from melancholy which, in a man of such wit and merriment, was sad to see. But, with only a little effort, I look beyond, to the sunlit days of our childhood beside the Water of Leith, to his love, his companionship, his cultivated intelligence and his lack of conceit or self-satisfaction. It is one of the delights of advancing years sometimes to see in my grandchildren, in a look or a laugh or a mannerism, sudden glimpses of both my father and my mother.

I suppose I have inherited some of his attitudes – his Francophilia and his belief, sometimes strained in the face of mindless crime or executive greed, in the possibility of social harmony. When I became an editor at *The Glasgow Herald* his influence was the most pervasive of all, perhaps because it operated unceasingly and often at a subconscious level. I was more than usually sympathetic to contributors and freelances because I had seen how my father, down the years, had suffered at the hands of the mediocre and the arrogant. As a freelance, he usually had to grin and bear it, although sometimes he didn't.

But, most of all, I think, he influenced my own rejection of Thatcherism. Its emphasis on the marketplace would have offended his concepts of social harmony and he would, I fancy, have detested its hectoring tone, just as my mother did. His premature death still fills me with a sense of injustice and every year by which my own lifespan exceeds his seems an ill-deserved bonus. Above all, like many Scots, I sense in myself that everlasting struggle between the bourgeois and the bohemian. In his case the bourgeois won but the bohemian was always there too, never crudely dressed but wrapped in wit and irony.

2

Newspapers

WHAT FOLLOWS IS AN EXTRACT from a memoir of Kemp's early days learning the trade.

When I joined *The Scotsman* sub-editors' room in 1959 I was given a seat opposite Don Miller, a gruff old communist from Caithness who specialised in foreign news and was especially punctilious about stories involving the Soviet Union. (He also was famous for his headings with double meanings, like 'Man performs on 150ft crane' and 'Russian virgin lands'.) He constantly sent 'signals' – wire messages – to Reuters correcting some looseness in nomenclature about the first Praesidium of the Supreme Soviet (I have probably got that wrong, come to think of it). One night he received a hysterical reply: 'You are right, you are always right, but for God's sake leave me in peace.' I had a vision of some poor Reuters man, worrying about his mortgage, his marriage, or both, for whom Don's latest signal was the last straw, rushing dementedly into the night.

Every night he sent the copy boy to the fish shop for a steak pie. Before attacking it he spread out sheets of copy paper on his desk. When he bit into the pie a great glob of gravy would dribble down into the paper. Then he would lick it clean before scrunching it into a ball and throwing it into the bin. Throughout the procedure his damp Players cigarette butt smouldered acridly in the ashtray, like a joss-stick for some northern god, to be smoked down to the last quarter inch after his meal was over. Every night I found myself waiting for and then watching this performance with a kind of repelled fascination.

At New Year he would bring beer into the office in an old antifreeze can and share it with favoured colleagues. For all his earthy ways, he was a kindly old chap without a hint of malice.

I suppose the word that comes to mind about *The Scotsman* of that period is august. The pages were grave and dignified, though well printed and with excellent picture reproduction. Multi-deck headings were then the convention in British broadsheets. Don was always writing ones like this:

THE FUTURE
OF CYPRUS
Thousands riot in
Nicosia
PM INFORMED

The old Scotsman building had a massive, sepulchral dignity. Now a hotel, it stands sentinel over Edinburgh, rising from the valley that separates Princes Street from the Old Town. The press hall was at the bottom, opposite the back door of Waverley Station, and the front entrance, four or five floors up, gave on to North Bridge. Behind, in Fleshmarket Close, in Cockburn Street and the High Street, were our favourite pubs: the Adelphi, the Jinglin' Geordie and the Halfway House. The editorial department was on the third floor, its corridors lined with the busts of proprietors and hung with the portraits of editors. (When a member of the reading room staff had a nervous breakdown he went along the corridor smashing as many of the busts as he could before he was restrained.)

The sub-editors worked in a gloomy room overlooking Fleshmarket Close into which the sun never penetrated, but the editor's office commanded a noble view of Princes Street and that acme of Edinburgh refinement, Jenners.

The management suite on the fourth floor, with its walnut hall, was richly panelled and until the 1970s the chief executive's room had a coal fire. The marble central staircase linked the management and editorial floors; here was the war memorial. But the rest of the interior, constructed round a well, was dim and secret, with mysterious corridors and dark stone stairs.

When Roy Thomson bought *The Scotsman* from Sir Edmund Findlay and his associates in 1953, he got it more or less for nothing because he immediately sold off the adjacent property in North Bridge. The equity hidden in these shops and office suites had been overlooked by the Findlay family's self-satisfied but somnolent professional advisers.

One evening in the 1970s I wandered through a forgotten entrance into the staircase of the surplus property next door. A disused lift shaft, enclosed by ornate metal, disappeared into the gloom above. There was dust everywhere and the marble tiles on the stair wall were grimy. I felt like a time traveller.

After acquiring *The Scotsman*, Thomson then set about reforming the commercial departments, introducing methods of selling advertising which revolutionised the industry in the UK. In the old days dignified clerkesses waited for advertising to be brought in through the front door; they would put aside their knitting to take the details. Now it was canvassed and pursued, by telephone and personal visitation. Thomson is supposed to have said that editorial was the stuff that went between the ads but he remained true to his promise that he would never interfere in editorial. In our ignorance we would rail against him over our beer, but in recollection he emerges as a newspaper proprietor *sans pareil*, shrewd but also principled.

The Scotsman had been founded in 1817. It remained Liberal until 1885 when Gladstone's Irish Home Rule Bill convulsed the Scottish Protestant middle class and it turned Tory. After World War II the paper sank into genteel decline and debt. Edinburgh and the staff of the paper almost entirely ignored evidence given to the Royal Commission on the Press in 1948 which made the situation clear: Sir Edmund had taken over his father's interest in *The Scotsman* on the assumption that profits would meet death duties, but slack management undermined his hopes.

There were apocryphal stories that Sir Edmund liked a drink and would sometimes dip into the petty cash before setting off for Monte Carlo but whatever the truth of that his advisers decided that he had to sell. Perhaps because he made them look like slow-witted hicks, Thomson was never forgiven by Edinburgh and he never was easy with its rigid gentility and entrenched snobberies.

When Thomson flippantly said he planned to introduce a page of comic strips, the town was aghast. It simply couldn't take the joke.

The editor Thomson inherited, Murray Watson, resisted all suggestions of change, refusing to put news on the front page. But after Watson's death, Thomson appointed Alastair Dunnett as editor.

Dunnett, a small, dark man, a shrewd, humorous and lively journalist, revived the paper and brought to it and its editorial proceedings the wit and warmth of the west, together with his own passion for home rule for Scotland. He sensed earlier than most what was to be the dominant theme of post-war Scottish politics but felt unable immediately to commit the paper to federalism, which he did half a dozen years later.

The incumbent deputy editor, John Buchanan, was a frosty, unsociable and pedagogic man who had expected the top job and was not easily reconciled to Dunnett. He maintained a long froideur.

One or two of the senior staff rallied to him and formed a disloyal opposition with which Dunnett had to cope for some years. Under Buchanan the leaders were opaque, with a Mandarin hauteur and a windy prose style. But there were signs of things to come.

Dunnett had appointed Eric B Mackay as London editor, a man of few words from the north-east but with a discerning eye for talent. Neal Ascherson and David Watt were among those who made their start in the old London office, then in Fleet Street. Dunnett was determined that the paper should speak for Scotland and be heard where it counted: if we don't do it, no one else will, he would say. It was a lesson he had learned during the war when he had served as information officer to the Secretary of State Tom Johnston. Given a free hand by Churchill, Johnston acquired a substantial amount of administrative discretion and is a father of modern devolution.

Dunnett hired Magnus Magnusson to lead an assault on *The Glasgow Herald*'s redoubt in the west, an attack, never successful, intermittently repeated down the years. Magnus's fluent and graceful writing came as something of a tonic – though with minimal sales gain – in a paper whose grey pages had the repressed and fluting tone of pan-loaf Edinburgh speech.

Some of the staff carried polite Edinburgh's distaste for sensationalism to the point of absurdity. One reporter, when he covered religious affairs, fancied himself a bishop and, when his beat switched to the centre of government in Scotland, St Andrews House, he adopted the mannerisms of a senior civil servant. He once rebuked me about a story we had run, saying 'we were very upset'. By 'we' he meant the senior civil servants.

Charles Graves, the dramatic critic, was an Olympian and erudite Shakespearean. One night, having completed an extended report on a poetry reading by TS Eliot, he put on his hat and then, as an afterthought, informed the chief reporter that a lion had escaped at the circus playing in Waverley market and mauled members of the audience.

'What, Graves? What?' barked the chief reporter in some astonishment. 'I can assure you that it's true,' replied Graves loftily. 'I saw it myself.' He had been commissioned, to his evident disgust, to drop in on the circus on his way to the poetry reading.

On another occasion, sent to review Cliff Richard at the Empire, he devoted most of his piece to the jugglers who were second on the bill, making many scholarly references to the history of their art. Cliff was mentioned in the last paragraph which was 'cut on the stone' (removed in the composing room).

There was a sweetness to his character which made others forgive his eccentricities. The agricultural editor, Robert Urquhart, was studying a map of Hampshire one day when he felt Graves at his shoulder. He pointed to a place where he had served in the RAF during the war. 'I nearly died there one day,' he said. 'Our bomber was so heavily laden that it barely cleared the church tower.'

Loftily Graves responded: 'That would have been a great tragedy; the church is one of the finest examples of Norman architecture in England.'

I learned my trade as a sub-editor in the oddest of ways. The production of the paper was a shambles – a word, I recall, banned by The Scotsman Style Book except in its correct sense of slaughterhouse.

Dunnett had decided that London must not be deprived of his paper; he also started an airmail edition for overseas. This meant earlier print times. But there was no compensating increase in the capacity of the composing room, and so every night's production was a bizarre exercise in improvisation and crisis management in which we all learned to think on our feet.

The composing room, with its smell of ink and lead, has gone from the industry now, but it was a place of genuine fascination. Surely no more beautiful or satisfying machine has ever been designed than the Linotype. Man and machine worked together in harmony, and the machine's long arm, grasping the brass matrices from the moulding pot and returning them aloft to the magazine in which they were stored, moved up and down in human rhythm. The lines of metal slowly grew into complete stories and were collated in galleys. If speed were of the essence then a story would be split into 'takes' and distributed for setting, and could be completed in a matter of minutes.

A man went round with a piece of tape measuring the metal as it accumulated. On the hour he would communicate the news that there was not nearly enough type to see the paper away in time. Some fairly desperate stratagems, for example running the same picture on different pages or putting the results of The Scotsman's staff golf tournament on the front page, were occasionally used.

I had a recurring anxiety dream in which I stood at the bottom of a page waiting for metal to drop to fill a hole, knowing – but not daring to confess I knew – that it would never come because I had omitted to send it down via the hissing compressed-air system of Lamson tubes which connected the departments. I stood in my dream doomed to wait for type into the depths of eternity.

Gordon Anderson, the chief sub, would draw the roughest of page plans. In the composing room we improvised, filling up each page as metal dropped. He emerged after the chaotic first edition carrying endless galleys of overmatter. The edition was padded with material – much of it from *The Observer* foreign news service, including the dispatches of one K Philby – set in the wee small hours during the previous day.

The capacity, in short, was there but not at the appropriate time. The result was that our readers in the far reaches of Scotland were extremely well informed about foreign affairs, if less so about their own country. The sub-editors then had to cut the omitted material into the next edition.

In this harem-scarem manner I acquired a remarkably useful training, learning to work under pressure, improvise, condense and rewrite. Page proofs were an unheard of luxury. We had to cut the stories on to the page by reading them, upside down and in mirror image, on the stone. The compositors – their trade has vanished now – were kindly, humorous and pawky men, slapping the metal into the page without ceremony as deadlines neared and passed.

As I poured over a galley of type and made my selection of shorts for the Scots news page, one of the upmakers called wee Davie Blyth would say in his sing-song Edinburgh voice: 'You're the boss, I hope you know what you're doing.' These words have stayed with me throughout my career.

We worked hard, but also had an enormous amount of fun. After the tempest of the first edition, the rest of the night was more spacious because at that time paper ran on two presses. The Glasgow edition went at 1am and the last Edinburgh at 3am, or sometimes later if there were new stories of significance. The late crew loved nothing better than to tear apart the first edition. Our idea of a good time was to make sure that the final edition bore only a passing resemblance to the first.

In between times we might nip along to the Press Club for a pint and, on our return, play a practical joke or two on colleagues who seemed to deserve it. One was John Campbell, our assistant chief sub, an able journalist who dreamed of the big time and, when excited, sounded like Walter Burns, the manic publisher in the play *The Front Page*, perhaps because he had come into the game relatively late after a career in local government and was smitten by its romance. He was a decent man, of whom I grew very fond, but if he were left in charge it went to his head. All evening he had been bossing us about in an unacceptable manner, ordering us to fetch him tea and perform other menial tasks, in his best Walter Burns manner.

Eventually the worms turned. It was a conspiracy of four – Ian Wood, later an outstanding sports columnist; Bill Watson later a novelist, playwright and, under the pseudonym JK Mayo, successful writer of thrillers; Alistair Clark, who outside journalism played a hot jazz trumpet, and myself. One of us slipped up to the wire room and persuaded the operator to type out on the teleprinter a series of bogus wire 'rushes', purportedly from the impeccable source of the Press Association, which were fed down the Lamson tube, landing with a soft plop in the padded basket. The first said: 'FLYING SAUCER LANDS AT BUCKINGHAM PALACE.'

Alistair presented the copy to John dead-pan. 'You'd better look at this'. We waited for John to see the joke. Instead he went red and barked: 'I've been waiting for this all my life; clear the front page!' Aghast, we watched as he phoned the case room to warn them of a big page change. By now our further rushes were plopping into the basket – the Prime Minister informed, the Household Cavalry mobilised.

John tried to phone London – but we had nipped through to the operator and told him to cut off the call. We had visions of ruined careers and instant dismissals. Eventually we got our fellow conspirator in the wire room to send through a final rush: 'KILL, KILL, KILL: please disregard previous messages.'

John's whole body sagged. Slowly he picked up the phone and stood down the case room. Covertly we watched as he wrote his overnight note, for the attention of the chief sub when he came into work the following afternoon. And then, a deeply frustrated man, he put on his coat and hat and left. We quickly took possession of the note, to which he had pinned the rushes, and amid relieved hilarity read its conclusion: 'I think we have been the victims of an establishment cover-up.'

Journalists are like policemen; their friendships tend to be with others of their kind. Ian Wood tried to teach me to play golf, with indifferent success. But we had many happy outings, to his club at Duddingston or to the links at Gullane where the larks sang and it never seemed to rain. After finishing a late shift, we would walk down the hill to my parents' house in Warriston Crescent, having purchased earlier a half bottle of whisky, and sit in the drawing room listening to records and chewing the fat. Ian would leave as the world stirred for breakfast, and I would put the empty bottle into a drawer in my bedroom. My mother was aghast, some months later, to discover what was by now a considerable hoard and accused me of being a secret drinker.

Her feelings were as nothing compared to those of Dunnett sometime later. He had invited Lord Clyde, then Scotland's senior judge, to lunch in the boardroom, and was showing him round the office. As they walked through the library, Lord Clyde spotted a legal work on the shelves – for argument's sake, let us say it was 'Rettie on the law of contract'. 'Ah, Dunnett,' he intoned, 'I am delighted to see that you have that excellent and substantive work,' and reached for the volume. As he removed it a shower of empty MacEwan's beer cans cascaded to the floor. What Dunnett did not know was that the library was a bit of a drinking den for the late staff and one – Pat Gaffney, a delightful man who in his cups would proclaim: 'Give me a stand of pipes and I'll play you the Black Bear,' stored his empties behind a book he felt confident would never be consulted.

The Guardian

When my friend Bert moved to London, to work at the Press Association, I began to feel restless myself. I was still living at home. It was time to move on. And so I wrote to Alastair Hetherington at *The Guardian*.

During Wimbledon fortnight in 1962 I reported for work to John Putz, the paper's night editor. At that time *The Guardian* rented a section of Thomson House in Gray's Inn Road, home of *The Sunday Times*, and ran off its southern editions on its presses.

The sub-editing department contained a mixture of old journeymen and young hopefuls, very friendly and sociable, spending rather more time than was good for it in the Lamb in Conduit Street or the Blue Lion in Gray's Inn Road. It was there I made my first acquaintance with the flat hoppy bitter of the south, a brew which has almost entirely disappeared.

Putz, an old hand, had known my father and appointed himself in loco parentis. He disapproved of our outings to the pub, and would praise the excellence of the canteen. (Which was execrable.) Eat your greens, he would intone in his lugubrious Lancastrian voice, and plenty of fruit; it keeps the blood clear. Later, early one morning, I gave him a lift home. As we waited for the lights to change, he would intone gloomily: 'Don't sit on the clutch, man, for heaven's sake! Leave that trick to tradesmen who don't own their own vehicles.'

But for all his foibles, he was a kindly man and a conscientious night editor, though some of our flowery writers suspected that he preferred the unvarnished prose of the Press Association to their more ambitious efforts. In those days the front page carried across two columns a brisk summary of the main story, running the dispatch itself immediately beneath it. Every night Putz sweated to produce the most polished and concise summary, wrinkling up his brow with the effort before pronouncing himself satisfied. And every night, as soon as he had done so, Ian Aitken, the brilliant political correspondent, would phone in from the parliamentary lobby with a new story that supplanted the lead. With a scowl and a muttered curse, Putz would scrunch up his little masterpiece into a ball and throw it into the bin.

At this time the paper retained a gentle, provincial air. Its editors and executives were exceedingly courteous, even shy, and did not care for confrontation. Hetherington himself, who in his first manifestation at *The Glasgow Herald* had acquired the nickname 'the boy scout' because of his earnest conscientiousness, worked extremely hard. He was fair, open and spoke his mind. When, as father of the NUJ chapel, I demanded the 'closed shop', as I had been mandated to do, he simply said 'no'. This left me at a loss since I knew my members would not wish to take the matter into the realms of a real industrial dispute. We sat and stared at each other for a while, and then we both started to laugh.

In all newspapers there is a tendency for peer groups to drink and socialise together. The subs therefore saw the writers and reporters from something of a distance, though they were always perfectly friendly. At the time the pay of these often very distinguished journalists was not munificent and many supplemented their income through freelance work. When leaving the office for an assignment, say, at Bush House and the BBC World Service, old hands at the game would leave their jacket over the chair, implying they were still somewhere in the vicinity.

One evening the Commonwealth conference came to an end late on with the issue of a communiqué at Lancaster House. It was to be the splash in the second edition. Patrick Keatley, our distinguished correspondent assigned to write the story, was nowhere to be seen. Hetherington, sitting beside Putz on the 'back bench', grew increasingly anxious as the deadline neared. We concocted the story from the news agencies and awaited Keatley's copy for the third edition.

Still there was no sign. Hetherington chafed and fumed. Then Keatley popped up on the newsroom television to give his expert analysis to the BBC. Hetherington grew very red with suppressed anger. I do not know what was said at their subsequent confrontation except that next weekend Keatley posted a defiant notice on the board saying that if anyone was looking for him on Sunday he would be at one of the following phone numbers – and gave a list of the great and good from the Prime Minister down. It looked like crass name-dropping but I took the real message to be that you couldn't make fabulous contacts like these by sitting at your desk. The real sub-text, I fancy, was that *The Guardian* didn't pay him adequately and his tardy performance had been a mild kind of industrial protest.

Another star of the paper was the Kremlinologist Victor Zorza, who provided many scoops about crises at the heart of Soviet government, but who was a turgid and verbose writer. One of his articles filled an entire page, with half a column of overmatter. In the composing room we pondered the problem. Studying the text, in which each paragraph was cunningly linked to the next, we decided that Zorza had better cut it himself. He came down to the 'stone', as the composing room was called, and surveyed the problem for a while. Cut his copy? Unthinkable. His face lightened. 'The solution is simple,' he said imperiously. 'Remove the advertisement'.

The print workers, skilled and unskilled, were at that time kings of the working class. Their earnings could be very substantial. Early one morning, as I was leaving to drive home in our little green minivan, I rode down in the lift with two printers who were studying brochures for new cars. 'You know, Fred,' said one, 'I don't think I could ever go back to a small car again.'

The compositors, however, were friendly and decent men, though heaven protect you if you dared to touch type, except when the composing room was festooned with tinsel and stacked high with drink. Once or twice they were clearly surprised when, as late sub and accustomed to the old Scotsman ways, I dared to switch the front-page lead in the light of breaking news. Their glances clearly indicated that they thought I was taking too much upon myself, but they were also impressed by my gung-ho attitude and rallied round nobly. The following afternoon, in typical Guardian fashion, nothing would be said, no rebuke issued; but somehow I sensed disapproval and I rapidly became more cautious: the words of wee Davie Blyth came back to haunt me. I wasn't really the boss and I might not be too sure of what I was doing.

Kemp saw the hardware of newspaper industry change dramatically, as this piece from 1991 shows.

I marvel at the rapid transformation in the way that news and entertainment are delivered to the public. Yet in their day the telegraph (invented in 1837), the modern typewriter (1867), carbon paper (1872), and the telephone (1872) were just as revolutionary. The arrival of the Linotype machine and the rotary press in the same period coincided with the removal of stamp duty and press censorship.

The use of pigeons to carry news also occurred around that time and is part of the folklore of the press. Though I have never seen it they say there is a pigeon loft in the old Herald building in Mitchell Street, which has stood empty since we left it for Albion Street in 1980. [*The building in Mitchell Street is now The Lighthouse, the one in Albion Street an apartment block called The Herald Building.*]

Sometimes, listening to the stories of old-timers, I have found myself feeling a certain scepticism, thinking that perhaps they were apocryphal. Certainly most of the yarns are risible. Yet the use of pigeons for news, documented in various histories of the press, must have seemed during its brief epoch as innovative as fibre-optics in our own time.

It is hard for us to imagine how slowly news arrived until the technological revolution of the 19th century. In 1815 the news of Napoleon's defeat at Waterloo took four days to reach London; the news of his death at St Helena six years later was brought by sea and took two months.

Telegraph lines began to spread from the 1840s and the use of pigeons sprang up to fill gaps in the chain. It is often thought that Julius Reuter was the first to employ pigeons in this way but this was not the case. In the field before him were Charles Havas, the founder of the French agency of that name (whose integrity was to be compromised by French Government subsidy), the Rothschilds and other financiers. The development of international news services was driven by the need for financial information as well as for political and diplomatic intelligence.

Reuter brought a high degree of organisation to the deployment of pigeons. In 1950 there was a gap of 76 miles between the German telegraph line linking Aachen to Berlin and the French system joining Brussels to Paris.

Reuter made an agreement with an Aachen pigeon-fancier who supplied 45 trained birds to maintain a service with Brussels, where they were sent each day by rail to fly back next day.

The first pigeons were released at dawn. To guard against loss or delay, three birds carrying identical messages were sent up each time. A trusted assistant received them in the pigeon loft in Aachen, placing the messages in a sealed box to be sent round to the office where Reuter sat waiting, smoking and reading the papers.

When the box arrived Reuter and his two clerks sprang into action to transcribe the densely hand-written sheets. Runners hurried them to the telegraph office for dispatch to Berlin.

Even in modern times Reuter men occasionally fell back on pigeons in emergencies (for example during the Normandy invasion) but their systematic use by newspapers must have persisted only for some years after 1850.

There was an anecdote in *The Manchester Guardian* about a reporter of the old school who was sent to cover a Gladstone campaign meeting. He went by bike from Manchester to, let us say, Altrincham, and was alarmed to see that a rival had brought pigeons. Full of despair, he set off back to Manchester as soon as he could, his shorthand notebook in his pocket. As he cycled, the sky darkened and it began to rain. To his immense relief he saw the pigeons of his competitor settle on the dome of the town hall. On that occasion, at least, he was first with the news. No date attaches to this story but it may have been some time before 1867, when Gladstone won a landslide victory and formed his first administration.

Another hoary old anecdote concerns the sports reporter who, towards the end of a local derby in Edinburgh, had written out the scoreline and inserted it under the pigeon's wing. Just before the final whistle, Hearts scored. The reporter (I fear he was biased) raised his arms in exultation, releasing the pigeon prematurely. As it flew off he shouted after it: 'Hearts 2, Hibs 1!'

In those days the pigeon and the telegraph were used to deliver news of national or financial import, of wars and treaties, of markets collapsing or prospering. Nowadays Reuters' worldwide system of computer-driven financial information and dealing systems is of first importance, a vehicle for the currency flows which so inconvenience national governments from time to time. In the sixties the volume of foreign exchange transactions was about $3 trillion a year. By 1987 it had reached $87 trillion, a staggering rate of growth.

Much of the new information technology delivers entertainment or trivia across frontiers, reinforcing American domination of popular culture. But even in the old days the cabled message could be vacuous, as we are reminded by the couplet on the illness of the Prince of Wales by Alfred Austin, whose appointment as poet laureate in 1896 aroused widespread derision:

> Across the wires the electric message came:
> He is no better, he is much the same.

Then, as now, the means to communicate provided no guarantee that there was anything to say.

As early as 1969, Kemp was looking at the way in which computers would affect the future of newspapers.

> This week in the Glasgow College of Printing, delegates to a seminar on computer typesetting stirred uneasily in their seats as the upheavals in traditional methods that the computer will bring were spelled out.
>
> 'This should be X certificate,' remarked one delegate gloomily as Charles Ross, director of International Data Highways Ltd, flapping his arms about like a bird of augury presaging doom, set out with malicious glee his vision of life with the electronic god.
>
> He saw a computer system which would eliminate nearly all the traditional areas of printing: typesetting, composing, proof-reading and so on. From the original copy he envisaged a combined keyboarding and correcting operation followed by printing without further human intervention.
>
> For a craft of high traditions, the thought seemed fairly shattering. And there was only temporary comfort from the view, expressed by other speakers, that as of now the computer is not necessarily of benefit to printers and the press.

As the delegates, somewhat bemused, emerged into the glaur of Glasgow, most of them took comfort from what seemed to be a central message: that the traditional skills of the industry will never die. The computer will take the drudgery out of them; it could be, in short, the great liberator.

Good typography should never draw attention to itself; it should be the servant, not the master, of the matter. The printer's ability to handle copy intelligently, and his knowledge and experience of good design, will always be a sine qua non. Similarly, the journalist's skills – writing, news gathering, assessment and presentation – will forever by needed even if the alarming concept of the instant newspaper, dialled up at breakfast time over a domestic receiver ever becomes reality.

In 1964, in a *Guardian* pamphlet, Kemp attacked the notion – widely accepted at the time – that TV would spell the end of the newspaper.

It was perhaps not foreseeable how hard certain types of newspapers would fight back.

TV can beat newspapers in terms of time alone. But newspapers are still indispensable to those who want a full knowledge of events – even of those events instantaneously shown on the home screen.

Secondly, so far newspaper reporting has been more enterprising than television reporting. 'Scoops' still happen and will do in future.

Thirdly, only in a newspaper can a mass of detailed information at present be put together. These are the reasons why *The Guardian*, along with other newspapers, believes that it has a vital future.

Some things changed – others did not. This editorial from *The Scotsman* of June 1973, on a move by Edinburgh District Council to use embargoes to suppress information, expressed a commitment to freedom of information that still resonates today.

We have become accustomed to the naïve critique which blames upon newspapers all the ills of contemporary society simply because they report them. We have come to expect the attempts that are made from various quarters to manipulate the news. Here the only protection resides in well-trained journalists with healthy scepticism and sturdy independence. It is tragic, however, that the democrats themselves appear to be as ignorant as any of the role of the press in a democratic society. Stanley Baldwin spoke for them when he called the press a harlot, enjoying power without responsibility. His descendants are alive and well and living in Edinburgh. Like him, they fail to grasp that the job of the press is not to administer, adjudicate or be responsible; it is to disclose information: no more, no less. This is no petty or unimportant task: it is the very lubricant of our democracy. Yet excessive secrecy is a characteristic of our civil service and our local authorities. We give notice that Edinburgh's embargoes will not be respected by *The Scotsman*.

In his *Observer* column (2002) Arnold looked back at some court appearances and analysed the outcome of the Lockerbie trial.

Once upon a time, with my old friend the lawyer Alistair Bonnington, I appeared in every court in the land, from a police court to the House of Lords by way of the Sheriff Court, the High Court and the Court of Session. I do not have a criminal nature: indeed my friends tell me I am tediously law-abiding. What brought me before the beaks were those hazards of an editor's life: defamation, contempt of court and the Official Secrets Act.

Sometimes the proceedings were slightly scary. Robert Maxwell sued me for £500,000 because of something I said on the Colin Bell Show on Radio Scotland, a sum which deeply impressed my bank manager: the case collapsed at the last minute, to the mortification of the judge, counsel and Pat Chalmers, boss of BBC Scotland, all of whom had been thirsting for battle.

Maxwell was not a vexatious litigant in the usual meaning of the phrase: although he had frequent recourse to law he subordinated it to his own advantage. He was menacing and powerful and used the laws of defamation and libel to silence critics. Against the individual of modest means he mustered an array of legal might that was designed to be intimidating.

In 1986 I implied criticism of his conduct during an industrial dispute with the journalists at the *Daily Record*. Colin asked whether press barons could be regarded as a benign force. My reply was sometimes yes, sometimes no – for example when they showed a disregard for the welfare of their staff.

Maxwell felt the reference was to him. In due course a grubby brown envelope arrived. It announced that he was suing me and the BBC for half a million pounds. Generously, the BBC picked up my personal liability and decided to resist. Eventually the case was settled in some bathos. A simple statement in *The Herald* ended the matter on the eve of the case.

Another case was absurd. Two fellow editors, who had suffered a painful strike in Aberdeen, sued *The Glasgow Herald* because of a diary paragraph reporting that the NUJ had sponsored two poison toads in Edinburgh Zoo, naming them Harry and Dick. I thought they were joking and offered a correction: the creatures in question were frogs, not toads.

The case went to court, causing general hilarity among the lawyers who couldn't believe their luck. One unintended consequence, I believe, was that the zoo thenceforth abandoned such sponsorship schemes.

I remember, too, attending an appeal hearing at the House of Lords and hearing an English judge sneer at the Scottish legal device of a 'caveat'. This instrument is of particular value to editors. For a modest fee it can be lodged at the Court of Session. It ensures no interim interdict can be granted against a party unless it is represented at the hearing. The English judge expressed astonishment, as if it were as remote a concept as the infinity of a circle's circumference or the expansion of the universe. 'Caveat?' he asked, deliberately mispronouncing the word. The unfortunate Scottish QC at the wrong end of the exchange, rather gutlessly I thought, did not correct him, but apologetically explained what it was.

Alistair and I used to joke that our unfulfilled ambition was an appearance before the European Court of Justice, a joke which our financial director considered to be in very bad taste.

But although I am now free of these legal hazards, Alistair has gone on to become a professor of law at Glasgow University, closely observing proceedings at the Lockerbie trial at Camp Zeist.

As Abdelbaset Ali Mohmed al-Megrahi began his sentence in Barlinnie, Alistair told me that he had very little doubt of his guilt. Indeed, in his view, few people who observed proceedings thought otherwise, although unanimity is not universal. An obvious exception is UN observer Professor Hans Köchler, who has called the verdict a 'spectacular miscarriage of justice'. Alistair suspects he has exceeded his brief, which probably was to make sure the proceedings were fair, and has extended it to analysing the judges' logic in a case which all agree is circumstantial.

Though there is no room for complacency; we are right, I think, to take some pride in the normal rules of Scottish criminal procedure. But this was an abnormal case. And even if the judges were correct in their analysis of the evidence and the proceedings impeccably conducted, the format is not really satisfactory. Such a court will always be open to the allegation that it is under political pressure. Lockerbie, and of course September 11, strengthen the case for the international criminal court.

Thoughts on William Roughead from 1992.

One of my prized possessions is a set of books by William Roughead, the classic chronicler of Scottish crime. He wrote or edited the definitive accounts of the trials of Deacon Brodie, Oscar Slater, Burke and Hare, William Porteous and many others.

He was himself a lawyer and historian. He was also an ironist and amused observer of the human condition. He was a writer of such distinction that he does not deserve the obscurity into which he has sunk. He is not mentioned, as far as I can discover, in any of the shorter modern dictionaries of biography.

Life was simpler for Roughead. He wrote his books in a more leisurely age. He was an essayist and historian rather than an investigative reporter. Crime had not become an industry. I thought of him this week when Lord Hope, the Lord President, announced that the supreme courts were to be opened to television cameras though in a tightly regulated way and only after successful experiments.

The cameras will not be allowed to cover criminal trials except for subsequent use in documentaries or similar programmes. Even that will be subject to the agreement of all parties, including the jury. The Judge will have to view and approve the film before it can be screened.

It is a pretty limited advance and re-asserts the judiciary's claim to control the press and live media at points where they impinge on the judicial process – a claim that has been carried to a more extreme point in Scotland than in most comparable jurisdictions.

Television will convey to the public the flavour and pomp of proceedings in some of the supreme courts but not much else. After the novelty wears off it will attract little attention except, perhaps, in appeals involving particularly notorious cases.

Will a modern Roughead emerge in the form of a television producer? Will resources be available to permit a crew to devote their time, as Roughead did, to one crime and follow it through all its judicial stages?

A dramatised documentary, using actors, would probably make

better television but in any case the question of resources is likely to be decisive. There is an underlying problem here which Lord Hope ignores (rightly, for it is not of his making).

The coverage by the media of the Scottish criminal legal system has become patchier than most of us would like. There is now so much crime that coverage of the courts stretches the resources of the media to the point where routine but serious cases may be quite widely ignored.

A small number of staff journalists and freelances cover the Court of Session and the High Court in Edinburgh. Our own Bruce McKain has achieved great distinction in this work but he and his colleagues cannot be everywhere at once.

A lawyer who wishes to avoid press publicity for his client requires only a little cunning to have a fair chance of achieving his purpose. As for the High Court, its sittings have multiplied and it seems permanently on circuit.

Of course there still are cases of exceptional interest to which a news editor can safely commit staff in the knowledge that they will yield copy (the luxury of being omnipresent is not open to him either). The recent acquittal of Paul Ferris *[b1963, former gangster who later became a crime writer]* for the murder of 'Fat Boy' Thompson produced some outstanding reporting, of an old-fashioned kind, from *The Herald*'s Carl Gordon and James Freeman. *[More than 300 witnesses were called in this trial which cost £4 million and was at the time the most expensive in Scottish legal history.]*

Here was the Roughead cocktail: authority, concision, irony and human observation.

It wasn't all hot dispatches from the high court as this piece from August 1994 shows.

The silly season is upon us. At this time of year news editors develop a strong interest in the mating habits of bats or infestations of snakes in the cornfields of eastern Europe.

A survey of the Scottish press of this August week shows that the spirit of recondite inquiry is still with us. The Glorious Twelfth saw much serious concern about the dearth of grouse; the Atlantic salmon has swum more obligingly into the news columns than into the nets of fishermen; and we are indebted to *The Daily Record* for the ghastly news that Marks & Spencer prefer German to British fish fingers.

The search for diversion is not hard to understand. The major foreign news is infinitely depressing. People confronted night after night by images of horror may be left with feelings of impotence or despair. It is not surprising that they should seek escape from so rigorous a diet.

Parliament has risen, and although a few ministers remain active, most have had the good sense to take themselves off to some sunny beach and switch off for a while.

Legal friends will from time to time complain at the lack of press presence at interesting cases, and some have contemplated employing agents to make sure that their efforts are brought to the attention of the hacks. 'Anything interesting on the go?' I asked one of our leading criminal defenders when I bumped into him the other week.

'No,' he replied, 'just a murder in Airdrie.'

Unfair to Airdrie, no doubt: but his reply implied another truth about crime. The more commonplace it becomes, the less newsworthy. When I was a lad, any murder would be destined for the front page, and probably make the lead. Now a low-life murder gets the briefest of mentions. The only cases that command the undivided attention of the media are bourgeois crimes, like the recent Newall case [*army officer Roderick Newall, found guilty of murdering his parents for a £1 million inheritance*], that seem to have come straight from the pages of Ruth Rendell.

Nevertheless, the many freelances now operating in our courts are providing a very useful service and, in the bygoing, some entertaining copy. I enjoyed Sheriff Thomas Croan's warning at Kilmarnock, to a man convicted of breach of the peace, to 'beware the slings and arrows of an outrageous woman' whose behaviour would soon have him back in jail.

And I relished the irony in the report of a case in Oban. One of three men convicted of attacking a policeman had the nickname of 'Slasher'. He claimed this was a reference to his bladder but 'was unable to produce a medical certificate to support this interpretation'. The odd bit of understatement does not go amiss.

Kemp presided over *The Glasgow Herald* when it was said to have 'more columns than the Parthenon'. One was a particular trial to him, as this piece from 1990 shows.

Nothing in *The Glasgow Herald* has given me more trouble than the Jack McLean column. Yet I would not be without it. Indeed, it is my belief that, long after we are gone, people will be reading Jack McLean not as a prophet but as a chronicler of his age.

When people complain about Jack's columns, I tell them that he is a satirist who uses the rhetoric of vituperation in order to achieve comic effects and deflate the pomposities and hypocrisies of the day. But I am also conscious that it is hard for people who have been the objects of his derision to take so Olympian a view. People have been grievously offended by Jack's column, people who themselves are engaged in the hurly-burly of journalism. Jack himself, however, is genuinely surprised when people take his remarks ill. His intention is to ridicule, to send up. He hurts but he is not malicious.

As a writer Jack is original. He went to no school of journalism. Indeed, he was educated at Edinburgh School of Art and then became a teacher. My impression is that his time at the chalkface was not happy and it must have come as a relief to himself and his employers that his translation into journalism slowly grew to the point where he could give up the teaching.

He was discovered when Harry Reid and I were colleagues on *The Scotsman*. We ran his 2,000-word essays in the weekend section there, and they were received with some pleasure in Glasgow. When I became editor of *The Herald* in 1981, and invited Jack to become one of our columnists, his work had a very different impact. In *The Scotsman* it had been like a sermon on a distant hill. Now Jack had entered the drawing rooms of the Glasgow bourgeoisie. Their first reaction was of shock: it was as if a drunk had staggered in through the French windows and had been sick on the carpet.

Slowly the shock wore off and Jack began to be accepted. He has written no more moving column than his tribute to his mother after her death. From that piece I date his acceptance by the family of Herald readers. Not that he will ever be their unanimous favourite. You either love the Urban Voltaire or you hate him. There seems to be no middle ground. You have to hand it to Jack: he dishes it out but he takes it too, for no Herald writer has been more publicly reviled in our letters column.

Once when I was a member of the judging panel for the Scottish press awards, Jack was in contention for the award of columnist of the year. For obvious reasons I fell out of the judging. The rest of the panel was split between those who voted for him enthusiastically and those who would allow him to win only over their dead bodies. So immovable were the opposing camps that the chairman had to break the deadlock with his casting vote. *[Jack won a special commendation and Feature Writer of the Year that year; the award went to another Herald columnist Brain Meek]*.

Jack's political progress has been typical of the age. Of impeccable working-class credentials he has moved progressively away from the Labour politics he inherited. He has slowly become a member of the bourgeoisie. He now even owns a flat, for goodness sake. He has drifted to the right. Some of his views seem to me to be positively conservative.

Yet he is uneasy with his bourgeois fate. His lifestyle may have changed but his class loyalty remains strong. He has evoked very vividly his own progression through the shifting strata of Margaret Thatcher's Britain and Pat Lally's Glasgow. What gives his work its merit is his clear eye, his refusal to be impressed by convention and authority, his honesty about himself and his disrespect for mere politeness. He has the capacity to voice what many people often think but rarely dare say. He has the courage to be wrong.

As editors we face problems with Jack's copy. Sometimes he pushes the limits. Sometimes we excise passages that will try the readers' patience too far. There is after all no victory in making someone turn the page in a spirit of rejection. Sometimes, we think, Jack puts in things for us to take out. Yet there is a limit for us too. We cannot take too much out or else we will destroy the very qualities that make Jack's writing what it is – the keen eye, the descriptive prose, the cadences of demotic speech which he so faithfully expresses. Jack does not invent the forceful language of the street but his prose is redolent of it, together with a strongly ornate quality which I can only describe as Edwardian.

Some people thought that Jack himself vaingloriously adopted the title of 'The Urban Voltaire'. The truth is that Harry and I invented the name in our Scotsman days and it has stuck. It was inspired by the Thurber short story about the Rustic Voltaire, a man who sat on a cracker barrel in a country store and had the answers to everything. Jack's omniscience is sometimes breathtaking but it is blessed by a sense of the ridiculous, not least about himself.

In an appreciation after Kemp died, McLean wrote:

Sartorially, he was shambolic. I once wrote that he was the only man in Britain who bought an incredibly expensive Chester Barrie suit and then paid three tramps to sleep in it for a fortnight. He sometimes got his hair cut. The inside of his head was a bit long-haired as well, and somehow cavalier: he was not a Roundhead in politics or personality.

It was Arnold, along with his lifelong friend and colleague, Harry Reid, who first titled me the Urban Voltaire. I am indeed urban, but not urbane, and I am not a Voltaire, and Arnold knew it. He delighted in irony.

Myself, I am in some distress, for I expected him to live long. My memories, and that of everybody else who knew this most gentlemanly of editors, writers, and citizens of his country, will live long enough. Tears in the Press Bar tonight and a toast to him to boot.

A role in a television advert for *The Herald* in the eighties brought Kemp a moment of fame.

If you are seen on the box, you somehow exist in a way that you did not do before. A few years ago my commercial masters made an advertisement in which some of *The Herald* journalists appeared and I was required to thump the table and say, 'Let's run it!', which I did in a hammy way.

While that advertisement ran, people gave me knowing looks in shops, or stared at me in the street (or so I imagined).

At such times ordinary mortals can get an inkling of what it must be like to be truly famous. It is a curious thing, fame: people hunger for it but it can destroy their privacy and their lives. Arthur Miller, in his autobiography *Time Bends* wrote movingly of the insecurities of fame undermining his marriage with Marilyn Monroe. The punter who watches from the gallery, or peruses his tabloid, gives fame but he takes away happiness.

The public memory, however, is short, and as soon as the ads stopped I was allowed to resume anonymity. The brevity of such celebrity explains the chronic insecurity of those who must make their living on screen or stage. They cannot be content with Andy Warhol's allocation of 15 minutes' fame to everyone.

Your friends and acquaintances may be impressed by a TV appearance and in some odd way think it proves and enhances your existence. But they also have a way of cutting you down to size should you make the mistake of contemplating your own performance with satisfaction.

Many moons ago I made my TV debut in the unlikely capacity of anchor for a series of religious broadcasts. After the first broadcast one Sunday evening at tea-time, I went down to the composing room of the paper for which I worked, that glorious, smelly, noisy, inky old crucible where journalism was turned into hot metal and the Linotypes whirred, sighed, and clicked.

An upmaker approached me. He had seen me on TV, he said. Oh, I replied, waiting for the inevitable compliment. 'Ay,' he continued. 'I was having my tea and the sound was turned down on the telly. I looked up and said to the wife, I know that bloke. You were wearing that green suit I've sometimes seen you in down here, and so I knew that the TV colour wasn't right. I fiddled around with it for ages but, ach, I couldn't get it right. So I just switched it off.'

Whether this was a criticism of the suit or my TV performance I was not sure; but I concluded that it was a justifiable attack on both. The chief embarrassment of that series was that people thought me a man of intense religious feeling; when I told them I was not, there would be a pause, and then a sniff implying a certain hypocrisy on my part. Mercifully my engagement was ended by a 'Dear John' letter whose true nature I did not at first recognise because of the extravagance of the compliments it contained.

That's showbiz, and it is a cruel business at that. But I have to say that our local broadcasters [BBC Scotland and STV], are invariably polite and considerate. Yet there is a certain television type who may make a number of condescending and irritating assumptions and relay them through a snooty secretary who sounds as if she has briefly left her ancestral estate to go slumming.

First, you will drop everything for the singular honour of appearing on screen; secondly, you won't mind hanging interminably about the waiting room until their lords and ladyships are ready for you; thirdly, once you are in the studio you are an object to be shoved around until the magic moment for your reanimation arrives. The assumption, in short, is that nothing else in your life has mattered beside this moment in the sunshine of TV.

But I should not cavil too much about television. I have spent many a happy hour chewing the fat in the hospitality suite. It is in the hospitality suite, in vino veritas, that the true egotism of the presenter-type may emerge. Once I took part in a political discussion where I found myself, rather to my surprise, defending the government against some otherwise unanimous attack on it from the fellow guests.

Perversity, I suppose, or simply a desire to stick up for the underdog.

The presenter, a well-known figure who had made a good job of concealing his right-wing prejudices on screen, supped his wine and grew expansive. 'Thank you,' he said portentously as if he were the head of the civil service itself, 'for what you have done for the state.' Think nothing of it, I replied, and disappeared back into obscurity.

In a lecture at Glasgow University in 1996, Kemp looked back and forward over the past and future of Scottish newspapers in a changing technological and economic climate.

The information industry is growing at an amazing rate worldwide. This is a fact that is beginning to reach into every household. How many of us now, if we wake in the wee small hours, will creep to the keyboard to tap our way into the throbbing electronic world without frontiers?

I cannot claim to be a surfer on the internet. I am a somewhat hesitant and timorous inhabitant of cyberspace, living in a little corner of the worldwide web. But I am aware of the enormous possibilities that have been opened up for the rapid exchange of information and images across the world. I am aware that every household, one of these days, will have access to the information and entertainment superhighway and will be able to transact much business without leaving the keyboard. I am aware too that this enormous technological leap forward is not necessarily accompanied by a similar increase in the sum of human wisdom. I may be able to communicate with people all over the world. But have I anything interesting to tell them?

My contributions to international enlightenment so far, have been confined to advising someone in Los Angeles about haggis: what goes into it and how to cook it.

Information seems as infinite as the universe. But infinity is incomprehensible and information is of no use to anyone unless it is organised and synthesised. A newspaper does precisely that: a newspaper is the selection and organisation of information into a user-friendly format. And since no newspaper can be all things to all men, the press is, and should be, varied: it should reflect the mosaic of human needs, interests, aspirations and abilities. Each newspaper has an agenda and that agenda is derived from the political and cultural agenda of the country or the locality in which it operates.

In more than 35 years in journalism, mostly in Scotland, I have lived through profound changes in the press, in its ownership and the environment in which it works. These changes have in the last few years gathered pace. The rapid development in information technology has destroyed the role of the press as a primary source of news, except as a messenger of scandal or disruptive revelation or as a purveyor of what might be called niche news, for example local news.

Secondly, the commercial pressure on newspapers to maximize the returns of the business have increased to an intensity which may not always be compatible with the public interest.

The period after the war saw the end of Scottish ownership of our two main important newspapers, *The Glasgow Herald* and *The Scotsman*. The latter was the first to go, the casualty of proprietorial incompetence. Lord Fraser saved *The Herald* from Lord Thomson and earned our everlasting gratitude by preserving two serious papers in Scotland. Thomson would have combined them into one and the evidence from newspaper mergers elsewhere is not encouraging. There is always a net loss of readership and editorial resource. It is too much to say that Lord Fraser's son then lost *The Herald* at the roulette table to Tiny Rowland; but it is uncomfortably near the truth.

The end of this period saw the retreat of the *Scottish Daily Express* and the *Scottish Daily Mail* from Glasgow and Edinburgh respectively. Older people will remember their dominance. Lord Beaverbrook lavished resources on *The Scottish Daily Express* of which he was immensely fond, with a complete contempt for the canons of profitability. But this period saw the decline of the philanthropic proprietor, like Lord Beaverbrook, content to tolerate a host of inefficiencies and to suppress profits because his primary interests and motive were not commercial. The Scottish editions closed and in their absence the indigenous papers, notably the *Daily Record*, *The Herald*, and *The Scotsman* were able to increase and consolidate their circulations at hitherto unimaginable levels.

The next period was characterised by industrial wars. Many people will remember the painful scenes at Wapping when Rupert Murdoch smashed the print unions. A decisive element in his victory was the disillusion felt by many journalists after years of being messed about by printers. Many crossed the picket lines. His victory was also made possible by changes in the industrial law and the committed support of the government in the shape of the Metropolitan Police. As a result, new technology was rapidly introduced through the British press and although journalists were given an increasingly important role in the production function the collective power of this and other key groups was undermined.

The proprietorial interest reacquired the right to manage without consulting the workforce. As in the rest of industry, there was an erosion of employment rights.

For the Scottish press, a much fiercer competitive environment emerged. This affected both newspaper sales and advertising revenue. London newspapers renewed their interest in the Scottish market, which in UK terms, they under-penetrated. They were able to do so at marginal expense. It cost much less to 'put a kilt' on a London newspaper with relatively few staff in Scotland than to publish a Scottish newspaper from start to finish. The Scottish newspaper found itself, for the first time, in a similar position to the independent retailers threatened by chain stores in the years after the war.

Above all these developments towered the figure of Rupert Murdoch. He revolutionised the industry by his victory at Wapping, but that was only the start. The Broadcasting Act of 1990 conferred on him a singular and significant advantage. The limits on the stake UK newspaper proprietors could have in television companies did not apply to him. Ostensibly this was because Sky used a satellite not within British jurisdiction but cynics were not slow to point out the close relationship between Murdoch and the Thatcher administration.

Murdoch's gamble in satellite television brought his companies to the brink of insolvency. It has to be said of Murdoch that he has shown courage and judgement. That does not mean that the consequences of his actions have always been beneficial.

The gamble eventually paid off and Sky moved into profit with profound consequences for the British press. Murdoch was able to cut the cover price of *The Times* and *The Sun*. This brought to the quality broadsheet sector something which it had never known, certainly not in my time; a price war. This made the battle for a declining market all the more costly and intense.

For the Scottish press, the price war has been an irritant rather than a disaster. There is still quite lively cultural resistance to London titles. But even though most of the Scottish papers have not cut their prices in nominal terms, they have been unable to increase them in line with inflation. At the same time their blue chip advertising revenues have come under threat from new competitors. For instance, solicitors in the Scottish cities, themselves under fierce competitive pressure from estate agents, have developed new ways of advertising properties so that this revenue stream is retained and not passed to the press. The emergence of new forms of advertising in the electronic media must be a source of serious concern to the Scottish publishing houses.

The effect of all this turmoil on the serious press has been the trivialisation of its agenda and the development of a prurience hitherto unknown in this section of the market.

There are a number of factors at work here, some of them quite puzzling. It is passing strange that in an age where divorce and single parenthood are common, where secular values are dominant, the press should have become obsessed by the private moral conduct of members of the royal family and the political classes. Is it the symptom or the cause of disillusionment with the establishment and the political system? What we can say with certainty is that it is commercially driven. Such stories sell newspapers.

The prurience of the popular press is no new phenomenon. The Matrimonial Proceedings Act was introduced in the 1920s to restrict the coverage of divorce hearings, such was the gusto with which the papers reported the salacious evidence. What is new, I think, is the relationship that has developed between the tabloids and the so-called serious media. A tabloid breaks a story of sleaze, perhaps by unscrupulous means, for example electronic eavesdropping or pandering to a blackmailer. Once the cat is out of the bag, however, the serious press makes just as much sport with it. In its po-faced discussions it spares the reader few of the juicier details. The tabloids do the deed but the qualities share in the proceeds. Not only the serious press pick up the story – but also the BBC and ITV. So the tabloids have become the slightly squalid gumshoes of the political system. They feed off resentment and jealousy and the desire for revenge. The modern blackmailer no longer needs to dun his victim for money; the press may pay him instead.

When I was editor of *The Herald*, I made a protest against hypocrisy of this kind by refusing to regurgitate next day a smear story about a local political figure *[lawyer Ross Harper]*. It turned out to be a futile gesture, for when he resigned office it became news anyway. And that is the point worth noting; the sleaze stories produced by the tabloid press produce a political reaction.

The respected American journalist Aubrey Lewis wrote in *The New York Times*: 'Humbug is alive and well in the British press ... An oily mixture of titillation and self-righteousness ... What is different these days is the extent to which the full-size papers have descended to the slimy and the sensational.'

Rupert Murdoch, continued Lewis, 'the dominant newspaper proprietor ... appears to have no interest in old-fashioned journalistic values. Thus when the Chinese government objected to BBC news broadcasts, Murdoch cut the BBC World Service off his STAR TV covering China.'

Lewis's conclusion was depressing: 'The prospect is for an increasingly nasty, irresponsible British press.'

When politicians argue for a new privacy law they are apt to claim they are doing so on behalf of the small man who has no redress against the media. But the drive for new restraints has not come from the public at large. On the contrary, it has come from members of the Establishment and the political class who are the most spectacular victims of what I might call 'the new voyeurism'.

It is worth remembering, before we rush to place new restraints on the press, that newspapers in this country have no entrenched rights. They have no more rights, in the eyes of the law, than any citizen. Already they operate under many restraints. The laws of contempt of court have been interpreted with particular strictness by the Scottish courts, making the journalistic investigation of crime very difficult. The laws of defamation can be a fearsome instrument in the hands of a rich man, as the life of the late Robert Maxwell reminds us. He used libel writs as a blunt instrument with which to silence his critics. The defamation suit is almost completely useless for the small man, since legal aid does not apply to it. The enormous legal costs turn a libel action into a game of Russian roulette, particularly in the English courts where such cases are heard by juries. I have always agreed with Alan Watkins' [*political journalist, died 2010*] view that it would be a good idea to have a fast-track procedure with limited awards, so that the small citizen could get satisfaction if he were treated unfairly.

Generally, however, I think there is no case for further regulation of the press, particularly the Scottish press. Perhaps because it is nearer to its audience, it has a relatively good record in terms both of its general veracity and credibility and of its conduct. But the most powerful argument against regulation is this: a free press capable of investigating the public conduct of those who exercise power is an essential part of democratic life. You will note that I refer to public conduct, by which I mean conduct relating to the exercise of power and authority, I reject the role of the press as some kind of moral policeman. Indeed the very idea is laughable.

The question of the press's ethical standards is inseparable from that of its ownership and unfair competitive forces have put the serious press under severe stress.

Where does that leave the Scottish press? The answer depends on whether it aspires to a quasi-national or merely local role. The first is demanding in terms of resources – requiring extensive political reporting and international coverage; and the second is a much cheaper option. In my time three daily papers – *The Herald, The Scotsman* and *The Daily Record* – could be said to be national. They circulate through the country and deal with national Scottish issues. A local role would have considerable economic consequences for the Scottish papers. It would imply modest aspirations and a low cover price. The national role is more ambitious and much more difficult. It implies greater editorial resources to justify a premium price. It means having the capital resources to develop, perhaps in the electronic media, new revenue sources to replace the old. It is the more demanding option – but it is the only one worth having. If we do not fight to preserve it, then the bleak conclusion for any serious Scottish journalist who wants to deal with the central policy issues of his time will be that he cannot do this in his own country.

I have spent most of my career in the Scottish papers. The editors I worked for were determined to resist this kind of marginalisation and they had to work hard to convince the proprietorial influence that this ethical component in their papers' lives had to be paid for. On the whole this commitment was given, if not always gladly, just as the readers of the serious papers have mostly stayed loyal. In the years ahead the prospect is that their loyalty will continue to be tested by premium pricing.

Perhaps it is too much to expect proprietors to share this ethical stance. We have no more Beaverbrooks and the proprietors now are men whose chief responsibility is the stewardship of other people's money or the satisfaction of the city commentators' expectations. They cannot reasonably be expected to hazard money on the principled support of a national Scottish press. For this reason, competition within Scotland between *The Herald* and *The Scotsman* is cru-

cial to the health of our Scottish national press because it forces proprietors to release resources. Had there been only one title as Lord
Thomson wished, then proprietors would have been able to ratio-
nalise, consolidate and withdraw. Study of evening paper mergers
makes the point.

Yet unless its revenues are sustained, a serious Scottish press cannot
exist. It is not the least of the jeopardies into which the confused regula-
tory environment has thrown us that the Scottish interest is never mentioned by the government in its considerations of the public interest.

This dilemma is not unique. It will exist in any small country
sharing the same language with a more powerful neighbour. The
Irish press faces similar problems and has to charge a premium price
that makes our own look modest. The Irish press is sustained by a
readership which accepts that a national press is an indispensable
part of nationhood.

Sometimes I have a dream that the serious Scottish papers will
not be driven along primarily by the needs of profitability. I dream
that perhaps they might be administered by trusts of the kind that
run *The Guardian* and *The Irish Times*. The ethics of these institutions are not to ignore the imperative of profitability and efficiency;
they cannot be ignored. But shareholders do not take first place in
the scheme of things; that primacy is given to the newspapers themselves. That, I think, is as it should be.

3.1
Europe: The East

AN IRON CURTAIN DIVIDED EUROPE for 40 years after the Second World War. But in 1989, the Berlin Wall was peacefully toppled and in 1991, the Soviet Union was dissolved. Kemp personalised these momentous changes for his readers by writing about the friendships he formed across the barrier. As the Cold War ended, he took pleasure in visiting the great European cities that had been hidden for most of his life behind its impenetrable folds.

A *Herald* column from 1991:

Dr Johnson said a man should keep his friendship in constant repair, but some can survive prolonged neglect. About 35 years ago a shaft of sunlight fell across our lives in the person of Stas (pronounced Stash). This week, after many years, it shone again.

Stas is Polish and in the late 1950s was, like me, a student at Edinburgh University. He arrived at our house in Edinburgh by a circuitous route. He had escaped from Poland and its totalitarianism, and made his way to Paris. There he had been befriended by Darsie and Cecilia Gillie.

The late Darsie Gillie, by then the Paris correspondent of *The Manchester Guardian*, had been the British news editor of the BBC's French section in 1940. It was through my father's friendship with the Gillies that Stas came to us in Edinburgh. He adopted the Gillies as parents and us as friends. He breezed into our family, carrying with him a cheerfulness and animation which made him an always-welcome guest.

I can see him yet, sitting in our sunlit garden beside the Water of Leith with his bushy blond hair and his infectious laughter. He was hostile to the Russians and disliked team games, smacking as they did of totalitarian demands for collective discipline.

What he studied at university I can't recall. I would see him in the distance in the Old Quad always with a woman in tow of an elegance and sophistication that I, as an immature 17-year-old, found slightly intimidating but exceedingly impressive.

Thereafter I caught glimpses of him in London in the 1960s. Once we spent an interesting evening together in an illegal roulette house in Notting Hill, run by a fellow Pole.

He never disappeared entirely from view and was a chatty if intermittent correspondent. He got into journalism in Montreal, ran a
flea market then emerged as the proprietor of the city's finest Polish
restaurant.

I came to hear the details of Stas's escape from Poland just before
Christmas 1990, at a house party near Loch Lomond, I met Ian
Harrison the brother of Ronald Harrison [sons of the ship-owner and
art collector Ion Harrison, patron of the Scottish Colourists] who had,
with a group of others, encountered Stas in Warsaw in the late
1950s. The idea of smuggling him out came to them quite sponta-
neously, as they were preparing to say farewell. Without too much
thought for the dangers, they hid him in the rack of their train compartment. The border guards were fooled. The casual insouciance of
it all still takes your breath away but given the sunny optimism of
Stas's personality it is not all that surprising.

Stas also featured in Kemp's father, Robert's Saturday column in *The Herald*,
in 1961. This piece gives a sense of the exhausting effect the war had had on
men like Robert and shows how ready many of his generation were to stand
aside and let youth have its day, as the 1960s began.

Of the many tragedies of modern times, the most intolerable are
those that continue from day to day in a living man. I cannot forget
the Polish soldier, a professional man called to the colours in 1939,
who had lost wife and family without even knowing how they had
met their end. Those who are uprooted from the farms and villages
of home and herded into camps for displaced persons seem to be
among the most miserable of our century, a perpetual reproach to
the inhumanity of some, the impotence of others, and the sheer
indifference of most of us.

Even in so dark a picture there sometimes appears a tiny candle of
light. In my case it is borne high aloft by a young Polish friend, who is
always good enough to visit us when he is near. Let me call him Paul,
for older members of his family remain behind the Iron Curtain.

Paul entered our lives by a curious and devious route. His parents
had been abroad before and during the war, when he was a boy, so
that to his native language was added a very fluent, inaccurate and
cosmopolitan brand of English.

Paul's formal education had been totally neglected. Even after his
family returned to Poland, during the amnesty, he made it a point of

honour to avoid education at the hands of the communists, with the first hour of every day devoted to Marx and Lenin, and constant indoctrination at points thereafter. The compulsory Russian he refused to learn although after he came to this country he did so, in order to gain some certificate or other.

But I anticipate. Safely out of the east he headed for Paris and some friends of his father, who were also friends of mine. They thought that he could catch up with his education in Scotland, and passed him on to me.

It was obvious that Paul's first need was to introduce some grammar and correct pronunciation into his turbulent Slavonic English. To this end, he used to come to me on Sunday afternoons, when we struggled together though an English grammar specifically designed for foreign students. I don't know how much he learned from this but it taught me humility. Seen from the outside as it were, English does seem one of the most lunatic languages imaginable. That much he forced me to admit.

I am devoted to this independent, adventurous, spirited young man, who seem to proclaim that youth has kept its soul and may yet triumph. But we never finished our book. After about seven chapters, Paul discovered some convincing reason why he would be unable to come on Sunday afternoon. I realised that I, as a teacher of English at least, had 'got a sack'.

Kemp updated Herald readers on Stas's progress in 1992.

After the end of the cold war Stas returned frequently to Poland to visit his in-laws. He and his wife found that no restaurants offered really good food and service and resolved to fill the gap.

They took over a rundown cafe, 'or rather a cockroach farm', and after 10 weeks of renovations reopened the Café Eulat. The sub-tenancy of the Polish-Israeli Friendship Society, it had an Israeli name.

In no time at all Stas was being denounced by the neighbours as a Jew from Paris (where he previously lived) who did not even speak good Polish. They complained to the health authorities and police that the restaurant was frying herrings, cooking garlic and onions and playing the piano 24 hours a day.

Eulat does not serve herring. Nor does it have a piano.

The Eulat, in 'embassy row', quickly found favour. The next problem was that, observing its success, the landlords proposed to increase the rent by 140%. Stas threw a spectacular tantrum and threatened to take his business elsewhere.

The landlords thought he was bluffing. But within a week he had reached agreement with the Actors' Club next door, once a fairly exclusive club for thespians, writers, journalists and artists but now a 'disastrous' restaurant. The landlords dropped their demands; but Stas found himself stuck with two establishments, one seating 70, the other about 120.

Next door had been a 'bugs' paradise', kept in business by regular bribes to the health authorities. Stas renovated and reopened. The bribes stopped; he sensed that the authorities might have then closed it down had it not been instantly popular with ministers, generals, writers and journalists.

At the time of writing Stas was organising the club's New Year's Eve ball. He also hoped to do the food for 500 guests at a new American-owned disco. He and his growing family are renting an apartment. The rent is four times the average wage but is regarded as a good deal. He reckons you could have a mansion on the outskirts of Paris for the same price.

As ever, Stas is unquenchably cheerful. Yet between the lines of his letter you sense the difficulties that have led to the political defeat of the economic reformers in Yeltsin's government. The new economy deals in hard currency and its light bathes only a few; in the darkness beyond remains a sullen population disenchanted by what the reforms have meant for it.

Here is the breeding ground of xenophobic nationalism and fascism. The illusion, irresponsibly peddled by some western politicians, that democracy is synonymous with prosperity, is long gone. The Chinese are demonstrating that economic success, for the moment at least, is not incompatible with totalitarian socialism. Democracy's merits are as much ethical as economic; better to live, as my mother used to say, in a poor country and a free one.

The reforms are going to take much longer than anyone thought. The leadership has changed but old communists are still everywhere in the administration. They watch, and wait.

In 2012, Stas was well and living in Warsaw, where he had set up the Radio Café, a co-operative, with former employees of Radio Free Poland.

Here Kemp sniffs the air of West Berlin a few months before the wall came down in 1989.

It is a curious experience to sit on a sunny bench in this city – Europe's supreme memorial to political failure – and read a series of essays on the unexpressed rights and will of the Scottish people.

Berlin is a terrible warning to all who do not count their blessings. If Scotland is the forgotten partner in the UK then how much more powerful must be the suppressed feelings of a great nation sterilized by formal political division.

From my hotel window I can see the ruined Gedachtniskirche which stands like a broken tooth in the centre of West Berlin to remind the fat, the prosperous and the complacent of the terrible consequences of the collapse of democratic consent.

Over the wall the eastern sector has been tarted up with signs of commerce that seem to be window dressing in both the literal and figurative senses. The economic divide remains so marked that the wall's immediate removal would unleash an unmanageable wave of emigration to the west. The East German leadership remains very hostile to perestroika.

Yet small nations have their rights too. The fact that a nation is not oppressed, that it enjoys the rule of law and that its citizens have freedom of movement, does not mean that it must yield the right of small countries to self-determination. Indeed, Berlin is a monument to the folly of crushing minority voices.

Kemp was one of the first Western journalists allowed by the Soviets to visit Georgia after the onset of nationalist unrest and a rail blockade in 1990.

Tbilisi: In search of its place in the sun.

It is a fine evening. Outside the headquarters of the Georgian Soviet authorities, near the spot where 20 people were killed in April 1989, when nerve gas was used on demonstrators, a crowd of about 100 has gathered. They have come not to demonstrate, although they are in favour of an independent Georgia, but rather to debate, exchange gossip and garner what little information there is. Although 240km to the north a couple of hundred trains and more than 2,000 passengers are reported to be stranded, blockaded by nationalists camping on the line, there is very little reliable information to be had.

Rumours are snapped up voraciously: the authorities are threatening to use force, workers at the Rustavi steel works are on strike, the train blockade will develop into a general strike, the authorities are escalating the crisis to give them an excuse to send in the troops. Small groups of debaters form and re-form. We are quickly caught up in one of them. On hearing that I am Scottish a few gather round me to try their halting English. Glasgow Rangers, says one. Another tells me he is a neuro-scientist. He has heard that Scotland has a great love of freedom. Do I think that Georgia has a European culture?

Yes, I reply, Tbilisi, with its tree-lined streets, its terracotta roofs, its sandy hills covered with scrub, reminds me of the Mediterranean. The people are passionate and Italianate. We think of the typical Georgian face and we think of its infamous son: Stalin of the broad brow, the dark looks, the moustache, the heavy jowls. But there is a great variety here – faces that are Semitic, faces with a touch of the Orient, tough and humorous faces that you could find in Scotland.

Monumental statuary gives Tbilisi the authentic stamp of a communist town. Lenin is the last Soviet icon: all the others have been discredited by perestroika, except in the eyes of the hardliners, 'flat-earthers' as they are scornfully known. Lenin still towers over streets innocent of advertising, sterile in their lack of commerce.

For men and women gathering in the evening sunshine, the communists are little less than quislings. Their demand is for full parliamentary democracy and free elections now. How long, asks the scientist wistfully, will it be before we can match your better standard of life? He answers the question himself: about 20 years. Another man says impatiently: We are sick and tired of communism. He draws his finger across his throat as if to cut it. We want our own money in our own pockets, he says. No, we are not afraid of the tanks.

Outside an art gallery, on the opposite side of the road from the government building, a group of widows holds vigil. Around the balustrades are hung about 40 portraits of young men and women, victims of crimes or accidents whose perpetrators have not been brought to justice.

Will you write about Georgia? asks a tall man with a long, sensitive face. He has been hovering at the edge of our group. Yes, I say. Thank you, he replies simply ...

As I write these words I hear of Ian Gow's [Conservative MP for Eastbourne] murder by the IRA. Nationalist terrorism could be the road Georgia takes too, because its tradition of gangsterism means the country is full of weapons. Nationalist brigades are said to be arming. The communists prevaricate, but time is running out for them. Free elections would sweep them away because only the gun keeps them in power. Surely the cold repression of Stalinism cannot return and Georgia can find its place in the sun at last.

Back in Scotland, Kemp continued to ponder the future of Georgia and other former Soviet countries. A column from 1992 on an article by Donald Rayfield in the *Scottish Slavonic Review*.

That Lavrenty Beria was a monster is well enough known, though the full extent of his activities is still dimly understood. Apart from developing state terror as an instrument of policy, he killed and tortured personally, for the pleasure of it. He became Stalin's secret police chief. When the Soviet Union finally acknowledged its responsibility for the Katyn Massacre of 1943 – when more or less the entire Polish officer squad was wiped out by the Soviet secret police – it named Beria as the guilty man, though his recommendation was countersigned by Stalin and others.

Stalin came to suspect him and towards the end of his life was moving against him to curtail his immense power. Beria is thought to have engineered Stalin's death in 1953. Beria then plotted to seize supreme power but was himself denounced and executed later that same year.

Beria, writes Rayfield, was fascinated by the arts and particularly by artists and writers. From 1927, when he won a dominant position in the Georgian Cheka, he built up dossiers on all the leading figures in literary groups, in the conservatoire and the university, targeting most for destruction. His work culminated in the mass denunciations, arrests, torture and executions of 1937.

The blow fell in May 1937 when Beria made his report to the party. A long survey of politics and economics ended with a cultural review. 'The list of works published or aborted was very like that of citrus and tea bushes planted or uprooted, coalfields exploited or abandoned.'

A member of the writers' union was entrusted by Beria with task of pursuing the unfortunates. All the writers mentioned in his speech were made to attend sessions where they incriminated themselves and others.

During one session a poet suddenly pulled out a hunting gun and shot himself. On December 10 the proceedings were over: a quarter of the writers were slaughtered. A year later Beria went to Moscow. There, concludes Rayfield with characteristic sarcasm, he found his workload 'enormous'.

It is an appalling episode even in the context of an appalling career. Yet are we doing enough to help prevent a relapse into so terrible a tradition? The other week I listened to a talk given by Tauno Tiusanen, professor of economics in the Institute of Soviet and Eastern Studies at Glasgow University. I must say I left feeling as if I had strayed into one of Ibsen's less cheery dramas. This year because of scheduled debt payments, the professor pointed out, the West proposed to exact a net capital transfer from East Europe and the former Soviet Union. 'This is catastrophe,' he said with a gloom that seemed entirely justified. History may prove that only Hungary, the Czech and Slovak Republics and Poland have managed a decisive break with the old empire. If Russia relapses into autocracy then we in the West will carry some of the guilt.

The economic meltdown of the former Soviet Union had all kinds of effects. Kemp noted one in a piece entitled: 'A Moscow spirit of free enterprise', in 1990.

Ah, said a friend. You are staying in the Rossia. You will have no trouble with prostitutes because there is no bar there.

The Rossia, a great factory of a hotel near the Kremlin, is one of the most charmless I have ever encountered. It has thousands of rooms. Its corridors run for hundreds of yards. Floor ladies, some pleasant, some dragon-like, preside at intervals. When you leave your room they exchange your key for a hotel card without which you are naked.

At either end of the hotel, on alternate floors, there are cafés at which you can buy meals of a kind, if you are lucky. They have a habit of closing just when you are hungry. But there is no bar and the notorious Moscow prostitutes leave you alone. Oh yes? At about 11.30pm on the second night of my visit, the telephone rang. 'This is Maria from Georgia. Shall I come to you?' When I expressed the wish to be alone, she sounded most surprised – a characteristic, I was told, of Russian prostitutes – and asked 'why?'.

There was no answer to that and I hung up. But it was only the start of a long campaign, the persistence of which would have done credit to any door-to-door salesman. There was a knock at the door. Outside were two girls – one short and dark (presumably Maria from

Georgia) and a tall blonde.

Both were very pretty but I closed the door and returned to my book. The phone was to ring at intervals throughout the next two nights. The last call came at 6.30am on my last day and the air of injured surprise was there to the last.

Friends told me that members of the staff, perhaps the floor ladies, sold lists of unaccompanied men to the girls who then tried to set up their assignations by telephone. The spirit of enterprise may be rare in the Soviet Union but Moscow's ladies of the night cannot be said to lack it.

In its impersonality and authoritarian air, the Rossia represents all that is worst in the Russian hotel. But I have to report that, on my first morning, and before I had had time to acquire roubles, I ordered breakfast in the café. I offered my hotel card, hoping to put the amount on the bill. This was unacceptable indicated the rather stern woman behind the counter. Suddenly an unexpected smile crossed her face and she allowed me to take the food. That morning, I ate for nothing. In Russia, they say, you won't starve because somebody will always feed you. That is the Russian way.

Moscow friendships, glasnost candour and communism on the wane in 1991.

This week I heard from my friend Dmitry in Moscow. Dmitry worked for Novosti, the Soviet equivalent of our Central Office of Information (COI). It disseminated official news about the Soviet Union, with branches in London, Paris, New York and arranged visits to the Soviet Union for foreign journalists. In the bad old days it carried its complement of KGB stooges. One was expelled from London only two years ago.

But by the time I visited Moscow, Estonia and Georgia last year under its auspices, glasnost had more or less eliminated the KGB influence and quite astounding frankness was the order of the day. Much more frankness, indeed, than you might expect from our COI. At the time Dmitry, with his excellent English, intimate knowledge of Soviet politics and sense of irony was an invaluable source of understanding about often puzzling events and tendencies.

On the final Sunday of my tour Dmitry, my guide Nikolai and their delightful wives took me for a typical Russian day out – a visit to one of those pre-revolutionary palaces which are so lovingly preserved and a walk in its extensive grounds. We rounded it off with a lavish meal in one of the then fairly new co-operative restaurants. We dined well that afternoon, with Russian champagne and Moldavian wine, and as I weaved back to the hotel by metro I was reminded of the great kindness of the ordinary Russian: several came forward to guide me through the correct turnstiles.

Even then the daily business of living was becoming exhausting. Masha, Dmitry's wife, spent most of her day queuing and hunting for the wherewithal of life. Dmitry, too, was expected constantly to be on the alert for food. As in fishing, there was an art in knowing when and how to strike. At the first rumour of a delivery, a queue would form. The summer at the dacha was spent bottling and preserving and their great anxiety was the deficient diet on which their little daughter Anastasia was being raised.

Inflation is steadily destroying the rouble. Dmitry's salary at Novosti was 600 roubles. The rate of exchange is now 40 roubles to the US dollar, which means that he would be expected to support his family on the equivalent of $15 a month. Goods are available in the free markets but at prices beyond the means of those on such salaries.

There have been reports of the wholesale collapse of the rouble, with barter developing as the basic means of exchange. The governor of the Bank of England has warned that hyperinflation is now a real and immediate threat in Russia. Dmitry and Nikolai must try to earn hard currency, but it is not easy.

Nikolai told me that in Russia you will never starve because people will always help you. Everybody relies on personal connections. You know a man who can get meat, or a doorman who will let you buy food in the hotel restaurant normally designated for foreign or out-of-town guests.

In our hotel I watched ordinary Russians hold up the queue while they loaded their bags with cheese, sausages and tomatoes. The best welfare system Russians can hope for is their family and friends. They share what they have. Masha and Anastasia are spending much of their time visiting friends and relatives. Despite his difficulties, Dmitry's latest fax is cheerful, even perky in tone. 'All is basically OK at this end apart from the remaining economic difficulties many of us are going through.

'Still, we are optimistic and full of hopes that we will find a way out of the situation. When answering to this fax please write a few words about your life and what are your plans for the future.'

His interest in us in the fat west touches me. I hope this gifted and charming man can make a new career in free-market Russia. His fear, and that of his friends, is that they will be a lost generation, caught between the frozen certainties of communism and the still unformed opportunities of a new economic order.

Hard times in Budapest for the secret policeman. From 1992:

It is a sunny spring afternoon in Buda. At the British Embassy they are giving a tea party. The guests are ushered through the magnificent old mansion, dating from the great days of the Austro-Hungarian empire. They admire the circular marble staircase and the Bluthner grand piano.

They gather outside on the patio where the ambassador's wife, who has injured her ankle, reclines in a chair to receive them. Beyond the balustrade the garden, lined by chestnut trees and bounded by a row of poplars, descends to a croquet lawn. Off to the right a hose plays water on the rose garden and signs of construction confirm that the British taxpayer is investing in a swimming pool.

Over the garden wall Buda falls away to the Danube and, beyond it, Pest: more mansions, more poplars and chestnut trees, the plonk of tennis balls. We could be in France, except for the very English spread on the patio.

There is a silver tea service, cucumber sandwiches, cakes, pastries, strawberries. The guests, as they engage in that restrained and cautious social intercourse which distinguishes English from more boisterous Scottish parties, eye the fare with anticipation.

A butler in a white coat moves between the house and table, carrying bits and pieces in penny numbers. He is a tall and impressive man with the sad look that is the natural expression of most Hungarian faces in repose.

But there is something going awry at the embassy this afternoon. An hour has elapsed and no tea has appeared. The butler continues to pass to and fro, going priest-like about his duties. The maid hovers and fusses. The gastric juices rise. But no tea appears.

Eventually the ambassador takes matters into his own hands. He summons us to table. He presses strawberries on us. Under his prompting the butler eventually appears with a brew in the silver pot. It has to be renewed from time to time, a lengthy and elaborate process. But eventually we are all served.

It is a trivial incident, adding a touch of eccentricity to a pleasant outing. But as we head back to Pest, we talk it over. It provides a straw on which to build a grand edifice of journalistic speculation.

The butler, someone says, has been with the embassy for 21 years. Ah, says another, he must have been the KGB man. And, adds a third, he must have lost his second salary when glasnost threw his trade on to the scrap heap. Therefore, concludes a fourth, he must have been on a go-slow, a work-to-rule. That was why the ambassador had been obliged to be mother.

This fanciful train of thought prompts a more serious question. What has happened to the old secret policemen? In some of the Eastern European countries, like East Germany and Czechoslovakia, they have become a redundant group, reviled and resentful and pursued by the law. Some have fought back and in Moscow you hear of ex-KGB men going into the new advertising industry. In Poland there is bitter controversy over the presence of former spies in the government.

No modern state can do without its secret police and no doubt the KGB will continue in some form or other. As capitalism brings its own accompaniment of crime, at least some of the secret policeman's energies may be turned to work of a more conventional kind just as, with the end of the cold war, our own MI5 is bending its mind to Northern Ireland.

Yet the spy is a professional like any other. He has his wages and conditions; he has his pension fund. Indeed it was because he was bitter over his pension that Peter Wright wrote *Spycatcher*, the book which the British government fought so hard and foolishly to suppress in the 1980s.

Since the war European literature has been obsessed by the Holocaust. Our own has dealt in themes of betrayal – emotional, sexual, political. The spy has been the hero both in substantial literature and drama (Le Carré, Alan Bennett) and in popular fiction cinema (Bond et al).

The spy, I fear, will be with us for some time yet. The industry will not disappear: it will be restructured and diffused more widely through our culture. Specialist shops sell the gear of executive espionage – remote listening devices, concealed microphones, machines to detect telephone bugs, recording briefcases that enable you to eavesdrop or capture what is said at meetings when you are out of the room.

It evokes a deplorable picture of mutual distrust; but spying is part of the human condition. The ambassador's butler may live in hope that better times for spies are sure to come again. If they do not the ambassador may have to add tea-making permanently to his diplomatic skills.

Dmitry and family came to visit Scotland in December 1993. Kemp described their stay below in a piece entitled, 'Inner thoughts of a Russian doll'.

The question: how do you entertain a five-year-old Russian girl in Scotland for the weekend? The answer, as it turned out, was: with ease and pleasure.

Stacy, as she translated her name Anastasia, does not have much English beyond please, thank you and hello but she pronounces them with an impeccable accent. Our first move turned out to be our best. As a present we gave her a glove puppet, a fetching invention combining the body and tail of a raccoon with the face of a koala bear. She and Stripey immediately became inseparable.

To the Tron Theatre's pantomime, Snow White and the Seven Dwarfs. The adults liked it only in parts: I found the show's talking loo unamusing and felt short-changed that we only had three dwarfs and that they did not sing 'Hey ho, hey ho, it's off to work we go.' But Stacy got the drift all right. She oohed and aahed and booed the villainous queen along with the best of them, and applauded enthusiastically.

Later that night she asked if we could go again the following day. From the critic who mattered the show could have had no more sincere tribute.

Next day was an outing to Loch Lomond. To break the journey, we were to feed the ducks and view the peacock reputed to inhabit the garden of the Inverarnan Inn. For this purpose a loaf was purchased at a filling station. The ducks of their eponymous bay had read the script. They squawked and splashed and quarrelled over the bits of bread. Seagulls came looping in and grabbed the morsels as they were thrown in the air.

A cold wind off the loch sent us on our way. Inverarnan was full of climbers and walkers supping beer before the roaring fire. This has long been the site of an inn. According to ARB Haldane's classic, *The Drove Roads of Scotland* (1952), the north end of Loch Lomond was the meeting place of three droving routes. The route to

Crieff lay up Glen Falloch, joining the route from Skye in Glendochart. A second route climbed the hills to the east of Ardlui. In 1948 Haldane reported that those living in Loch Lomondside remembered seeing droves from Argyll climbing to the watershed from Glen Falloch on their way to the Falkirk Tryst. The third route lay down the west side of the loch to Dumbarton.

The sun that had begun to disperse the mist on the hills had retreated again, and it was getting chilly when we left the inn's welcome fire and went to find the peacock. There was the bonus of a Highland coo, a donkey and a pony. Only the pony showed much interest in the proffered bread. The peacock was nowhere to be seen but eventually, after a persistent search, was discovered huddled miserably in a corner, its tail folded, in the company of a plump hen (of the domestic, egg-laying kind).

I have never seen a bird that looked so obviously fed up. When it observed our approach its body sagged, as if to say: Oh no, not another lot; why don't they leave me in peace? And when we threw bread at it, it scuttled off in disgust and disappeared among the parked cars. The hen, comfortable and untroubled, snaffled the crust.

On the way home Stripey was put back into his house and Stacy fell asleep. That evening, refreshed, she dined out with us in the Ubiquitous Chip. She ate her mussels with the elegant aplomb of an 18-year-old, and happily let the conversation flow round her.

Things are not easy in Moscow. You can buy goods in the market but they are very expensive; if you want to buy things at a reasonable price in the state sector you still have to queue for hours. Nowadays Stacy's parents double-lock their front door because of crime and the fear of political disorder. The rich 'new Russians' have steel plates on their front doors.

Our friends' daughter has something that often seems elusive in the pampered west – good manners and an inner repose. Perhaps these qualities come from long hours spent at home in the sunlight of her mother's attention. Perhaps they are the gifts of nature. But they are assets beyond price.

Postscript (a later column, also from December 1993).

Dmitry, Masha and Stacy are back in Moscow now, and when we hear of that city's privations we think of them. They came to my mind again last week when, at a dinner in London, I listened to a speech by ex-President Ronald Reagan that dripped with complacency and self-satisfaction.

He remains in remarkably good shape, slim and even boyish. But his speech consisted of a triumphalist review of the collapse of communism in the Soviet Union and Eastern Europe. You'd have thought there were no social or economic problems of any kind in the free world, a surprising thought for anyone who has visited Washington DC, for a start.

In ex-President Reagan's review of events in the East there was too much schadenfreude for my taste. Now is the time to help – not to crow.

3.2
Europe: The Union

A PASSIONATE EUROPHILE WHO OPENED a *Herald* office in Brussels and read *Die Zeit* and *Le Monde*, Kemp was at times a critic of the way the institutions of Europe functioned – but he also saw the creation of the democratic institutions of modern Germany, and then of the European Union, as the key achievements of his post-war generation.

Setting the scene: Kemp lived with the fractured history of 20th-century Europe in the front of his mind, as in this piece from 1991 'Out from under the burdens of sorrow'.

The images of a liberated Kuwait (1991) have been filling our television screens these last few days, images of joy and a sorrow that at first was remarkably free of vengeful spirit. The Kuwaitis seem an unusually placid people, more concerned with rebuilding their shattered city than exacting punishment for the torture, abduction and killing carried out by the Iraqis, about which many of our peaceniks have been so lamentably silent.

Even in the grimmest setting humour may surface. One image of the week that will stay with me, because it made me smile, was of a vox-pop interview conducted with two Kuwaitis by Michael Macmillan of the BBC. Macmillan was clearly exhausted after a terrifying journey to the city, but gallantly complied with the studio's request to 'find a few Kuwaitis' and 'get their reaction'.

As they earnestly talked, a fat and jolly looking Arab, wearing a red kaffiyeh on his head, started passing in and out of shot. On each pass he simpered at the camera, and began to have a profoundly distracting effect on the interview. Finally, he stepped boldly between the two Kuwaitis talking to Macmillan, smiled broadly, gave a Churchillian V-sign and then, satisfied at last, went cheerily on his way. Macmillan appeared oblivious of his presence throughout.

Apart from a sense of comic timing of which Eric Morecambe would have been proud, the anonymous Arab seemed to express the feelings of the Kuwaiti people as eloquently as anyone. There was joy here, not rancour.

As the week wore on the images grew grimmer, the rancour more evident and more understandable. The horror of Kuwait has been so profound and immense that it is curious to reflect that this city, for which the allies have gone to war, is about the size, in population, of Glasgow and that the state of Kuwait has fewer people than Strathclyde region. Yet the agony of Kuwait has been on a scale that makes you think of other great cities that have suffered occupation or bombardment.

We now know that the London blitz reduced the morale of its population much more than contemporary propaganda suggested. The systematic bombing of German cities by the Allies remains a thorn in the Western conscience, and the images of Hiroshima and Nagasaki still summon revulsion.

Berlin, with its wall, remained the most enduring monument to the suffering of war. I certainly found that city, with its still manifest evidence of sorrows, more congenial than Vienna, with its sickly cream cakes, its overblown buildings from the Austro-Hungarian epoch, its cruel Spanish Riding Academy and its revolting tradition of anti-Semitism which still furtively survives.

How lucky, by contrast, has Paris been. It cannot, I think, claim any moral superiority over other great cities, although it has, like London, been a refuge for the persecuted. It has been as self-indulgent as any city, more ready than some to compromise its soul in the interests of self-preservation. Yet it stands as one of the world's finest human artefacts and that gives it some sort of special power over the minds of men and women.

The other day I found myself in one of the world's great hotels, the Meurice in the Rue de Rivoli. I hasten to add that I was not staying in its marbled splendour, amid its Louis Quinze furniture in salons opulently decorated in trompe l'oeil, but was being entertained to breakfast there by a friend.

During the war the Meurice was the German HQ. There, over three harrowing days in August 1944, the German commandant of occupied Paris deliberated whether to obey Hitler's orders and raze Paris to the ground before withdrawing from the city.

The Allies were closing in fast. The general, Dietrich Von Choltitz, was tempted to obey his orders to destroy Paris because the Parisians, many of whom had been collaborators, suddenly started attacking Germans, particularly on the Left Bank where the ancient narrow streets run behind and between the boulevards.

It was the Swedish consul-general, Raoul Nordling, who dissuaded him and who effectively saved the city. Nordling had a series of tense meetings in the general's first-floor suite at the Meurice. They would sit on his balcony, overlooking the Tuileries, and apart from the Swede's arguments the most eloquent witness for the defence must have been the incomparable city itself.

Last weekend, when the Gulf ground war was joined, French television went out into the sunlit streets of Paris for a bit of vox pop, that expedient of any television producer short of inspiration. A woman interviewed in a café on the Champs Elysées said honestly: 'It is very sad. But here I am in Paris enjoying a drink. Life goes on, happily.' That is a fair motto for a Parisian.

Britain initially tried to join the European Economic Commmunity in 1963 but was rebuffed by Charles de Gaulle. It did not join until 1974. In a *Scotsman* editorial from 1971, Kemp examined the effect membership was having on Ireland. 'Irish Lesson for Scotland'

Some interesting lessons for Scotland are to be found in Ireland's first 15 months of Common Market membership. Ireland's dependence on the United Kingdom market has been diminished, with exports to EEC nations other than Britain rising. Obviously, in a country where 24 per cent of the population are still on the land (in Scotland farming and forestry employ less than 3 per cent of the workforce), the common agricultural policy is a particular attraction.

There is a tendency, however, to identify political desires and movements too closely with economics. Nationalist sentiment springs from deeper, philosophical roots, and it is therefore significant that one important cause of Irish satisfaction with EEC membership derives from unquantifiable factors of prestige and international influence. Five new Irish diplomatic missions are soon to be opened and accreditation with 20 more countries will take place this year. The Irish Foreign Minister, Mr Fitzgerald, said in a recent interview with the International Herald Tribune that increasing intimacy with other countries had given Ireland a self-confidence it never had before.

Scotland, which Europe regards as a region and insults further by designating as 'peripheral' and 'maritime', may justifiably look on with some envy. Ireland, after all, has a population of only three million; but on the international stage this is the era of small countries in that their lack of ambition and their acceptance of a modest destiny make their judgements less open to suspicion than those of major Powers anxious to preserve or extend their influence. The Scottish Council in their report 'A Future for Scotland' argued for direct Scottish representation at Brussels and the conversion of Mr James Sillars and other Labour MPs to the idea of devolution owes something to a similar conviction. The growing demand for Home Rule combines with European political evolution to offer Scotland the best prospect of reasserting her national identity and of moderating English hegemony while retaining intimate and friendly relations. For such reasons SNP opposition to the Common Market is one of the party's more misguided policies.

In a 1972 *Scotsman* editorial, Kemp argues that countries at the edge of Europe should expect subsidies.

The view that free-market forces must be left to operate regardless of social consequences is as unacceptable within the EEC as it is, *pace* the Monday Club, within the British economy. The Agricultural Fund demonstrates the need to subsidise a social transition that might otherwise be agonising. Scotland, and those like her on the periphery of the market must have permanent compensation for their distance from the economic heartland. If Scotland were independent, this effect could be achieved by an adjustment in the parity rate of her currency: this, of course, is not possible.

After Britain joined the EEC, those familiar arguments about sovereignty began. The paradox of sovereignty, from *The Scotsman*, 1975. Brussels.

Sovereignty is a lovely word. It means, says the dictionary concisely, 'supreme and independent power.' In the world that has seen the United States humbled in Vietnam it may no longer exist.

It has become the big issue in the Common Market referendum campaign. Through it politicians may appeal to the deep-rooted insularity of the British people, their suspicion of foreigners, and even in these post-imperial days their conviction that they are the best.

This reassertion of the British Parliament's right to enjoy supreme power comes at a curiously interesting time. This month the Government have insisted that the process of devolution must not involve the division of Westminster's sovereignty.

This means that a return of sovereign power to Scotland cannot be contemplated. Yet the Treaty of Union invested the sovereignty of the Scottish Parliament in a UK Parliament and did not transfer it to the English legislature.

So, what is sauce for the English goose is not sauce for the Scottish gander.

Those who play the sovereignty game portray the Market as a centralised monster depriving the people of the power to influence their environment. A visit here this week produced a rather different picture.

First, the vision of a supranational European identity, which informed the men who built the Community out of a continent ravaged by two world wars in a century has grown dim and is almost extinguished.

It has not been forgotten, however, that those wars and the suffering they caused arose in part from that national pride which is now called sovereignty.

'I have no wish,' said an official of the Commission, 'to see a Europe goose-stepping behind a European flag while a European band plays the European national anthem.'

Rather the tendency is in the opposite direction in recognition of the realities in a continent encompassing such disparate groups as the Irish farmers, the Sicilian peasant, the West Highland crofters and the disenchanted Walloons of Belgium.

Now the whole thrust of the Community is away from a monolithic centralism and towards flexibility. This is reflected in all the major areas of policy.

The idea of a central bureaucracy imposing unacceptable regulation does not bear examination.

Rather it is the centralised, bureaucratic nation state that has proved itself incapable of responding to the needs of cultural minorities. The devolutionary movements in Scotland, Wales and Belgium and the discontents of Brittany represent a response not to the Common Market but to metropolitan dominance.

So in the Common Market devolution down – and up – is the name of the game.

'Surely that's federalism?' I asked several officials.

All winced at the word with its connotation of bumptious supranationalism of which the Unites States is federalism's greatest example.

'We are looking for something new,' said one official, 'something that has not been tried before.' Its aim will be to fulfil the expectation of all Europeans of high economic and social standards and yet permit them to express their essential differences.

Sovereignty resides in the Council of Ministers representing the collective sovereignty of the individual members. The development of the Market can take place only by a process of consent guaranteeing members' rights.

Since the Market's actions will affect Britain whether she is in or out, a decision to leave the EEC will mean a loss, and not a recovery, of sovereignty.

Luncheon with the count and the dowager dog prompted reflections on the European project. A *Herald* column from 1992.

Burgundy
The fire, extravagantly set by Patrice with old fencing for ignition, pine for aroma, chestnut for endurance, and hazel for fireworks, sparkles in the stone hearth. Outside, milky clouds move slowly across the sky. A Barbary white duck stands like a policeman in the farmyard, immobile until at last it slowly flexes its wings before resuming its conscientious watch.

The countryside is soft and rolling, well timbered, the green fields stocked with white Charolais beef cattle. The little lakes and ponds are full of pike. The sandy soil is poor and vines are not cultivated here.

Farm incomes, as elsewhere in Europe, have been falling and forestry is gaining the upper hand. In Scotland the sitka spruce has disfigured many acres but here there is a pleasing balance – mature stands of Douglas fir and Sylvester pines; oak, poplar, chestnut, beech and hazel; cherry and apple in blossom.

In the chateau Patrice's much loved uncle, the Count, sits with his treasures and his memories. There are paintings by Ingres, Raphael, and Breughel, and nursery furniture from Versailles. He has a housekeeper and a cook but sleeps alone in the chateau – fitfully, for he has been burgled three times. On the last occasion he put the intruders to flight by threatening to shoot them. He has a revolver. He keeps his bedroom door locked at night, but he is unafraid.

Most of the rooms are in darkness, with the shutters closed and furniture covered. He receives visitors in his cosy sitting room which has a log fire, an enormous television set and, in a glass cabinet, a collection of elaborate court costumes.

He is a stickler for punctuality, not just because the lack of it causes anxiety and is therefore thoughtless, but also because he hates to spoil his meals by keeping them waiting. We are careful not to be late and he greets us with great kindness.

There is time for an aperitif, a glass of port, before we go downstairs to the kitchen where, for reasons of warmth, meals are taken. The housekeeper and cook join us at table where we are seven plus dog. We rapidly dispose of two enormous and delicious omelettes made with rich country eggs and morilles (wild mushrooms) which Patrice came upon with a delighted cry during a walk in the woods the day before. Their crinkly brown heads make them hard to spot against the moss and leaf mould on the forest floor and I would have walked past them. To have found them is a great triumph and the place where we did so is a secret of the kind you do not tell even your best friend.

At table we move on to a regal dish of Charolais beef, sanglant or blood rare in the French manner, with a medley of six vegetables fresh from the walled kitchen-garden still tended by three men. The dog is a model of decorum. Lulu is a King Charles Spaniel and she sits on a raised chair with her chin on a dainty little plate. From time to time she is given morsels which she eats slowly with the dignity of a dowager. The Count, a tall and impressive man with an ironic sense of humour, explains that for his part he eats merely to give himself the strength to die.

Afterwards, on a tour of the chateau, we are shown family mementoes. The Count and his father, mother, and brother were imprisoned by the Germans in a concentration camp in 1943. Their crime had been to help escaping Jews. The father was condemned to carry bricks and died of a heart attack in captivity. We are shown a memorial to him – a framed collage containing poignant snapshots. Across the bottom runs like an ugly brand the crudely lettered number allocated to him by the German authorities.

The Count does not much like to be lured from his own table and fireside but that evening he pays us the compliment of joining us for dinner. On the menu are the three pike Patrice has caught in one of the ponds. They are not fish with which I am familiar but, poached slowly in butter, herbs, and white wine they are pronounced delicious.

What do you feel about the Germans now? I asked the Count. He cannot pretend affection, he replies, but he tries to forget the past and acquire tolerance with age. Perhaps this is the true impulse behind the European Community.

Next day Patrice takes me fishing in the rain. To approach the pond we cautiously skirt some cows. In spring they can be aggressive, especially with calves at foot, but today they are merely curious. On my third cast of the spinning rod the spoon parts from the line and lands on the far bank. Patrice is a Parisian now but dearly loves his ancestral landscape. He wades thigh deep to recover the spoon, showing complete contempt for his own comfort (I would have gone the long way round).

On my fifth cast, by great good luck, I catch a half-pound pike. We carry it home in a bucketful of water but, in the interests of gas-tronomic variety, are advised to liberate it. As we pour it into the farmyard pond, where it will terrorise the resident fish, the sentinel duck watches gravely.

Is there no end, he seems to ask, to the eccentricity of humankind? He himself is destined for the pot in September.

On the introduction of the Euro in Ireland, from *The Observer*, 30 December 2001.

The currency may change but life goes on. Ireland, as it prepared for the euro, fell about the Christmas feast as if it hadn't a care in the world. The free-range Wexford turkey was the least of it: the ances-tral Irish festive board is not complete without a ham and a hunk of spiced beef as well.

Given Ireland's respect for its traditions, the fatalism with which it is giving up so powerful a symbol of nationhood as its currency is an impressive sign of its political will. The Irish coinage, first struck in 1928, was one of the first creations of the Free State.

Yet from the table-talk this Christmas, with euro 'starter packs' already available, the topic was largely missing and the country seems extraordinarily relaxed about the switch. There are tales of second-hand car dealers trying to unload punts from their hip pockets with-out attracting the attention of tax inspectors or money laundering regulators. Criminals, so goes the myth, are offering interest-free loans in punts to those willing to pay back in euros. Cash sales of lux-ury cars and other goods are said to be soaring, and 'mattress money', say some estimates, accounted for 14 per cent of the Christmas retail boom.

In Scotland, there is a sotto voce counterpoint. We are standing aside from the euro, of course, but we are celebrating, if that is the word, a new right conceded by the authorities: next year motorists will be able to embellish their number plates with the Saltire or, if they are English or Welsh, the St George's Cross or the Dragon. And in the meantime those who fail to display the regulation plate, with the European flag and GB below it, will not be prosecuted.

This is a sensible sop to nationalism and europhobia, all at once. The European Union, while a powerful idea and already a substantial historical achievement, remains politically at best a weak confederation, with sovereignty vested in the Council of Ministers representing states still gripped by powerful national emotions. If the Government is to lead us into the euro within the next two years, as appears increasingly certain, then it seems shrewd to remove petty irritations which give fodder to the Europhobe press. The idea that the European Union is a rigid centralist superstate, or in immediate danger of becoming one, is as absurd as believing that the heart of European culture is to be found in a Dieppe urinal.

But those who support the European project, as I do, must confront a worrying paradox: we have never had so many elections to so many parliaments. Yet our parliamentarians are held in lower esteem than I can remember and the public votes for them in ever declining numbers. HL Mencken [the American journalist known as the 'Sage of Baltimore'] found nothing so abject and pathetic as a politician who had lost his job, 'save only a retired stud-horse', but now the public would spread its contempt to those who still practise the black arts. Part of the explanation, perhaps, is the growing enfeeblement of parliaments as institutions. The Strasbourg parliament has a great power – to reject the commission's budget – which is about as practically useful as the nuclear deterrent, and many minor powers which are of little account. The commission proposes, the council of ministers determines, and the national parliaments rubber-stamp.

Westminster, too, is suffering from a loss of public esteem, perhaps because Tony Blair has, if anything, intensified Thatcher's presidential style. In Scotland, the parliament remains largely unpopular, or at least among the people I've bumped into lately. Some, particularly West of Scotland Tories, never wanted it in the first place and are irritated by what they perceive as its provincialism. And we have to admit that in some respects the new parliament has not broken resolutely enough from the bad habits of Westminster.

Enlargement will raise the constitutional debate in Europe more keenly. It is unrealistic to dream, with the Germans and the Dutch, of a fully federal arrangement, of a European parliament with teeth holding the commission to account. Indeed, even in a mature federation, like the US, tensions between the centre and the states continue to be a dynamic part of the political process.

Another paradox of our politics is that we hold our politicians to account with increasing energy while despising them more. Once MPs took prostitutes into the Commons, from which the press was excluded. Lloyd George made a pass at anything in a skirt while remaining a political giant. The private lives of many other leading figures did not bear examination – and, generally, did not receive it. Europe must grow. It will probably do so, as it has always done, through crises and their mediation. The euro's introduction will not be without dangers and complications, and stresses will undoubtedly emerge, particularly at a time of world recession. Yet it is another giant step on the road to European political maturity.

PART II
SCOTTISH IDENTITY

4
Religion and the appearance of the secular society

WITCH-BURNING IN SPOTT, EAST LOTHIAN

Spott is what its name implies, a little place. The writer William Roughead said that it lay remote from the high road of history; yet it looked down on stirring events and was occasionally touched by them. The journey from the Tyne to the Forth was across difficult country and hostile troops came by sea to Dunbar. Agricola, Edward I of England, and Cromwell used this route. Edward won the first Battle of Dunbar in 1296 quite near where the kirk stands, and in 1650 General Leslie lost the second to Cromwell. He pitched his camp on the summit of Doon Hill before confronting Cromwell but abandoned his strong position, Roughead tells us, 'at the command of the prophets who accompanied his army'.

The parish was the scene of the last witch-burnings in Scotland (though there were executions elsewhere as late as 1727). In October 1705, only two years before the Union, the minutes of the Kirk Session, cited by Rev Duncan Turner in a parish history, recorded: 'Many witches burnt on the top of Spott Loan'.

Much has been written about the exceptional ferocity with which witches were persecuted in Scotland after the Reformation. A belief in witchcraft was, wrote Roughead, a foremost article of the new faith. The Reformed Church took upon itself the rights and duties of the moral and spiritual policeman. Knox lumped witchcraft along with the Mass and the Devil as manifestations to be expected in the 'utterly corrupted' religion of his country.

Historians at one time estimated that between 1560 and 1707 more than 3,000 people, and perhaps as many as 4,500, were horribly murdered. In England, with a population about five times greater, only about a thousand people seem to have been killed in this way. Later work, notably by C Larner in *Enemies of God*, has revised the Scottish total downwards to 'something over a thousand'. She showed, too, that acquittals were quite common. In *Waverley*, Scott gives a particularly ludicrous example of a woman accused of being a witch on the grounds that she was 'very old, very ugly, very poor, and had two sons, one of whom was a poet and the other a fool'. The charge against her collapsed.

The first statute against witchcraft, imposing the death penalty, was passed in 1563. It was the murder, not the superstition, that was new, wrote the historian Professor Christopher Smout. In Scotland the Reformation seems to have added virulence to the persecution but it was a Papal bull of 1484 which first advocated the extirpation of sorcerers and there was no difference between the Roman and Reformed Churches on the point that the old pagan deities were the great fallen spirits of the Scriptures. Around this time German priests systematised the deep-seated superstitions of the countryside as a coherent conspiracy organised by the devil. The scriptural justification for the killing of witches relied on a passage in Exodus; Calvin himself wrote that all witches and enchantresses must be put to death. Scottish intellectuals travelling to Europe were influenced by such work, and ruling circles adopted its ideas too. It was what we would call politically correct not just to believe in the reality of witchcraft but also that it should be rooted out without mercy. The king himself, James VI, published in 1597 his own *Daemonologie* to confound an English view that witches did not exist.

The important thing to remember, wrote Thomas Davidson in his book *Rowan Tree and Red Thread*, was that the conversion to Christianity was a slow and long drawn-out process. By the middle of the seventeenth century it applied to the townspeople and the upper classes.

In the country, it made little impression on the minds of the peasantry, who continued to adhere to the old beliefs to which they were accustomed. There were hardworking but grossly ignorant, simple and superstitious, and their conception of a witch was one who represented the perpetual attraction of the secret and dangerous, of fairies and spirits, and of auguries, good and bad. To have spoken doubtingly of witchcraft to a peasant would have caused him to produce his Bible – and who dare doubt the evidence of heaven! ... [The peasants] were too simple and superstitious to grasp that all their old accustomed rites and ceremonies were iniquitous, since they constituted an appeal to and worship of evil spirits.

The ignorance of the peasantry flourished under the pre-Reformation church which neglected the parishes and their priests;

its resources were concentrated at the top, its energies went into the foundation of collegiate churches and universities, and its benefices were corruptly distributed. The ordinary vicars were underpaid and incompetent and, in some case, barely literate. Churches were falling down and there was no money for their repair. Periodic attempts were made to stop them engaging in commerce to supplement their income and there were episodes of priests demanding payment before administering the sacraments.

Professor Gordon Donaldson, in his history of the Reformation, believed that parochial decay, rather than licentiousness of the kind Sir David Lindsay lampooned in The Three Estates, was the true scandal of the Church. Attendance at Mass seems to have been fitful and public behaviour sometimes ribald and irreverent. John Knox complained that people went to church only at Easter and then were not seen again for another year. In such circumstances the old super-stitions lived on; sometimes, when reading of some suburban séance or seeing the gullibility with which the public swallow the pro-nouncements of astrologers, I think they have never died out.

John Buchan set his own favourite novel, *Witch Wood* (1927), in Broughton in Peebles-shire, not so far from Spott. A young minister comes to a parish where a witch cult is in full cry. Buchan describes a witch-hunt, the activities of the witch-prickers, and a trial before the presbytery. For Buchan the cult, with its pagan ritual, was a reac-tion against the repressive moral code enforced by the new religious order. The new kirk and its ministers, he wrote in his biography of Montrose (1928), by condemning natural pleasures and affections, drew a dark pall over the old merry Scottish world where, Professor Smout implies, the chief pleasure of the common people was forni-cation (as it continued to be in the time of Burns and beyond).

Some modern historians explain the persecution as arising from the animosities, jealousies, and hatreds of a countryside sunk in poverty. The denunciation of women as witches – and less frequent-ly of men as wizards or warlocks – was often motivated by spite or greed. The denouncers might want to settle a score; they might covet land or cattle from which the owner might be prised by a charge of witchcraft. Single women living alone and unprotected by husbands were particularly at risk, especially if they had engaged in hitherto harmless pursuits like herbal medicine or fortune-telling. The perse-cution has been compared to the outbreak of score-settling that fol-lowed the liberation of France in 1944 when collaborators were hounded and abused. No single reason suffices; it was from the combination of many ingredients, social, intellectual, religious, political, that the Scottish persecutions formed so lethal and poisonous a brew. Yet the modern mind tends to filter history through the prism of its own rational and secular perspectives, and I prefer the explanation of Buchan and Davidson – that the reformed Church was in competition, for the hearts and minds of the common people, with the old beliefs and rites, and pursued their extirpation, and its own dominance, with ruthlessness.

Outside the door of the church at Spott is preserved, as a souvenir of cruel times, a hinged iron punishment collar, or jougs, to which those guilty of moral offences were chained by the neck to a wall or post, a tool of ecclesiastical discipline like the cutty stool and the sack gown. They were mostly used in the early eighteenth century and the *Scottish National Dictionary* gives this example:

John Roy to stand at the jogs on the Sabbath day at the kirk of Cromdale for the scandalising of Janet Calder.

But by the 19th century, the culture of Scotland had changed, as described in this column on Hugh Miller from *The Herald*.

During a visit to Cromarty the statue of Hugh Miller provoked in me a sense of guilt that I had never read the work of this extraordinary nineteenth-century Scot. By one of these odd coincidences that keep up the credibility of astrologers a copy of his book, *First Impressions of England*, came into my hands the same week.

Miller, born in 1802, was a polymath. When he was five his father was lost at sea. His schooling ended abruptly after a violent clash with the dominie and he became apprenticed to a stonemason at the age of 17. He was an excellent workman and after three years began travelling round Scotland as a journeyman. He grew interested in the stones and fossils on our shores and became an accomplished geologist.

This he combined with a strong religious tendency. After working as a bank accountant in Cromarty, in 1840 he was appointed editor of *The Witness*, a bi-weekly paper published by the independent wing of the Church of Scotland.

To his journalism and scientific interests he added considerable skill in theology and he spent much intellectual energy trying to reconcile the emerging scientific explanations of the Creation with those given in the Bible. Unusually for his time he believed that they were not incompatible. He published many books, pamphlets, and articles. In 1856 his mind gave out under these exertions and he shot himself.

It is hard for our secular age to imagine how obsessed Scotland was, until quite recently, with religion. But it was a faith based on legalism, on the idea that Scripture is the supreme authority. As ever, religion became caught up with politics and nationalism.

The rejection of episcopacy and the English prayer book in the seventeenth century was essentially a political rebellion uniting all classes but it encouraged a dogmatic adherence to presbyterian principles as if they were of universal truth.

This led the Scots presbyterians into what history must judge to have been an overweening attempt to impose their system of church government on the English, though there is, paradoxically, no biblical support for any one system or another (nor did Calvin himself prescribe any).

In the nineteenth century legalism, and the insistence that the church had supreme spiritual power, led the Kirk into conflict with the state on the question of patronage and the authority of temporal courts.

The controversies of the Disruption absorbed Scottish intellectual energies for generations. The bout of church-building produced by the schism must have, at least, stimulated its economy. In Miller's judgment, theological obsession also stimulated the national intellect.

Miller sets off for England in 1845, two years after the Disruption. He takes his seat at Edinburgh on the top of the Newcastle coach, crosses Carter Fell a little after noon, and finds himself in an England drenched in the prolonged rains of a disastrous harvest season.

He lodges in a modest but respectable house in Newcastle and immediately is embroiled in a theological discussion with his fellow guests. There are a few smart commercial gentlemen from the Midland towns; two Sheffield mechanics who earn good wages and take care of them; and a farmer or two from the country.

The mechanics are talking theology. The men from the country say nothing. The commercial men seem amused to hear so much talk of religion. The mechanics are Methodists but, says Miller, are wild nondescripts in their theology. A man in black enters. It turns out he is a Calvinist – not, however, 'of the most profound type'.

The discussion centres on the doctrine of atonement, the reconciliation of God and man through the incarnation and death of Christ. The Wesleyans say there is really no such thing; it is mere orthodoxy. The Calvinist adduces evidence from Scripture to prove the opposite.

A tall and respectable man has entered the room and has been listening. He intervenes against the Calvinist. 'Can it really be,' he asks, 'that the all-powerful God – the being who has no limits to His power – could not forgive sin without an atonement?'

Miller can barely conceal his contempt for such amateurish forays into theological debate. The arguments would make little impression on the skilful Scottish peasant controversialists of his time, 'so unwisely satirised by Burns', or on those 'grave-livers' of the parish in some country churchyard gathered for a spot of theological debate before the service begins.

He is curious to see how the metaphysics of 'our Scotch Calvinism' will tell on such an audience. He presents a closely argued proof of the doctrine of atonement. He pleads with the skill of an advocate, exemplifying the legalist tendency of the Scottish religious mind.

Not surprisingly, he silences his audience. Then one of the commercial travellers says: 'You Scotch are a strange people. When I was in Scotland two years ago I could hear of scarce anything among you but your church question. What good does all your theology do you?'

To the modern mind, that remains a pretty good question. Miller's reply is arresting: 'Independently altogether of religious considerations, it has done for our people what all your Societies for the Diffusion of Useful Knowledge and all your Penny and Saturday magazines will never do for yours: it has awakened their intellects and taught them how to think. The development of the popular mind in Scotland is a result of its theology.'

It is also connected with our political impotence as a country, our love of disagreement, our tendency to schism. In the nineteenth century the English could not understand the Scottish mind at all. Miller's English commercial traveller expresses that puzzlement eloquently and I am not sure that Miller's response will wash.

Scotland's obsession with religion largely supplanted any domestic political debate. It gravely weakened the Church of Scotland, a vehicle of a cohesive national identity. The Disruption was as much concerned about political power as about religion. Theology was a surrogate politics and speeded our assimilation into the British state by sowing division and distracting us from political affairs.

Today, if you checked in to a modest guest house in Newcastle, the conversation might be about football, television, the royal family, or the weather. It would be extremely surprising to come upon a debate on the doctrine of atonement.

The peasant philosopher, the theologian tending his flocks, was a figure beloved of Scott and Buchan. Burns's Cotter knew his Bible inside out. Now Scotland is ignorant of all four but is expert on the plots and characters of television soap operas.

Can that be progress? As you look around the world and its wars of resurgent nationalism, or consider the tragedy of Northern Ireland where people live with history in the front of their minds, you may decide that it is a lucky country that can live in cheerful ignorance of its own tortured past.

By the late 20th century, things had changed again.

These fine, or not so fine, spring mornings have found me walking in Kelvingrove Park for constitutional purposes, and I have stopped once or twice to admire the splendid fountain, by the architect James Sellars and the sculptor John Mossman, erected in 1871-2 to commemorate the inauguration of the Loch Katrine water scheme.

It is richly carved in Scottish Gothic and since its restoration a couple of years ago it spouts voluptuous jets of water behind which can be glimpsed the bright pink blossom of the Japanese cherry trees. Much of the detail piously commemorates Lord Provost Stewart, whose civic genius created the water scheme, but its crowning inspiration is Sir Walter Scott's Lady of the Lake.

With my shoe I clean the inscription set in the ground and think it apt that Sir Walter's name should be covered with mud. The neglect not only of Sir Walter Scott but of its own history is a striking aspect of contemporary Scotland. There can be few other countries that are now so cut off from their own past as is Scotland, so forgetful and so careless of it.

Of course, Scott's work is now found old-fashioned, wordy and slow. The romantic novels do have the fustian air of the historical curiosity. Literary criticism has faulted his characterisation and found much of it wooden. Gradgrind historians have quarrelled with his grasp of factual detail. Others have objected to his snobbery, his Toryism, his hobnobbing with royalty, his part in creating the romantic myths with which the modern Scottish spirit is so impatient.

Yet Scott was one of the very few international geniuses Scottish literature has produced. His influence on the European novel was profound. He is still read with respect and enjoyment in France and Russia. Without some knowledge of Scott's greatest works, those which reflect, however subjectively, the social and political history of Scotland, no Scot can have much hope of understanding the past. Yet in modern Scotland he is read hardly at all.

There are, of course, explanations for the neglect of Scott other than the encumbrances that have made his work seem difficult and remote. In modern Scotland he is not politically correct, and debunkers have denounced him as some sort of toady greasing up to his English masters.

This has always been unfair. Edwin Muir pointed out that Scott shared the dilemma of every Scot since the Union. He adored and celebrated the traditions of his own country and as a Tory was committed to their preservation. He keenly felt the paradox that the Union, rooted in history and sanctified by the past, would undermine those very traditions which he valued so much. On one occasion the inevitable dilution of the Scots legal tradition made him weep.

The neglect of Scott is perhaps understandable, given that we live in a visual and disposable culture where the fast-forward button is king, but an equally striking phenomenon is the embarrassment with which Scotland now regards John Knox.

He has been put out of our minds because our society has been so rapidly secularised and he stands for a collection of cultural baggage which we have tried hard to discard.

Knox in particular and the presbyterian tradition in general have been blamed for Scotland's neglect of theatre and music, for making us a repressed and unimaginative nation, and for countless other failures. The schismatic tendencies of the Church, our most significant national institution to survive the Union, and its defeat at the hands of politicians after the Disruption, was certainly a defining moment in our history, and perhaps does much to explain our incurable failure to achieve any kind of political coherence.

Perhaps most of all in the modern era Knox was unfairly represented as standing for an outdated bigotry that could not be sustained
in an urban, materialist, pluralist and open culture. In Scotland, if
not in Northern Ireland, religious turbulence is a distant echo and
our new and largely secular society has brought many benefits. I for
one would not wish to return to the dreary Scottish Sundays of my
youth, when the only bright moment in the morning was 20 minutes
with 'Oor Wullie' and the 'Broons' before Kirk, when the highspot of
the afternoon was the dreary and maddeningly repetitive radio programme Down Your Way, and when bona fide travellers drank
furtively in suburban hotels so as not to scandalise the lieges.

The pace of secularisation in Scotland has been faster than in
either the rest of the UK or in Ireland. We shop on Sunday without
much thought, whereas in England the very idea is still resisted. A
couple of Irish visitors, over for the rugby international last month,
were amazed, on their first visit, to find how much Scotland had
departed from the stereotype of Calvinist gloom which they had
believed still to be the truth.

I cannot regret the fact that the Scottish people have found
release from a preternatural sabbath gloom but in this great change
there has, of course, been a loss. Knox cannot be erased from
Scottish history as if he were some newly incorrect figure in a Soviet
official encyclopaedia. That an attempt was being made to disinvent
him became clear when, in the seventies, the authorities in
Edinburgh renamed the John Knox Steps, running down from the
Mound beside the National Gallery, the Playfair Steps. The greatest
Scot had been supplanted by the architect of Edinburgh's New
Town, who died in 1857.

Was it a fair exchange? I think not. Playfair gave us one of
Europe's finest architectural passages in Edinburgh's golden age.
Knox gave Scotland something even more profound – its democratic temper and its respect for universal education before such ideas
took root elsewhere. These ideas were later to suffuse its special
brand of socialism.

Modern Scotland may desire to set Knox in a different light. We
clearly have wished to strike in new directions from those in which
presbyterianism led us. We have sought liberation from a tradition
that was in many ways oppressive. Our age is ecumenical and pluralist, as it must be. But that does not mean that we should forget our
history and our great men.

Sectarianism and Old Firm rivalry from *The Observer*, October 2001.

Bigotry arises from a tribal need to create a community to which to belong and to create an enemy on whom to vent festering resentments. It may deploy logical argument, but is essentially irrational. Partisanship at Old Firm games became extreme only after 1912, when Harland and Wolf of Belfast opened a shipyard on the Clyde and brought a Protestant workforce to man it.

During the seventeenth and eighteenth centuries, about a third of migrants from Ireland to Scotland were Protestant. Anti-Irish sentiment in Scotland reached a peak in the Twenties and Thirties, when a political party was formed on sectarian lines to defend the Protestant working class. Anti-Irish prejudice was an important component in the multiple prejudices of right-wing nationalists like Andrew Dewar Gibb.

But in the years after the Second World War, my recollection is that the bitterness had faded, though not entirely. People of Irish descent penetrated the professions and took an increasingly significant role in politics; the expanding local government system also gave new opportunities.

But the bile rose again with the Troubles. The Orange Walks, which had seemed in terminal decline, revived, though their adherents are a ragged bunch. But every marching season in Northern Ireland sees the ferries full of Scottish foot-soldiers; and every Old Firm game sees a large exodus of fans from Northern Ireland, mixing their religious prejudices in strong drink, reminding one of Mark Twain's dictum 'that the earliest pioneer of civilisation, the van-leader of civilisation, is never the steamboat, never the Sabbath school, never the missionary, but always whiskey'. The truth is that over the centuries, the Scots and the Irish have been in a continuous process of interchange.

Bigoted employment practices were still in evidence in Glasgow in the early 1980s, as Kemp recalled many years later in this *Observer* column.

When I was appointed editor of *The Glasgow Herald* in 1981, the then managing director of the publishing company came to me in great embarrassment. A board member, evidently confused by the fact that I was a Hibs supporter, had insisted on knowing whether I was a Catholic. When I answered in the negative, a cloud lifted from his brow.

Some days later, I was visited by a rather sinister member of the personnel department, who wished to assure himself that I would observe the company's traditional recruiting policies. This meant that applicants' letters would be placed in three piles – probables, possibles and 'those you won't want to see'. This last was a euphemism for those whose name or educational history betrayed their religious affiliation.

The editorial and commercial departments abandoned the old ways, but they lingered on in the composing and machine-rooms. The old caste system, generally to be found in West of Scotland industry, applied: the skilled occupations were in the hands of Protestants, the unskilled open to Catholics. When Rangers won, we moved more swiftly to press start than when they lost.

Differentials drove pay bargaining, a nightmare for negotiators, though, as production unions sensed their growing weakness, they increasingly left the journalists to lead the attack each year.

The internecine jealousy in the mechanical departments reached a ludicrous pitch when Mrs Thatcher visited the office on the occasion of the paper's bicentenary. Union officials in the machine-room advised the management she would not be welcome there. Instead, she went to the composing-room where she was feted by the camera-happy operators. After her departure, the machine-room men sent a formal complaint, asking why she had not visited them.

The new personnel management junked as many of the old ways as it could and drastically reduced the number of negotiating groups. But it wasn't until Rupert Murdoch broke down the unions' fierce rear-guard action against computerised composition that the old elite groups began to be wept away. In London, the first women and the first blacks entered the production side of the industry. In Glasgow, the men themselves accepted the change philosophically enough. They had always known that some day the game would be up. Some left, some retrained as journalists or advertising men. All around us, as the old heavy industries contracted or disappeared, much the same process was going on. And so the end of the old technologies loosened the old loyalties. Now desktop publishing skills are part of the new literacy.

But the newspaper and publishing industries are a treadmill. Without unions, people are easily exploited. Casuals on short-term contracts are sometimes treated with an indifference I find disgraceful, and some managements play on their insecurities as a control technique.

Perhaps the unions will have their day again. I just hope they stick to representing their members' professional and industrial interests, and leave the nepotism and sectarianism at the door.

A hard, industrial past had left its mark on Lanarkshire manners, Kemp noted in an *Observer* column: 'God bless Lanarkshire, home of hot tempers and warm champagne'.

As a county, Lanarkshire does not always have a good press, though it contains New Lanark, the Falls of Clyde and some delightful countryside. But its industrial belt has become synonymous with the hard political world of Old Labour. Sectarian enmity festers between Coatbridge and Airdrie, and in Larkhall where the tensions of Northern Ireland are faithfully mirrored.

Not all of its political traditions are to be despised. The leader of the Labour party John Smith had his constituency here, though he believed in letting sleeping dogs lie. Lanarkshire councillors dominated the Strathclyde region, abolished in the last days by the Tory Government which had grown jealous of its power and influence, and acquitted themselves pretty well. Its first Labour leader, the late Dick Stewart, ruled it with a rod of iron but was universally respected. He was an unusual example of the political type. He had little oratory but extraordinary, even feline, skills of control.

He told me that the key to Lanarkshire politics was housing, and he first made a reputation by his effectiveness in that field. He and his brothers worked in the coal mines which dotted the county. Life was hard, absenteeism commonplace. During the war, the men were often rebuked for it but when some were allowed to join the forces, Dick caught the bus to Edinburgh. He met his brother coming down the steps of the recruiting office – he had beaten him to it and Dick had to go back to the pit. Both thought life in the forces preferable to life in the mines.

Without the expansion of the Lanarkshire industrial base in the eighteenth and nineteenth centuries, Scotland's rapid economic growth of that period would not have been possible. The need for labour sucked back into Scotland the religious animosities of Northern Ireland. It is often forgotten that a substantial minority of those migrants were protestant.

After the Second World War, the expansion of employment in local government diminished some of the worst effects of systematic economic prejudice and people of Irish Catholic descent began to penetrate the professions; indeed they now dominate some of them in the West of Scotland.

Scottish Office papers recently released recall the struggle that was carried on in the late Sixties to maintain a Scottish steel industry in Lanarkshire and elsewhere. Later Ravenscraig became a symbol of the old industrial order. Ravenscraig is gone, but something of the hard old culture survives.

A few years ago, a party of us went to the Saints and Sinners race meeting at Hamilton and afterwards for dinner to an Italian restaurant nearby which enjoyed a considerable reputation. Flushed by our winnings, we ordered champagne. When I had the temerity to point out that it had not been chilled, the wine waiter said suavely: 'Why don't you come outside so I can kick your head in?' To my head he of course applied the usual Lanarkshire expletive.

That robust tradition has survived in South Lanarkshire politics. Most of the ills of old Labour arise from its long years of domination in the councils of the central belt. It is not yet clear whether Holyrood will improve the quality of Scottish legislation. But it will surely raise the tone.

5
Scottish nationalism

KEMP TOOK AN ENTHUSIASTIC PART in the debates on nationalism and devolution in the last decades of the 20th century. In his view, nationalism evolved during these years from what he regarded as 'hairy nonsense' to anglophile pragmatism. Below is a Saltire Society Fletcher of Saltoun lecture he gave in 1990.

This is the age of nationalism. It has proved to be a much more resilient vehicle than communism. In his biography of Charles de Gaulle, Regis Debray distinguishes between ethnic and elective nationalism.

The first arises because of the homogeneity of a people. The second is a solution to the opposite condition: peoples of different origins may choose a common nationalism because they have to invent workable institutions and instruments. Elective nationalism is found in its most obvious form in the United States, which is a melting pot of races. Despite its evident racial tensions the US has achieved genuine national coherence.

Scottish nationalism arises from the concepts of ethnic nationalism, but can it survive in this form in the later part of the twentieth century? Inexorable and irreversible changes are affecting the character of Scotland, as indeed they are of all comparable parts of the world.

Scotland has few means of resisting these forces. Most of our important institutions have been anglicised since the war. Chief among these have been the universities, which are organised on a UK basis. You will remember that our universities were among the leading opponents of devolution in the seventies. In a country with a scientific and intellectual tradition such as ours, this was a bitter pill for many of us to swallow.

Scottish working-class culture has proved surprisingly robust. It is the mainspring both of modern Scottish writing and drama. By contrast the bourgeois tradition has grown feeble because it has been more open to anglicisation. The middle classes have been heavily exposed to the assimilative process. In the last couple of decades many people have come to Scotland from the south. They work in the new industries or penetrate the professions or are part of a growing population of rentiers and second home owners.

Such people may be seeking an enhanced quality of life; they may be making a career move into what they perceive as a provincial arena in the hope of distinguishing themselves in it and returning to London eventually. They may be retiring on investments gathered from a commercial or professional life in the much richer south. Whatever their motive, many of them make a genuine commitment to Scotland. Their presence among us is a fact of life and is often an adornment of it. Indeed, if you go to comparable non-metropolitan regions of Europe or the US, you will observe that exactly the same tendencies are taking place.

Even the local institutions guaranteed by the Union, the church and the law, are in various kinds of difficulty. The protection of Scots law has made it largely resistant to English infiltration. But this is not in every way beneficial. It has protected our criminal tradition but it has sidelined mercantile law. For example, the suppliers of the *Glasgow Herald*'s new presses insisted that the contract be written in English law. There seems a danger that Scots law will be driven into a rather squalid ghetto of criminal practice, trust work, domestic law and conveyancing. It comes as no surprise to be told that London is also the point at which Britain's European legal expertise is developing.

That Scots law has become something of a backwater was the theme of an article in *The Herald* by Lord McCluskey. He warned that it was in danger of being excluded from the development of European law.

The idea that because its roots were in the European tradition it had some sort of advantage was, he said, a fairy tale. On the criminal side Scots law has indeed been influential in influencing English practice but it seems to have become a machine for putting people in jail. Recent scandals in the judiciary suggested that this protected and sheltered elite had surrendered to some kind of complacency.

The Kirk's dominance of our national life began to wane with the Disruption, when it was lured into a contest with the temporal powers which it could not win. The contrast in the twentieth century with Ireland is again interesting. De Valera, in his drive to consolidate independence, appointed the Catholic church to a position of national guardianship. The result was indeed consolidated independence. But there was a heavy price to be paid in the form of an oppressive literary censorship. In Scotland we live in a secular age and the church's influence is feeble. It no longer attracts so many people of the first intellectual rank to make a career in it – though that is not to say there are not able people in the Kirk.

A balance sheet of sorts begins to emerge. The price of close Union with England is cultural assimilation and dominance. The Scottish economy, on the edge of Europe, has to be an open economy; so too must be its culture. Closing the door to external influence is a recipe for stagnation and mediocrity. That is the dilemma faced by modern Scotland.

These forces all make it difficult for us to develop a convincing ethnic nationalism. Apart from the new Scots (who may still perceive themselves as English or British, though some become more Scottish than the Scots), we cannot cut ourselves off from the wider polity and economy. The Balkanisation of the UK would be a nightmare. This difficulty is made worse by the fact that, even without its new population, Scotland is itself culturally diverse. We are not one country with a dominant metropolis. We are a very curious country – our real capital city, London, is not within our boundaries. We have four cities with extensive hinterlands, and caught up in rivalry with each other. We have vast, thinly populated rural regions which are deeply suspicious of the central belt.

During the devolution referendum in the seventies, these differences were skilfully exploited by the opponents of change, and indeed they explain why Scotland has found it difficult to combine politically. The Republic of Ireland is highly centralised, with its economy and political system based in Dublin: it would be impossible and indeed dangerous, to replicate such a system in Scotland. If Scotland were to gain its independence within the European Community, then its own constitution would have to reflect its personality and balance its regional interests. Without such safeguards,. Scotland would quickly fall apart.

There are interesting differences between our historical experience and that of other small countries like Ireland or Georgia, (which I recently visited). Chief among these is the fact that Scotland has not been oppressed. Oppression is perhaps an essential precondition for active nationalism. England's attitude to Scotland has been benign if sometimes patronising or arrogant. It has left Scotland to its own devices and has accepted the need to equalise the resources available for public services.

This means that public expenditure in Scotland exceeds the amount raised by taxation in Scotland. Generations of Scots civil servants have quietly achieved that result by their patient and subtle diplomacy in Whitehall. This so-called advantage needs some qualification, because the higher figures of public spending per head in Scotland do not reveal the enormous concentrations of wealth in England, which remains a much richer country. The figures arise partly from the higher proportion of public housing in Scotland. They also reflect the higher unit cost of delivering public services to a country with the lowest population density in Europe. England's wealth is rooted in its property and its invested wealth, and the Thatcher regime discriminates heartily in favour of the property owner through mortgage relief. Scotland was also more highly taxed than England through the rating system, and it has been amusing to hear the English outrage as this anomaly has been corrected through the introduction of the poll tax.

Even if much of the English criticism is simplistic, it's an ill wind – for among some of the excessive and indeed abusive statements are more sensible reflections. Among these is the observation that the Tories' root and branch opposition to devolution has distorted political life in Scotland. Mrs Thatcher has bound us together to a remarkable degree. Labour's dominance is artificial in that it arises from a genuine Scottish dislike of the values of Thatcherism rather than a universal commitment to socialist principles. Indeed, Labour's dominance is somewhat exaggerated, since it has only one MP north of the Highland line.

The unpopularity of the Conservatives does not just arise from the popular perception that they are now an anti-Scottish party. There are grievances that are real and specific. Some of our great assets – our universities, our teaching hospitals – are perceived as liabilities and attacked. On the contrary they clearly have an economic value since they provide a service in great and growing demand – it is the way they are financed that causes endless difficulties. Indeed they must form the basis of our future economic prosperity: for this must depend on high-value intellectual-based services and industries. Our scientific and intellectual community must not be eroded. Our medical excellence is a precious resource since health care too is a growth industry in which Scotland by dint of its native tradition has a leading position.

If that is a bourgeois grievance, then the decline of our heavy industries bears disproportionately on our working classes.

The case for Scottish independence within the European Community would have to be justified by the perception that Scottish interests are genuinely different from those of England and that a Scottish Parliament could express them and safeguard them more effectively. It is ironic that we owe to an English backlash the fact that Scottish independence is, for the first time, truly on the political agenda.

If it were negotiated with goodwill, and within the constitutional, political and economic framework of the European Community which removes the prospect of separation and exclusion, then we have nothing to fear from it. Indeed that development of federal relationships within the United Kingdom has long been the best hope of modernising the Union.

What we are hearing from the south, in increasingly strident tones, are the first cries of distress as the Westminster Parliament begins to sense its own supremacy under threat. The European reality is beginning to be felt at every level and is indeed working as a compensating force against the indifference of the Thatcher Government to such questions as public health and safety, and minimum guarantees for employees. If genuine political union does develop in Europe, then the Council of Ministers, subject to sovereign national Parliaments, must in time be superseded by federal European Institutions.

After the devolution fiasco in the seventies, I despaired of ever seeing a Scottish parliament in my lifetime. I am now more hopeful than I have ever been that it is coming before too long. My vision is not that of the romantic nationalist: the well-being of the people of Scotland must be an important constraint on the wilder impulses of constitutional visionaries. But Scotland is not alone in Europe as a small nation which feels emotionally frustrated. The European spirit is genuine, and the small forgotten nations now perceive that they may find their place in the sun – without the evils of Balkanisation. The idea of Scottishness cannot be based on romantic historic concepts. In the definition of Regis Debray, Scottish nationalism must be elective because it is reasonable and conforms to the reality of modern Scotland. Anything else would be romantic tosh. But it would be odd if the new punitive spirit of some English commentators, who would cut us off without a penny, were to produce a new bloom in a forgotten garden, for an oppressed or insulted nation will put the recovery of its dignity beyond the realms of petty calculation.

Scottish identity was a theme too in Kemp's journalism and he often surveyed developments on the scene in his *Herald* and *Observer* columns. What follows are a selection.

The origins of nationalism. Scotch myths:

The failure of Scotland to develop a full-blown nationalism in the nineteenth century distinguishes it from Ireland and other smaller European nations. For this there are many explanations; the connection with England opened many doors to prosperity and improvement and Scots successfully operated within the context of imperial expansion; the country was absorbed in industrialisation and religious schism.

But an important and rarely appreciated factor was the work of Scottish historians of the Enlightenment. They inflicted lacerating wounds on the historical assumptions on which Scottish patriotic pride had been based.

Chief victim was George Buchanan (1506-82), on whose history was based a school of political thought favoured by Presbyterians and Whigs until the end of the eighteenth century.

It asserted the right of aristocratic resistance to monarchs and rested on an interpretation of an ancient Scottish constitution from the legendary beginnings of the Scottish monarchy under King Fergus MacFerquhard in 330BC. In fact, this line of kings may have been a mere propagandist invention with which to refute English claims of sovereignty, and the historian John of Fordun may have been an early equivalent of the modern spin doctor.

The cruellest conclusion of the new historians was that Scotland had been liberated from backwardness and the petty despotism of its overweening nobles and lairds by the Union with England. Far from being a noble tradition protecting Scotland from military conquest, the Buchananite concept of a king elected by nobles who could remove him if he did not fulfil his duty of defending Scottish sovereignty was shown to have been a recipe for corruption, disorder, weak central rule and the survival of feudalism long after its sell-by date.

According to this view, the Scottish Parliament was corrupt and malleable; the legal system was arbitrary and despotic. Commercial advance allowed England to outstrip Scotland not only economically and culturally but in the establishment of liberty. Scotland was as backward as Poland, than which no European country was more retarded because of the grip of its aristocracy.

The new historians perceived that through the Union England conferred rights on Scotland which it had not enjoyed, that the Union had propelled it rapidly out of the darkness. They questioned the association of the Presbyterian movement with concepts of liberty and highlighted its dogmatic nature and violent history. This argument is put convincingly by historian Colin Kidd in his book *Subverting Scotland's Past*.

It was perhaps inevitable that the age of reason which flowered in Scotland would destroy the mythology of the kind on which every nation falsely rests. Historic error, wrote Ernest Renan, quoted by Kidd, is indispensable to the creation of a nation.

Scotch myth or Caledonian zeugma?

As a figure of speech the phrase the Scottish identity is not so much an oxymoron as a zeugma, since it unites widely disparate elements in a concept which, no matter how irrational, has persisted.

The iconology of the oppressed and dispersed Highlander has been adopted by Lowland Scotland, itself largely of teutonic origin although its place names, mostly Celtic, testify to an older order.

My mother, who was brought up in an Aberdeenshire fishing village, recalled that in the broad Scots she spoke were German words, like *fremd*, meaning a stranger.

Elizabeth Grant of Rothiemurchus, in that marvellous book *Memoirs of a Highland Lady*, recalled that when George IV wore a kilt of the Royal Stuart tartan during his visit to Edinburgh in 1822 the 'Anglo-Saxons', the local bigwigs, were much offended.

A revulsion against tartan kitsch, memorably trounced by Murray and Barbara Grigor, became fashionable in the Seventies and returns in Carl MacDougall's book *Painting the Forth Bridge, A Search for Scottish Identity*.

The book does not spare us the darker side of a Scotland hooked on drink, drugs and domestic violence. MacDougall argues: 'the romanticised Scotland is far more palpable, far more easily digested, remembered and understood than the cruel and often vindictive reality and the guilt that caused the birth of our romance with ourselves and the ways in which we have emulsified our past'.

This judgement is a little harsh. In the music halls of my youth arcadian visions of Highland scenes offered real escape to people locked in desperate slums. Our myths soothe and console as well as mislead.

As Sam Goldwyn is supposed to have said, no one went broke underestimating public taste. MacDougall quotes the producer Arthur Freed, who came looking for locations for the film Brigadoon and reported: 'I went to Scotland and found nothing there that looks like Scotland.'

The tourist industry needs its amiable inventions if it is to survive. The Scotland of drug abuse and domestic violence would not sit well in the promotional literature, and a few harmless liberties are perfectly excusable.

I recall the *New Yorker* film reviewer's sense of shock when he encountered the Edinburgh of Trainspotting, so brutally different from the city of the international festival and noble Georgian vistas with which he was familiar.

Perhaps the real answer to the question is that we should stop worrying about it, and instead embrace the contradictions and complexities of our history as a rich distillation of which we can feel reasonably proud.

The poem by Iain Crichton Smith read at the opening of the Scottish Parliament exhorts this 'three voiced country' to sing in a new world with friendliness to all, without dogma and with respect for its own origins, 'inventive, original, philosophical'.

The poem ends: 'Then without shame we can esteem ourselves.'

The Goschen/Barnett formula. (1992)

We start with a confession. *The Herald* has, these past few weeks, been mis-spelling the name of the formula by which Scotland's share of UK public expenditure is decided.

In our error we have at least been consistent, referring throughout to the Goshen/Barnett formula. This must have set up an irritation somewhere in my subconscious. No-one had complained or questioned us. But for no particular reason beyond a vague conviction that something was amiss, I looked it up.

My suspicions proved correct. The formula – the Goschen Proportion as it inevitably came to be called – was named after George Joachim Goschen, the Victorian statesman and banker. He introduced the formula in the 1880s when he was Chancellor of the Exchequer in Lord Salisbury's Government.

The best account I could find of it is in a book by Olive and Sydney Checkland. It was a curious circumstance, they wrote, that the Conservatives did more to recognise Scottish claims than the

Liberal Party so favoured by the Scots. By the 1880s Scottish national sentiment had revived and the formula was one of a series of measures designed to placate it.

RB Cunninghame Graham and Professor J S Blackie were notables of this period. Graham was a romantic figure – author, South American rancher, and gold prospector. He argued that Scots had a right to waste their own taxes.

Blackie was the first chairman of the Scottish Home Rule Association. He was professor of Greek at Aberdeen and Edinburgh, and founded the chair of Celtic at Edinburgh. The Checklands wrote drily that he was 'aggressively attired in plaid and bonnet' and carried a staff. He argued that Gaelic was derived from Greek which reflected 'the tenuousness of his grip on both languages'.

From the early 1830s the Home Secretary in London had been responsible for Scotland, drawing on the advice of the Lord Advocate. A series of boards was set up – on prisons, poor law, lunacy. The Scottish Education Department was founded in 1872 and the Crofters Commission in 1886.

The Goschen Proportion, introduced in 1886 according to the Checklands and 1889 according to the Scottish Office, was among a whole a series of concessions. Electoral reforms raised the number of Scottish seats. In 1885, largely under the influence of Lord Rosebery, the office of Scottish Secretary was established, superseding the Lord Advocate save in legal matters.

This, of course, was only the beginning of administrative devolution. The Scottish Secretary had no real power. He answered in Parliament for the Scottish boards but had little control over them. Appurtenances of government, they continued to be based in Dover House (where today Scottish Office Ministers have their elegant offices, with splendid views of Horse Guards Parade).

And what of Goschen himself? The son of a banker, the grandson of a Leipzig publisher, he had the sort of career in politics that would be difficult if not impossible today. He began as a Liberal MP and made his mark at the Board of Trade and elsewhere.

But he fell out both with Chamberlain (for his radicalism) and Gladstone (over Home Rule). He was elected for Edinburgh East in 1885, and was a founder of the Liberal Unionist Party. He helped to defeat Gladstone's Home Rule Bill in 1886. This was a watershed in Scottish politics: the *Glasgow Herald* and the *Scotsman*, both Liberal, turned Conservative amid much public uproar.

He succeeded Lord Randolph Churchill at the Treasury in Lord Salisbury's Government and it was as Chancellor that he introduced the Goschen Proportion. He later became the first Viscount Goschen and died in 1907.

As the Scottish Office grew in powers and importance, Scottish civil servants operated with growing skill in Whitehall. Without anyone really noticing it, they began to build up Scotland's share of spending. At ministerial level the partnership between Harold Wilson and the late Lord Ross was particularly fruitful.

In 1958 the Goschen formula was replaced by a system by which the Scottish Office bargained for a share of individual functional programmes. Officials liked this method. The late Sir Douglas Haddow, the permanent secretary at the Scottish Office, described it as 'very rewarding' since it gave his department the ability to retain unallocated funds.

Ironically, the devolution debates of the seventies brought Scotland's favourable treatment to more general attention. In 1979 the Barnett formula (named after Joel, later Lord, Barnett) restored the principle of a fixed proportion of new spending being allocated to Scotland, England, and Wales.

But this time the terms were less favourable. Even so, while conceding Scotland's relative advantage, some commentators believe it to have been exaggerated by per capita figures published by the Government. This is the calculation that causes the resentment in the south, although it is politically disingenuous. It has the mathematical effect of exaggerating the disparities because of Scotland's much lower density of population. Scotland has only 66 people per square mile compared with 362 in England.

You don't have to be a mathematical genius to work out that a mile of motorway in Scotland would cost much more per head than in England. (The low-cost version would work out at 59p per head in Scotland. The equivalent cost for England would be about sixpence.)

But relating expenditure to revenue raised in a particular geographical area is a system of derivation rather than equalisation.

To assign income tax in this way is a novel proposition in Britain. Indeed, few devolutionary schemes have envisaged it. Most give the Assembly marginal tax-raising powers – and even those would cause the Treasury angst on the grounds that they might distort UK economic policy.

In the 20th century, the Scottish nationalist movement took shape.

Roland Eugene Muirhead (1868-1964) who for 75 years 'relentlessly campaigned' for an independent Scottish parliament is now very largely forgotten in the country to which he devoted so much energy.

He was one of a group which formed the Young Scots League around 1900. It sought home rule through the Liberal Party. He turned then to the ILP, and practised what he preached in 1914 by transforming his family business, the Gryffe Tannery in Bridge of Weir, into a co-partnership with model conditions and a 40-hour week.

He and Tom Johnston, later Churchill's Secretary of State for Scotland and father of the modern Scottish Office, were among those who set up the Scottish Home Rule Association in 1917. Its efforts produced several home rule Bills. The Bill of 1924 fell with the Ramsay Macdonald Government and the 1927 Bill, giving Scotland dominion status (this was the year the Statute of Westminster set up the Commonwealth), was talked out by a Unionist.

The SHRA's activities were part of the pattern of agitation which led to the formation first of the National Party of Scotland in 1928 and then of the Scottish National Party in 1934.

Johnston wrote of him with evident affection in *Memories* (1951):

Almost as far back as spans the memory of living man Roland Muirhead has been a notable standard-bearer for self-government in Scotland ...

Half a century ago he packed his bag and walked out of the family tannery business in Renfrewshire to live the free life, first in an Owenite colony in the State of Washington (USA) and then in a non-violent anarchist colony in the same state.

I never rightly got the hang of what happened during his brief sojourn in these oases in the wicked world, but he was soon back in London organising a co-operative tannery, and shortly thereafter he was engaged managing the old family business in Renfrewshire, which – lest you think he is simply a starry-eyed dreamer! – he has managed for years and still does with conspicuous success.

The SNP in 1934 fused the National Party of Scotland and the Scottish Party, created by a group of dissident Unionists after the Cathcart breakaway of 1932. The party was immediately riven by splits over pacificism and fascism. Germany was trying to seduce nationalist movements throughout Europe and the consul in Scotland sent an emissary to Arthur Donaldson (SNP chairman in the sixties). The approach was repulsed.

When the war broke out, Johnston wrote, there was an energetic police round-up of the few – if any – subversive pro-Nazi and Mosleyite elements.

At the time somebody took it upon himself to hint to the police that Roland might be a sympathiser with Hitler, or at any rate was sufficiently anti-English to warrant a raid upon his house.

A raid duly took place and after some locks had been forced there was borne off in triumph a sporting rifle of last-century vintage which had belonged to an uncle or a brother, plus a few rounds of revolver ammunition, but no revolver.

Fortunately there existed at the time in the offices of the Crown Prosecutor and the Lord Advocate a sense of humour, and the engines of war referred to were hurriedly ordered to be returned, so that Roland Muirhead was deprived of a martyr's crown. But he complains that he has never yet been compensated for the damage to his locks.

After the war, as described in a slim volume dedicated to Muirhead, *Scotland's Constitution*, Muirhead came to the conclusion that the parliamentary route would not bring independence. In 1950 he formed a group called the Scottish National Congress to pursue independence Gandhi-style, by non-violence and non-co-operation, but he could not accept by the rule, introduced under the chairmanship of Dr John McIntyre, banning dual membership of the SNP and other parties.

He thus set up the Scottish Secretariat at Elmbank Crescent. Here would meet the Committee of Articles. It examined the constitutions of the world and prepared a Scottish constitution. Noted lawyers helped. They included Andrew Dewar Gibb, professor of Scots law at Glasgow, a founder of the Scottish Party and the Saltire Society, and the author of a book about Scotland's contribution to the Empire. It contains one of the most eloquent and lucid explanations for Scotland's recurrent dissatisfaction with the Union: the Empire, which could not have been built without the Scots, made the name of England great.

In his foreword to the new edition of the constitution, John Murphy writes that it was still incomplete when the 'Scottish Constituent Provision Assembly convened in the George Adam's Ballroom in Edinburgh on April 21, 1962'. A hundred and eight delegates turned up to 'hold Scotland's first Assembly since 1707'. Murphy himself was a delegate. The 97 articles, with illustrations by Matthew McKenna, are published at last.

We return again to Johnston for a portrait of Muirhead in old age:

He maintains an office in Glasgow which he calls the Scottish Secretariat, where there is stored many thousands of Home Rule cuttings, pamphlets and books, and to that office there wends daily this pioneer, still rosy-cheeked, but now, alas, ageing and bent under the weight of years, all the pockets of his homespun tweed suit stuffed and bulging with memoranda – this voluntary, this anti-compulsionist, this resolute and determined opponent of all bureaucracy and centralised government, with his eyes fixed upon the, to him, essential condition precedent to any beneficent or worthwhile change, a Home Rule Parliament for Scotland.

A leading figure in the war time and post-war nationalist movement was Wendy Wood who famously threatened in the 1970s to fast until death in the nationalist cause. But was she what she seemed? In 1998, Kemp looked into the past for *The Observer*.

The revered Scottish patriot Wendy Wood, wreathed in honour when she died in 1981 aged 88, may have been an agent provocateur in the pay of MI5. She is said to have planted gelignite on nationalist students to incriminate them and to have procured the imprisonment of an SNP leader under wartime regulations.

These extraordinary claims, long current in a small circle, gained wider currency in 1998 with the death of Robert McIntyre, 84, the SNP's first Westminster MP and later its chairman and president.

Senior nationalists gathered in Stirling for McIntyre's funeral recalled two episodes in which Wood may have been implicated.

In the first, Arthur Donaldson, later SNP chairman, was held for five weeks in Barlinnie prison in 1941 on suspicion of being a German spy. He was released because MI5 did not want its source compromised. In the second, the folklorist Calum Maclean, the poet

Sorley Maclean's brother, spent the war in Ireland after almost being compromised by planted gelignite.

Wood, born in Kent of a Scottish mother and Northern Irish father, campaigned for Scottish independence from the 1930s.

Before his death, at the age of 84, McIntyre said Wood had left a suitcase at a student flat in Edinburgh, asking its occupants to look after it for her. They were horrified to discover it contained gelignite. Maclean, then taking an honours degree in Celtic studies, asked McIntyre for his help. That night McIntyre arranged for the suitcase to be dumped by boat in the Firth of Forth. Next day police raided the flat. Maclean went to Ireland, ostensibly to pursue postgraduate studies. However, Sean O'Sullivan, the Irish folklorist, said before his death two years ago that Maclean had told him that he had left Scotland to avoid the war.

Arthur Donaldson's widow, Violet, who lives in Forfar, met her husband in the United States when he was working there. In 1937, they returned to Scotland and took up chicken farming at Lugton in Ayrshire, where Wood and her male companion – she had divorced her husband, Walter Cuthbert, in 1940 – visited them. They boasted of their exploits – raids 'over the border' and 'acts of sabotage'.

Mrs Donaldson said: 'She did the dirty by Arthur. We came to the conclusion she was a paid government agent. We heard from a third party that she was saying we lived so well that we must be living on Nazi money.'

At that time Donaldson was on the executive committee of the anti-war Nationalist Mutual Aid Society, which assisted conscientious objectors and helped people evade national service by fleeing to the Highlands.

On 3 May 1941, police visited the homes of 17 nationalists in Glasgow, Edinburgh, Aberdeen, Renfrewshire and Ayrshire, taking 12 in for questioning. One was Muriel Gibson, who had joined the National Party (a precursor of the SNP) in 1932. She was later commissioned in the Auxiliary Territorial Service and after the war left the WRAC a lieutenant-colonel.

She said when I talked to her: 'The police were trying to get us to say that Arthur Donaldson was a spy, which I denied and I know it was totally untrue.'

Papers in the Scottish Record Office include a note from the Crown Office saying there was a 'considerable body of evidence (against him) demonstrating highly subversive activities extending over a long period'. It added: 'Donaldson, like other quislings, uses a local Home Rule movement as the basis of his subversive activities.'

The authorities suspected that Donaldson might have been recruited by German intelligence while in the US. The SNP had been twice visited before the war by a known German agent. He is named in the public records as Dr Von Teffenar of Berlin. However, German documents uncovered by Douglas McLeod of BBC Scotland name him as Dr Gerhard von Tevenar.

The public documents make it clear that the 1941 operation was ordered by M15, authorised from its wartime headquarters at Oxford and co-ordinated by MI5's Scottish commander, Lieutenant-Colonel P Perfect.

Secretary of State Tom Johnston released Donaldson after the intervention of James Maxton MP. A note from the Crown Office dated 4 April 1942 said Donaldson was released 'because MI5 would not allow essential witnesses to give evidence before the advisory committee which might have led to the disclosure of their identity'.

Ms Gibson said Wood was a 'funny individual'. 'I would never have relied 100 per cent on Wendy Wood, because she was an odd-ball,' she said.

Mrs Donaldson said: 'She was a clever, clever woman but she wasn't stable at all. She wasn't a nice person.'

By the 1960s, the Scottish nationalist movement had become 'a bibulous and disputatious demi-monde of mad poets and paranoiac activists', Kemp wrote in his *Observer* column.

Every so often, amid bills and junk mail, something delicious comes through the post. John Herdman's account of an era in Scottish politics – Poets, Pubs, Polls and Pillar Boxes – conforms delightfully to the dictum that brevity is the soul of wit. Herdman was brought up, a bourgeois boy, in Edinburgh. His father accepted the Union, and English domination, as a fact of life but Herdman, who sensed a 'whiff of falsity' in the Scottish history primers of his time, embraced nationalism while a student at Cambridge and never changed his mind. Chiefly known as a writer of novels and short stories, he has also published a much admired book on Bob Dylan's lyrics.

This little memoir is a labour of love. Through its 48 pages, Herdman parades a succession of characters, describing them with a keen eye for the ridiculous but nearly always with an amused affection. For all their eccentricities, they played their part in the creation of the political consensus that has now led to a Scottish parliament. He joined the SNP towards the end of the Sixties, when oil stirred nationalism out of its doldrums, and became involved in a bibulous and disputatious demi-monde of mad poets and paranoiac activists, whose taste for vicious infighting was out of all proportion to their political importance at the time. He briefly edited *Catalyst*, the magazine of the 1320 Club, the ginger group proscribed by the SNP, and gives us a vivid portrait of the enigmatic major FAC Boothby, thought to have been an agent provocateur (a judgement Herdman sees no need to revise).

Boothby was a cousin of the maverick Bob Boothby. He served in the British army and had to flee the Home Counties after the press published stories of satanic cavortings in the woods with naked girls and boys. He turned up in the Borders, sometime in the fifties, as a fearless nationalist leader in search of troops to lead. In 1971, Herdman attended a seminar at which he saw Boothby deep in conversation with Matthew Lygate of the Scottish Workers' Revolutionary Party. 'I was surprised because Lygate was as far to the left as Boothby was to the right.' The following week, Lygate was arrested on charges of bank robbery in furtherance of his political aims and sentenced to 24 years (he was freed in 1983). When, a couple of years later, Boothby, as leader of the 'Tartan Army', was convicted after a bungled bank robbery – the chosen branch had closed – he received a much lighter sentence, three years, of which he served only 18 months.

At the centre of this curious scene in which the literary nationalists moved stood the figure of Hugh MacDiarmid. His poetry had stirred Herdman's nationalism at Cambridge. His only rival was Norman MacCaig, since his other great contemporary, Sorley Maclean, wrote in the Gaelic tradition and therefore was no threat. Maclean, a lovely man whom it was also my good fortune to know, was magically unworldly, and in a hotel was once found by his wife Renee trying to make a telephone call with the hairdryer. Here Maclean is giving a reading:

'His personal idiosyncrasies only added to the delight of his performances – the hums and haws, the pointed yet rambling introductions, the tightly screwed-up eyes, the shuffling of mixed-up papers, and the obsessively repeated glances at the large watch lying on the table – which he was somehow able to achieve without in the least compromising the passionate outpouring of language.'

Herdman's own verdict on MacDiarmid, who died in 1978, is perhaps a touch hyperbolic: 'His inspiration dominated the national movement in the broadest sense form the 1920s onwards, and while no momentous shift in the consciousness of a nation can be attributed to the influence of a single individual, none the less if one man can be said to personify, to embody a national aspiration which, while long largely unconscious, lived on subliminally and slowly struggled into self-awareness and self-articulation, then that man can only be Christopher Murray Grieve.'

An age of innocence has gone. The SNP, in the serious business of power politics, must prove its competence. A dull virtue, indeed.

In the 1980s, a leading figure in the nationalist movement was Willie McRae. His death from a bullet wound sustained after a car crash in 1985 gave rise to many conspiracy theories, as Kemp recounted in 1993.

Senior Government sources now accept that an error of judgement was made when it was decided not to hold a fatal accident inquiry into the death of the leading nationalist, Willie McRae, in 1985.

The decision let conspiracist theories bloom. Largely fed from exile by Adam Busby and David Dinsmore, these claimed that McRae was murdered by agents of the British state or even by Mossad, the Israeli intelligence service.

The truth was much less glamorous. McRae, 61, already in a suicidal frame of mind, knew as he sat trapped and injured in his crashed car that he faced almost certain imprisonment.

The probability that he shot himself with his own .22 pistol, a memento of his India days, is overwhelming. His brother, Dr Fergus McRae, in 1990 issued a public statement accepting that this is what happened and calling for his brother's memory to be left in peace.

An inquiry, however, would have opened the police and the health authorities to charges of indolence or incompetence. The failure promptly to recognise that McRae had been shot retarded the collection of evidence at the scene of the crash, on the A87 near Loch Loyne.

At first it was assumed that here was a road accident with no third parties involved and that McRae's injuries had been caused by it. By the time the gunshot wound had been discovered and police sent back to the scene, much of the evidence had been destroyed or moved.

McRae had been a former vice-chairman of the SNP. An outstanding lawyer, he was also a vigorous anti-nuclear campaigner. War service had taken him to India and he had joined the Congress Party. He also had close connections with Israel, where he worked and taught after the war.

The conspiracy theory has been fed by a steady flow of dubious circumstantial evidence from Busby and Dinsmore, two members of the SNLA who have been in exile since 1983.

In June 1985, three months after McRae died, Dinsmore issued a statement claiming he had been in regular contact by mail and telephone with McRae until two days before his death.

He named surveillance vehicles with Special Branch registrations which he claimed had been seen on the road the day McRae died. The authorities do not deny that these were Special Branch numbers. These have been disseminated widely in London. Car numbers provided by Dinsmore were first published in the *Morning Star*.

Dinsmore's claim unwittingly disclosed his manipulative intentions, it is claimed. One of the numbers was indeed of a Special Branch car: but it was of a car that had been used for the surveillance of Dinsmore, and it had been sold before McRae's death.

McRae's crashed car was noticed by passing tourists about 100 yards below the Invergarry-Kyle of Lochalsh Road near Loch Loyne at 10am on Saturday, April 5, 1985. One of the first on the scene was SNP member David Coutts, his wife, and a friend, who happened to be passing. (Mr Coutts fought Dundee East for the SNP at the last election.)

McRae at first appeared to be dead from the injuries sustained when his Volvo left the road and crashed down the bank. But signs of life were discerned and he was taken first to Raigmore Hospital, Inverness, as the victim of a road accident.

There was congealed blood on his temple. Underneath was a perfectly round bullet hole. It is not clear whether this was discovered at Raigmore or not. The conspiracist case rests on the proposition that it was and that this fact was suppressed.

The doctors more probably feared that McRae had suffered neurological damage. Raigmore had no scanner at the time and they would have sent him to Aberdeen Royal Infirmary as a matter of urgency, disturbing him as little as possible. At Aberdeen an X-ray showed that a bullet had lodged in his brain. He died later without recovering consciousness.

By the time police returned to the site, the car had been removed. An empty half-bottle of whisky had been found in it. It was not immediately clear, in the rough and broken ground, where the precise location of the accident had been. Evidence had been trampled on and disturbed. The pistol was found on April 7 in a burn directly below where, it was surmised, the driver's door had been. Two bullets had been fired, of which one was not recovered.

In 1990, Lord Fraser of Carmyllie, then the Lord Advocate, in a letter to Sir Nicholas Fairbairn said that the post-mortem showed the pistol had been pressed firmly against the skin.

According to senior Government sources, the decision not to hold an FAI was influenced by political considerations but mostly by a desire to spare the feelings of the McRae family. The decision was endorsed at the time by Gordon Wilson, then chairman of the SNP. McRae, a man whose early brilliance had been somewhat dissipated, was in a highly neurotic condition before he set off from Glasgow on his last journey on the Friday evening, bound for his cottage in Kintail. He had severe drinking problems and issues around his probable homosexuality.

His brother had taken his pistol away from him on a previous occasion, fearing the use he might put it to. In his statement in 1990 Dr McRae said that three days before his death Willie had spoken to a close friend about suicide. Others recalled that he talked of it frequently and had made inquiries about voluntary euthanasia.

William Wolfe, the former SNP chairman and president, had a business association with him and recalled, when we spoke earlier this year, that at a meeting shortly before his death he had clearly not been himself. Wolfe, incidentally, had become converted to the conspiracy theory because of a TV documentary which disseminated Dinsmore's claims and the general confusion surrounding the forensic evidence.

McRae had a black sense of humour. Some of his claims were so outlandish that they suggested they flowed from the mind of a fantasist. On one occasion in 1964 someone, perhaps he himself, inserted in *The Herald* a bogus notice of his own death. To the letter of condolence, he replied: 'Dear me, when did I dee?'

On the night before his departure from Glasgow he had, according to some accounts, set himself on fire through smoking in bed. This is a classic symptom of drunkenness.

As he journeyed north, his junior partner was phoning police stations – before the probable time of the crash – because he was worried about him. He apparently stopped to change a tyre, and the conspiracists have adduced evidence to support the idea that he was forced off the road.

The official theory is that McRae was depressed, had been drinking and had driven north with the general aim of suicide. He went over the edge, by accident or design, and found himself down the bank, trapped in the car, perhaps unable to get out even if he had wanted to.

To his depression, of which there was ample prior evidence, would now be added another grim calculation. Had he survived the crash he would almost certainly have faced imprisonment as a persistent drunk-driver. He already had one conviction and another charge was pending. Even a layman knows that a third drunk-driving charge means prison, and McRae was a lawyer. According to this view, he discharged his pistol once to see if it was working and then shot himself.

The law officers of the day were Lord Cameron of Lochbroom, Lord Advocate, and Peter (later Lord) Fraser, Solicitor-General. Friends recall that they debated the question of a fatal accident inquiry thoroughly.

On the one hand they were keen to cross-examine those who had made statements about the odd circumstances. Some of these statements were full of inconsistencies and had been changed with the passage of time.

On the other hand there were political considerations. Peter Fraser at the time was MP for Angus East, in desperately close competition with Andrew Welsh of the SNP, who in fact ousted him in 1987. An inquiry would embarrass the SNP and open Fraser to the charge of opportunism.

But the clinching argument for Lord Cameron was the family's wish that there should be no FAI and his desire to spare their feelings, for he knew that the seamy side of McRae's life would have to be paraded in public.

Around Willie McRae has grown a legend from which propaganda may be fashioned. Members of the Willie McRae Society gather every year around the cairn on the A87 which commemorates his death.

He is an unlikely saint. Somewhere, perhaps, he is having a sardonic laugh to himself for having caused all this trouble for the state.

Maybe the curious circumstances of his death were the last and blackest joke of all.

On the death of nationalist poet and folklorist Hamish Henderson.

The idea of 'writing' folk songs, rather than plucking them untouched from the oral tradition, seems something of a paradox. Yet that is exactly what Hamish Henderson did, as indeed did Robert Burns and Allan Ramsay.

Henderson's death at the age of 82 in 2002 removed what seemed a geologically entrenched feature from the Scottish landscape and brings to an end a life rich in achievement and contradiction. Henderson himself acknowledged the proselytising nature of the folklorist when, citing the work of Ramsay and Burns, he wrote that it could be plausibly argued that the Scottish folk tradition was nothing other than the sum total of a succession of revivals from the eighteenth century onwards. His apprenticeship began in Aberdeen as a boy, with the manuscript notebooks of Gavin Greig, containing 3,000 songs collected by the Buchan poet. Henderson's first thought was to transcribe some of the ballads and try them out at the 'bothy nicht' song sessions at the Imperial Hotel.

But while acknowledging the magnificence of Greig's collection, he noted that there were omissions. The first was the absence of songs from the travelling folk whose 'joyous exuberance' he remembered when they picked berries around Blairgowrie, where he was born in 1919. The second was the sound of the songs themselves. And so when he and the Gaelic scholar Calum MacLean founded the School of Scottish Studies at Edinburgh University in 1951, they set out on a life's work of collecting words and music in the field.

The process was dynamic: not only did Henderson discover talents such as Jeannie Robertson, but his work stimulated folk singers to investigate ancestral styles.

A conspiracy between artifice and the folk tradition lies at the heart of all great music. The result was the folk revival of the fifties, which rejected the polite cloak which had been wrapped around the Burns canon and ran counter to the overwhelming influence on popular music of the blues-driven black tradition which later produced such artists as Ry Cooder and Captain Beefheart and His Magic Band.

Henderson's alternative festival, the Edinburgh People's Festival, staged from 1951 to 1953, was the forerunner of the Festival Fringe. During the war, he had been an intelligence officer, serving in North Africa and with the Partisans in Italy. His book of war poetry, *Elegies For the Dead in Cyrenaica*, won him the Somerset Maugham award, a travelling scholarship which he used to visit Italy, from which he was expelled because of his left-wing views. And herein lay another paradox which he cheerfully confronted. He was a nationalist, intensely proud of Scotland, its achievements and its traditions, but he was also an internationalist. His *Freedom Come All Ye* has been suggested as a national anthem. He was very moved in 1992 when it was sung at the Democracy Demonstration during the European summit in Edinburgh: an enormous crowd of 25,000, perhaps the biggest political rally ever held in Scotland, turned out to indicate that Scottish politics was at last emerging from the long winter that had followed the failure of the 1979 Scotland Act.

The song's uncompromising Scots make it less than accessible, nor is it as easily sung along as *Scots Wha Hae* or *Flower of Scotland*. But its sentiments make it an apposite text for a modern Scotland. It stands for social justice, denounces imperialism and racism and asserts, with Aesop, that a crust eaten in peace is better than a banquet partaken in anxiety, or as Henderson put it:

In your hoose a' the bairns o' Adam
Can find breid, barley bree an' painted room.

Henderson is a father of what has come to be called 'inclusive' nationalism. This powerful notion has helped the SNP to marginalise its anglophobic elements. (Incidentally, Alex Salmond dropped me a note to rebuke me for associating the name of the late Willie MacRae with the SNLA, which he regards as entirely publicity-driven, the work of one or perhaps two fantasists.)

Salmond, I suspect, would agree that until he got hold of it and made it anglophile the party was prone to the odd bit of hairy nonsense. But in his task he was helped by the internationalism of Henderson, who was not much of a political-party animal, just as he was inspired by his songs.

6
Devolution road

THE 1970s IN BRITAIN WAS a time of political upheaval: oil crisis, strikes and short-lived governments. In Scotland, it was the first period of electoral success for the SNP, culminating in the failure of a referendum on devolution in 1979. Below is a timeline of some key events in the devolution story.

1967   Winnie Ewing win the Hamilton by election for the SNP.
1968   Opposition leader Edward Heath commits the Conservatives to a devolved Scottish Assembly in the Declaration of Perth.
1969   Labour PM Harold Wilson appoints Lord Crowther to head a commission (Kilbrandon) on the constitution.
1970   General Election, the Conservatives win under Heath, the SNP lose Hamilton but take the Western Isles.
1974   February, General Election, Labour win under Wilson, the SNP take seven seats. Labour have a tiny majority. Labour become a supporter of devolution.
1974   October, Labour win under Wilson, the SNP take 11 seats.
1976   Wilson replaced by James Callaghan.
1979   March 1: the devolution referendum in Scotland is narrowly carried, 52% for and 48% against. But an amendment to the Bill says 40% of the electoral roll have to support the measure for it to stand.
1979   March 28, Callaghan loses a vote of confidence, initially tabled by the SNP, and then formally proposed by the Leader of the Opposition Margaret Thatcher. The government falls.

This is a shortened version of a full account of those years in Kemp's book *The Hollow Drum*.

The devolution years really began for me in 1967. It was after midnight and on the *Scotsman* we were holding the Glasgow edition for the result of the Hamilton by-election. Seconds after the declaration – a stunning victory for the SNP candidate Mrs Winifred Ewing over Labour – David Bradford, one of the political editors, came on the line and bawled out the intro which I took down in long hand and sent to the composing room. I can remember that it began with the phrase, 'The rising tide of Scottish nationalism ...' and it expressed the mood of excitement. Mrs Ewing, though she lost the seat later, launched the SNP into the stratosphere of concentrated London media attention and from her victory is often traced the party's modern prominence.

Hamilton was not the beginning. It was a flowering. But its impact was dramatic. For the first time the party received sustained attention from the London media. Mrs Ewing arrived in London in triumph. Dover House was besieged by her supporters most of whom had patriotically driven down in Hillman Imps built at Linwood.

She herself had a lonely row to hoe. Scottish Labour members were rattled. Some subjected her to personal abuse of a kind that made her deeply unhappy.

Back in Scotland, Hamilton produced a flood of new members. The fissile tendencies of the party reasserted themselves. (After Muirhead's death the 1320 Club was formed to carry on his work but became associated with extreme fundamentalism and infiltrated by would-be terrorists. It was proscribed by the SNP in 1971 and, a decade later, merged with Siol nan Gaidheal, the raggle-taggle army of activists from the housing schemes, marching under the flag of caricatured celticism, which was itself banned by the party in 1982.) The 1970 general election was regarded by the party as disaster although it doubled its share of the vote from 5 to 11.4 per cent. The SNP had got itself into another classic nationalist scenario, that of heightened expectations punctured by reality.

Gordon Wilson, former national secretary of the party whom I first met at university in the 1950s, remembered: 'We had hopes not in the urban areas but in the rural areas. We hoped to keep Hamilton. That was Verdun, that had to be defended, *ils ne passeront pas*. In the event they did'.

On the Sunday morning after the election, Wilson recalled, they had gathered in an atmosphere of despair. 'As we waited for the Western Isles result, Douglas Henderson suggested that we might resort to prayer. Anyway, Donald Stewart sneaked in and kept our parliamentary presence and credibility alive. He was the first nationalist to win a parliamentary seat at general election and he kept us in the game. That was crucial.'

The period of 1970-74 saw the increasing agony of the Heath administration. The SNP capitalised on a growing loss of public confidence in the competence of government.

It was a time of genuine ferment. The 7:84 Company's satire on the economic exploitation of Scotland, *The Cheviot, the Stag and the Black, Black Oil*, was the theatrical expression of contemporary nationalism and it struck a deep chord in the public mind.

In 1973, Margo MacDonald surged to victory in the Govan by-election with 42 per cent of the vote. She was sensational, a 'blonde bombshell' charming the nation on television.

In the general election of February 1974 the SNP caused further consternation. It got 22 per cent of the vote and seven seats.

Between the elections of February and October, Douglas Henderson, the parliamentary whip, sustained the Labour Government almost single-handed.

The SNP was now ready for its greatest moment. On 7 September 1974, the first Labour White Paper on devolution proposed assemblies for Scotland and Wales. On 18 September an election was called for 10 October. The SNP achieved 30 per cent of the vote and acquired four more MPs.

The SNP's advance was almost a decisive breakthrough. But in it lay the basis of the party's later difficulties. The electoral wheel of fortune determined the composition of the group that was summoned to Parliament and the group that stayed behind. Into Parliament went 11 disparate personalities of uneven abilities.

John Smith, when we talked, said:

'The SNP group was pretty hilarious. There was a constant party. They were well known on the Terrace. They affected disdain for this Parliament but when you have 11 people you become an important force. I don't think they understood the role they were playing, the importance of it. They weren't unintelligent people but there was a festive mood about them.'

By the time that parliament limped to its end in 1979 very severe tensions had broken out between the parliamentarians and the thinkers and publicists back home.

One question was whether devolution was a prize, or a trap. There were those who believed in the 'big bang' theory and those who believed in the 'slippery slope', a progressive devolution. The party was ambivalent.

After the second election of 1974, the Labour government retained office, owing its majority of four to its Scottish seats. No further evasion was possible.

The Harold Wilson Government pressed ahead with devolution

despite serious misgivings. The Cabinet Office began to work on the details and devolution spread like a blight, pervading all branches of government.

Wilson abruptly resigned in 1976 for reasons that have never been satisfactorily explained. James Callaghan became Prime Minister. Michael Foot as Leader of the House and Lord President of Council took charge of the devolution legislation and John Smith, as Minister of State for the Privy Council went in to do the hard work of detail.

The first Bill died in March 1977 when 22 Labour rebels voted down a timetable (or guillotine) motion to curtail debate and secure the Bill's progress.

Smith recalled that when winding up the debate in March 1977 which killed the first Bill on the guillotine motion, he was handed a note from the Chief Whip saying the Government had lost. 'I had to pretend we were going to win. We were defeated and that was it.'

Enoch Powell said, 'There's a terrible stench in the chamber. Will someone please take this dead Bill away?'

The following month the Lib-Lab pact was announced, promising the Liberals regular consultations on policy, and the Government survived a no-confidence motion by 24 votes.

This moved the leverage from the nationalists to the Liberals. It took the SNP out of the limelight. The longer the Parliament continued, the weaker the SNP grew.

The crucial parliamentary session was that of 1978-79. The Government ploughed on with separate Bills for Scotland and Wales. But the Labour rebels found a way through. On 25 January 1978, George Cunningham, an expatriate Scot who sat as a Labour MP for Islington South-West, successfully introduced an amendment inserting the 40 per cent rule. This stipulated that if less than 40 per cent of the registered electorate endorsed the Scotland Act an order would be laid before parliament to repeal it. The amendments incorporating the rule were carried against government wishes.

After the indecisive devolution referendum of 1979, a new parliamentary game began. The failure of the Yes vote to achieve 40 per cent in the referendum meant that under the terms of the Cunningham amendment the Government was obliged to move an order repealing the Scotland Act. Cunningham estimated that 200 Labour back-benchers would not follow the party line. The 11 SNP MPs made their demand that Callaghan proceed with the motion and put on a three-line whip.

The refusal of the Callaghan Government to move the repeal order lead the SNP to table a vote of no confidence. 'This was not done with the intention of bringing down the Government,' said Wilson. It was done in the hope that the prospect of a hanging would concentrate the mind.

When the Callaghan Government fell, it did so on the Conservative motion of no confidence which had, in Henderson's phrase, hi-jacked the resolution tabled by the SNP.

Perhaps Callaghan came close to blaming Cunningham for his Government's defeat in the 1979 election. But the industrial troubles of the winter of discontent more gravely damaged confidence in its competence. Strikes by lorry drivers and 1.5 million workers in the public sector coincided with a winter of exceptional severity. The nation's television screens were full of apocalyptic visions of anarchy and incompetence.

It was a pivotal moment in British politics.

When the vote of confidence took place on 28 March, according to Henderson, Callaghan had been advised he would win the vote or at least tie. The whips calculated that two SNP doubters might abstain.

In the circumstances every vote was vital but Labour's Deputy Chief Whip Walter Harrison decided that the Labour MP Dr Alfred Broughton, who had heroically offered to be present was too ill to travel from Yorkshire; he died the following Saturday.

Michael Foot believed that Dr Broughton's absence and the failure of the SDLP member Gerry Fitt and the Irish Republican MP Frank Maguire to support the government was the 'double blow' that brought it down.

Maguire made a rare excursion from Fermanagh to London. According to the account of Henderson and others, the whips locked him up in their office with liberal quantities of whisky. They escorted him into the chamber in time for the division. He was smiling broadly and all seemed well. But when the time came he stood behind the Speaker's chair with his arms folded and refused to move. Henderson recalled that the whips tried to pull him into the lobby but he stood firm. Through his bluff, according to this account, he had the satisfaction of bringing down the government. Later he told Henderson; 'I came to abstain in person!'.

Something more serious may have been in question. According to some accounts, the real explanation for Maguire's failure to support the government was that he was intimidated by terrorists. Robin Cook in 1993 recalled that on the day of the crucial vote he was followed to Westminster from Ireland by his wife and 'two men in raincoats'. They never left his side.

Harry Ewing had no recollection of this but found it perfectly credible. In those days security in parliament was still relaxed. Fitt himself dismissed the idea of IRA intimidation. He did say that Maguire was close to the IRA. The men in raincoats, I infer, could have been IRA 'minders'. Cook's view that their presence was minatory was corroborated by deputy chief whip Walter Harrison. On the night the Government fell, Harrison had hidden away somewhere in the Palace of Westminster – even 14 years on he would not tell me where – two Ulster Unionist MPs. They voted with the Government. He had been given the promise of their votes and was trying to prevent the operation of what whips call 'the revolving door'. A whip may secure the vote of one MP but his support may repel another. Harrison feared that if Maguire or Fitt found out about the Ulster Unionists there was no chance of their supporting the government. There was little chance anyway, as Harrison recognised early in the day. He never tried to wheedle Maguire or Fitt. He took no for an answer from Fitt without further argument and conscious of the men in raincoats, marked down Maguire as pretty doubtful. Foot had an enormous regard tor Fitt's courage but thought when we talked in 1993 that it would have also been more than his life was worth to have supported the Government.

Harrison advised the Chief Whip that he thought the Government was about three short. But he took his two Unionist birds away to a secret nest while his colleagues worked on Maguire and Fitt. Sufficient ambiguity may have then entered the calculation to encourage Callaghan to take the gamble but his dismissive reference to the SNP also suggested that he was pretty fed up anyway and did not much care if it worked.

Smith said: 'I think it was true Callaghan was fed up. He thought we might win the vote. Maguire was supposed to come. It was close enough to gamble.'

But he continued 'He thought there was a price you did not pay, a kind of unseemly hanging on to office with all sorts of curious deals. That sort of thing, trying to be a Smart Alec, did not appeal to him.'

The motion of no confidence was carried by 311 votes to 310.

Harrison who had hoped for the votes of at least two nationalists – Hamish Watt and George Reid and perhaps another, recalled that there had been much whispering among the SNP. He had addressed them as a group three times during the course of the evening.

Watt told me that he spent an absolutely miserable evening. His constituency party had mandated him to vote with the Government. He had been elected in Banff by Labour voters and knew they would reject him, as indeed they did, should he help to bring Mrs Thatcher to office. Watt had the impression that Walter Harrison thought the Government had sneaked through and did not so much care what the SNP would do. After the division some SNP and Labour members thought the Government had just won. A teller gave a misleading thumbs up. When Watt realise the truth, it is said he tried to cancel his vote – permissible if you can get to the other lobby in time. He made a dash for it but it was locked just as he reached it. According to the folklore, he beat despairingly at it, demanding entry in vain. In conversation he told me this was not true; he did discuss reversing his vote with the Labour whips but the lobby door closed before any conclusion could be reached.

John Stradling Thomas, Number Three in the Tory Whips office, apparently dined out an anecdote from that night. Using a pre-arranged code he indicated to Mrs Thatcher that they had won by one vote by raising a finger. He used to remark that he was forever grateful they had not won by two.

The death of a man who had a minor role in the dramas of 1970s devolution inspired this column: A Burns Night 'Massacre'.

Sir Myer Galpern, who died in September 1993, was a Lord Provost of Glasgow and a Labour MP. But he will be remembered because of his time in the chair of the House of Commons as Deputy Speaker.

On Burns Night, 1978, he presided over the humiliation of the Callaghan Government when it suffered a series of defeats in the division lobbies. The result was the 40% rule which turned the devolution referendum into a mountain too high to climb.

The Labour Government, with no majority, had to rely heavily on the Whips. It is generally accepted by parliamentarians that the Labour Whips of that period brought the black arts of their calling to a high pitch.

Thoughout that Parliament, sustained in its last few years by the Lib-Lab Pact, the Whips cajoled, bluffed, threatened, bullied, pleaded, did deals. And, in tight divisions, they would hang about the division lobbies. Euphemistically they were there to make sure that members went into the correct lobby. In reality their task was to bully them into it if necessary.

That night, things got out of hand. Michael Foot and John Smith, in charge of the devolution legislation, had been ill advised of the mood of the House. A timetable or guillotine was in operation, and they calculated that the amendments would not be voted on at all but talked out.

The then MP for Islington South-west, George Cunningham, heard of what he later called their skulduggery, and rushed to the Chamber. By chance a number of people had drifted back into it, and it was one of these rare parliamentary occasions when a member actually sways the House by what he says.

In two divisions in rapid succession the Government was defeated thanks to an informal cross-bench alliance. The amendment – stipulating that unless 40% of those entitled to vote endorsed the Scotland Act an order for its repeal would have to be laid before Parliament – was carried by 15 votes.

The Whips were mortified, and sought to prevent a third amendment from coming to the vote – the Jo Grimond amendment which would have excluded Orkney and Shetland from the devolutionary scheme.

The Whips knew that if they could delay this division it would fall under the timetable. There seems no doubt that they resorted to excessively robust tactics. Cunningham later wrote: 'But they reckoned without Myer Galpern, the ex-Lord Provost of Glasgow, who was in the chair that night. Myer dispatched the Serjeant-at-Arms into the division lobby, sword in hand, to sort out the Whips.'

Walter Harrison, Labour's deputy chief Whip at the time, sorcerer's apprentice to the chief wizard Michael Cocks, recalled that he found himself 'pinned against the wall'.

Cunningham continued: 'As Big Ben started to strike eleven Jo moved his amendment and the Government went down to another heavy defeat. As one member of the press lobby said, it was a Burns Night massacre.'

The Cabinet's acute embarrassment is recorded in Tony Benn's diaries. There were other forces at work, of course. But the 40% rule became an insurmountable hurdle, confused an already troubled Scottish public and created the scenario in which the Callaghan Government, exhausted and demoralised, finally went to the wall.

The referendum was held on March 1, 1979, and Scotland voted Yes by a majority miles short of the 40%. Callaghan failed quickly to table the repeal order and require his MPs to oppose it – Cunningham reckoned that up to 100 would have disobeyed him. The SNP tabled a vote of no confidence, the Conservatives hijacked it, and the Government fell by one vote. Devolution disappeared in a puff of smoke; Mrs Thatcher became Prime Minister, Labour descended into a pit of internecine strife, and the Conservatives came to power.

What would have happened if Sir Myer had let the Labour Whips away with it? Probably not much. The 40% amendments had been passed by the time the Whips got rough. Thanks to his intervention, the Grimond amendment was passed; but it was removed at a subsequent legislative stage anyway.

It remains a glorious example of impartial chairmanship, without which no democratic chamber can work.

When the news of Sir Myer's death came on Thursday, they brought out the picture file. There were three envelopes showing Sir Myer in his various manifestations – Lord Provost, MP, Deputy Speaker – and in the company of various dignitaries.

It gives you a spooky feeling, to leaf through old pictures like that; there is a sense of hovering shades and spirits. Life was more orderly then. The 'photo-opportunity' had not yet been invented. The photographers were still in a subservient role and the public figure was seen in all his greatness.

Nowadays lords provost jump through hoops for the snappers: for every celebrity who shuns the camera there are 10 who woo it and 'media skills' have become a necessary item in the portfolio not just of politicians.

Sir Myer did not sacrifice his dignity for the camera. Today, no doubt, some PR man would advise him to take a course in camera presence. As a politician he never really made the top grade. But as a parliamentarian he cut himself an honourable niche in history.

The table-thumping years.

Down the 1970s, Kemp wrote many hard-hitting editorials or 'leaders' – the columns which appear unsigned beneath a paper's masthead – for The

Scotsman. Space in those days of hot metal was tight and he expressed his often passionate views succinctly. It was a turbulent time.

Battles Ahead for the increasingly ailing Conservative administration, *The Scotsman*, Wednesday 1 Nov 1972.

> *Reculer pour mieux sauter*: that could be the motto of the Conservative Government as they enter the new session of Parliament, although their enemies might phrase it rather less kindly. Much that was destroyed in the name of a purer Toryism is being brought back to life. Lame ducks have survived and are learning to walk again. There is a welcome acceptance that development aid is not a handout to ne'er-do-well regions too feckless to participate in a free-market economy but rather an essential attempt to fight decay and remove the disadvantages of distance from the marketplace. And as the lights burn late in Downing Street a statutory prices and incomes policy seems more and more the only available answer to the problem of inflation to which the Queen's Speech referred with the necessary vagueness.

Miss Wood's Fast was the heading of this editorial on 8 December 1972.

> Miss Wendy Wood was beginning her fast until death last night. Her purpose is to force the Government to honour its promise of a Scottish Convention. Many will share her sense of impatience and frustration. The tempo is decidedly andante. Nor are the cogitations of the Kilbrandon Commission on the Constitution likely to accelerate matters. Rumour has it that the commission is so seriously split that its final report will lack authority and thus consign itself to the dusty shelves of Whitehall.
>
> Miss Wood fears that strife will arise from Scotland's impatience and that she can prevent it by laying down her own life. One of the many tragedies of Northern Ireland is that violence has been seen to secure political change where the normal constitutional powers were inert. What made the terrorism of the Provisionals potent, however, was that they enjoyed like Grivas in Cyprus and the insurgents in Algeria but unlike the Angry Brigade, the support of some of the people on behalf of whom their vicious campaign was conducted.
>
> By contrast, Miss Wood is acting in isolation; and despite her fears there is thankfully no sign that the Scots are about to resort to

the gun and the bomb in pursuit of objectives about which they can muster little harmony. The fight for devolution should be conducted rationally and within the bounds of legality. Miss Wood adorns and enriches the Scottish scene. None doubts her courage or determination. But she must not rob us of her presence with a gesture that is almost certain to be futile.

Oil-fired debate: oil was changing the terms of the debate on independence, as Kemp argues here in December, 1972

Political power may indeed, as Mao said, grow out of the barrel of a gun. In Scotland and elsewhere it is increasingly a by-product of oil. The strategic importance of oil is that it has totally changed the grounds upon which the debate about Scottish independence will be conducted ...

To say that an independent Scotland could not support herself is now patently absurd. The debate will now increasingly return to the philosophical and political plane on which it began. Nationalism is about more than balanced books and prosperity; first of all it derives from a desire to express and in Scotland's case reassert, a national identity ... A new chapter in the progress of the devolutionary movement is about to begin.

Central logic from London is not in Scotland's interests, Kemp argues, in June, 1973.

'The existence of Scotland and Wales is, of course, very real indeed in terms of regional policy ... It is irrelevant in the context of the efficient operation of the national Government.'

At least he knows we're here; but with these cool words (rather incompatible with the treaty of union, as they are) Sir Henry Hardman sinks Glasgow's campaign to secure more Civil Service jobs for Glasgow ...

It is surprising that Sir Henry found himself able to recommend dispersal even as far as Potters Bar, so emphatic is he that centralised government implies centralised administration.

The moral for Scotland is clear. Britain, the report points out, is not a geographical federation (more's the pity). London is the only decision-making centre, the argument runs, and Scotland and Wales are concerned only with regional issues. The report is not only a statement of centralism; it is also a powerful argument for Scottish self-government.

Beeching's attack on the railways is not good for Scotland either. June, 1972.

After the Hardman report, Mr Richard Marsh's interim strategy for British Rail's next ten years is like a good deed in a naughty world. Because it recognises that profitability is too crude a test of the rail-way's value to the nation, it holds out hope for places like Scotland whose lines have rarely balanced the books. It runs counter to the centralist view that life and railways begin and end in the South-east. Above all, it marks a fundamental departure from the Beeching diag-nosis that British Rail's prospects of a valuable future lie in contrac-tion.

Scotland is a nation living at less than its full potential. July 1973.

'If she succumbs to the canker of centralisation, the Scottish nation, with its ancient geographical limits and its clearly defined historical and polit-ical personality, will be increasingly reduced to the second-rate role of branch management.'

This question from the report of the Scottish Council's European Economic Community Committee is refreshingly explicit. So too is the committee's call for the devolution not merely of institutions but of political power ... This report, in its rejection of Hardman central-ism, its reiteration of Scotland's crying need for a legislative focus, and its demand that our voice must not go unheard in Brussels is a courageous and even seminal document.

Whatever the practical impact of the document, its importance resides in its eloquent statement of Scottish nationhood. Despite the Kilbrandon Commission's inordinately long period of gestation, despite the pusillanimity of the Scottish Tories and their blinkered supporters, the demand for devolution cannot be left unsatisfied for much longer. What the committee call the 'canker' of centralisation has drained us of our power, both political and economic, and the best and most inventive of our people; it has also sapped our belief in our own abilities.

The lesson is plain: if we sit at home and bemoan our fate then we will lapse into provincial obscurity. If we use our native enterprise for once in our own service rather than for others, then there is nothing we cannot do.

Strikes and inflation were the order of the day as the unions took on a government incomes policy aimed at limiting inflatio. From February, 1973: 'The Bully Boys'.

The public should make clear their contempt for the bully boys, and the unions must come down from the battlements to seek a modus vivendi with the Government ... The revolutionaries may not be at the gates but they feed voraciously off real injustice and real grievances. The country needs conciliation and statesmanship, and it needs them now.

March, 1973, on Scots law.

There is a tendency for the law of England to be presented to Europeans 'as if it were the law of the United Kingdom'. This is not entirely surprising, since it has always been a characteristic of English lawyers either not to admit that a separate discipline exists north of the Border or if they have to borrow from it to do so without acknowledgement.

In a world of big battalions the small, sane voice of Scots law may go unheard; this would be tragic. Scots law is one of our small nation's most extraordinary achievements, reasonable, equitable, undogmatic, humane and strongly rooted in commonsense. It is also expeditious and as Professor Andrew Gibb has written, 'a certain elegance may be ascribed' to it. The Lord Advocate already has some important achievements to his credit, notably the appointment of a Scots judge to the European Court of Justice. Our law is a precious heritage and Mr Wylie must now listen to the polite but urgent warning from the commission.

This leader from 13 June 1974, looked at issues of ethnicity and nationality that would resurface later.

Old-fashioned liberalism is nowadays attacked by the Left as a bourgeois indulgence and by the Right as namby-pamby pusillanimity. The Liberal Party's report on immigration and race relations, therefore, in its attack on the 'callous foolishness' of policy since the 1962, is a ghostly reminder of the passionate debate that raged then about the justice and morality of immigration restrictions; and its assertion of the enrichment immigrants bring to our life and economy, together with the reminder of their rights to citizenship, are thus welcome correctives to the doom-laden prophecies of Mr Enoch Powell, who has done so much to keep fear and irrational prejudice alive. The document is mainly notable, however, in its emphasis on aspects of the multi-racial society that have not so far figured in the political debate.

The assumption of much of our policy has been that the aim of complete integration is necessary, desirable and possible. But how does a Sikh become a Scot, even if he wants to? The Liberal document, by contrast, talks of a society in which discrete groups adhere to their ethnic inheritance while subscribing to a common social will. The intellectual pessimism of apartheid holds such a goal to be impossible, believing that order, in the post-Colonial era, can be imposed only by a dominant group necessarily indifferent to certain human rights and aspirations. Our approach rather must be to offer equality before the law and in employment, while respecting difference of race, custom and religion.

The opportunity of immigrants to aspire to higher occupational categories must be a key factor in their willingness to subscribe to the wider social order and participate in its institutions.

As the Liberals remind us, the qualities of compassion, justice and respect for individual rights are not things upon which we may smugly congratulate ourselves, as is our wont; in the context of a heterogenous society, with the constraints of which we demand universal compliance, we must practise them too.

When Strathclyde's labour majority voted against a Scottish Assembly. June 1974: 'Regional visionaries'.

Further evidence of the conservatism, unionism, insensitivity and dedicated self-interest of the North British Labour Party was provided yesterday when 66 of the 103 members of Strathclyde Regional Council voted against the creation of a Scottish Assembly.

On Sunday the Scottish Council of the Labour Party pronounced that an Assembly or other constitutional tinkering was irrelevant to Scotland's needs; socialism was the answer. (Since more state control is likely to mean more London control, they seek not merely to conserve the union but to pull the bonds much tighter.) ... The first obvious consequence of Strathclyde's creation is that we have a powerful vested interest against reform of a far more important nature.

Left-wing times. In 'Watchers on the Warsaw Warpath', Tuesday 1 October 1974. It is interesting to note that Kemp found it worthwhile to ask whether 'in the fashionable scenario', there might be a possibility of military overthrow of a democratically elected left-wing British government.

> From the flat countryside over which the low-level attack and reconnaissance aircraft roar out on countless training sorties, the personnel of RAF Germany are watching the election campaign with some anxiety.
>
> Their concern is natural since the jobs of some of them may depend on the result; but added to that is a puzzlement about events at home which sometimes amounts to a sense of hurt.
>
> On a visit to RAF Germany last week I became aware of an almost universal feeling that the country had more or less forgotten the men and women in Rhineland whose job it is to protect those freedoms which we are exercising on October 10. [*The second UK general election of 1974*]
>
> Worse than that, some thought, the country had fallen into apathy and had become negligent of the threat which Nato was formed to resist.
>
> Yet officers to whom I spoke are convinced that the threat from the East has never been greater. Every day they receive intelligence of the continuing build-up of the Warsaw Pact's conventional forces ...
>
> But could it not be, in the fashionable scenario, that the fear of Communism inculcated in training, together with the naturally conservative bent of the serving officer, will turn anxiety about contemporary Britain into something altogether more sinister?
>
> I put the question to a senior officer. He smiled and replied: 'It's not the way we're brought up.'

In 1979, Scotland faced the first referendum on devolution. As well as inflation and a long, unusually snowy 'Winter of Discontent, the backdrop was the Iranian Revolution which having first been greeted with optimism was rapidly turning sour.

March 8, 1979, 'Revolutionary Justice', *The Scotsman.*

There are few phenomena more nauseating than the infallibility claimed by those who issue and administer sentences inspired by a revolutionary sense of justice. The smugness, self-righteousness and, doubtless, mere prurience of the mullahs and revolutionary militia-men who watched 120 lashes administered to a married woman and her lover caught in adultery in the small town of Kelarabad must cast doubt on the values underpinning the Iranian Revolution. Homosexual offenders are being summarily executed. Who knows what offence might next qualify for an appearance before the firing squad?

There may be a massive endorsement by the people of the Ayatollah's Islamic Republic in the March 30 referendum. But the seeds of a future revolution are being firmly sown.

The run up to the devolution referendum, 'Why we must vote Yes', *The Scotsman*, 23 February 1979.

The handsome neo-classical lines of the old Royal High school in Edinburgh have over the years acquired layers of reek. For all the complaints about its cost, the Scottish Assembly will be an intimate parliament and the modest symbol of a small nation finding its soul again. Calton Hill is a fitting place from which to begin a process of revival, renewal and change. The harmony of the old building's design speaks not of false hope or vainglory but of rational ambition, its exterior grime of realism. Do not let us pretend that the Assembly itself will solve anything. It will cast no spells and distil no magic potions. It is an instrument for our use, a great opportunity which must not be missed, not only for the sake of Scotland but for the health of the British Constitution at large.

The first argument for the Assembly is in the interests of good government. The tier of government which it will supervise already exists. The Secretary of State for Scotland deals with about ten major functions of government which in England are the tasks of separate Ministries and the expenditure for which he is responsible amounts to more than £3000 million a year. The price of subjecting most of these programmes to closer democratic scrutiny will be less than half a percent of their annual cost. The Assembly is not expensive; it is cheap at the price.

But the 'good government' argument applies with some though not as much force to the regions of England, and does not entirely explain why Scotland needs the Assembly so badly. Let us take as a premise that it is desirable to sustain the unity of the United Kingdom. Indeed, our close and cousinly links with the English, our affection for them and respect for their culture, the degree of domestic, social and economic intercourse between us – these facts make separatism (a perjorative word for independence) unthinkable. This unity can survive only if our institutions of government can renew and adapt themselves.

Far too much has been made of the West Lothian question. The idea of Scots MPs decisively affecting English questions should not unduly surprise a parliament which for years has loaded Scottish committees with English MPs (who regard this task as Parliamentary Siberia) so that they reflect the composition of the whole House.

We have no written Constitution. As a nation we may have a temperamental aversion to anything too rigid and restrictive. We also have a distaste for systematic constitutional change, though we are perfectly capable of writing constitutions for other people, sometimes, as in the case of West Germany, with considerable success. Therefore, we must thank our stars that our society is sufficiently mature and stable to produce change without violence.

Thus the Assembly offers more democratic control and helps sustain unity in diversity. It opens avenues to peaceful change. It begins the renewal of our democratic institutions. But the final argument is both psychological and perhaps emotional. The lack of national democratic institutions has grievously sapped Scottish self-belief. Standardising forces have eroded the external signs of our nationhood, speech, custom, dress, and left us confused and adrift. The deferential philosophy of dependence on English largesse attacks the qualities of enterprise, invention and self-reliance in which we once took pride. Dependence is in any case something of a myth, though a powerful one. There is hardly an area of Scottish life that cannot be uplifted and quickened by an Assembly.

The Assembly is the first stage in the journey towards a place for Scotland in the modern world. A small country living in close intercourse with its cousin England and it is a step from which we must not shrink.

The failure of the devolution referendum in 1979 was a huge personal and political disappointment for Kemp as for many of his colleagues at *The Scotsman*. He wrote later, in *The Hollow Drum*:

> As deputy editor of the *Scotsman*, I was one of those members of Edinburgh's chattering classes who deluded themselves that Scotland was impatient for change; journalists and political scientists, keen to create a polity to enrich their own lives, were accused of inventing the devolutionary movement of the time, although they were merely the descendants of a long line of campaigners.

In Kemp's later writing, he sometimes looked back at the fervid politics of the 1970s when nationalists and socialists clashed over Scotland's future. In 1997, Kemp covered the funeral of Jimmy Airlie, a union leader who co-led the famous Clyde work-in in 1971.

One last bevvy for hero of the Clyde.

Inside the crematorium, a hundred or more mourners say their farewells to Jimmy Airlie. Outside, as the body of the tough trade unionist who humiliated a Tory government is consigned to the flames, a couple of hundred more stand in the rain.

Family apart, entry has been first come, first served. The crowd outside includes Shadow Chancellor Gordon Brown, Labour MPs and old comrades from when the Communist Party, not Labour, was the power on the Clyde.

Outside too is Jimmy Reid, Airlie's co-leader in the 1971-72 work-in at Upper Clyde Shipbuilders, which won a temporary reprieve for its workers and £40 million of new state investment in the yard. Reid finds he is rubbing shoulders with an old acquaintance – Robert Courtney Smith the UCS liquidator. Together they listen to the orations and songs, which avoid Reid's name almost as much as they snub God's.

The scene serves, remarks a senior politician, as a metaphor for a society that has lost faith in Airlie's vision of justice. Glasgow's Craigton crematorium is run by the Co-operative Society, but the cemetery is owned by a private company. It has difficulty in raising maintenance fees and has tried to sell it to a city too broke to pay for it.

Grieving over the loss of his old friend, cut down by cancer in the first year of his retirement, Reid lets the ceremony's rewriting of history pass without comment. Only the oration by Campbell Christie, general-secretary of the Scottish TUC, mentioned Reid's role in an event that defeated Edward Heath, only to presage the legislation with which Margaret Thatcher crushed union power.

Airlie and Reid drifted apart after Upper Clyde, but they never fell out. 'He was a smashing bloke,' says Reid, 'a dear friend, great fun to be with. He had a sharp and streetwise intelligence. It was bloody delightful to know him.'

The mourners gather at the Dean Park Hotel in Renfrew where, over whisky, tea, sandwiches and sausage rolls, they piece together their memories of one of the greatest trade union leaders of his generation. Perhaps, if you take as the true test of leadership the ability to make followers do things they would rather not, Airlie was the greatest of them all, though he never became president of his union. It is true that Airlie was chairman of the UCS Co-ordinating Committee – Sir Gavin Laird, former general secretary of the AEU, said in the *Glasgow Herald*'s obituary that he was its prime mover – but he depended more than a little on others. Laird himself delivered the support of the Singer workforce, a major factory long gone, and the dispute could not have been won without secondary action of the kind later outlawed by Thatcher. And the committee could hardly have impressed national and international opinion, as it did, without the beguiling eloquence of Jimmy Reid.

What impressed the mass TV audience was the rigid discipline. The committee did a deal with the police, who stayed out of the whole affair in return for guarantees of good order. When Harold Wilson, as leader of the Opposition, came to visit they sent his police outriders packing. In a famous soundbite from a mass meeting, Reid ordained that there would be 'no bevvying' (no drinking).

In London around that time, I remember meeting Airlie, Reid and the committee when they came to lobby MPs. They were friendly, sociable men, yet they could hardly have been more different. Airlie was apprenticed as an engineer and joined the Communist Party because he was attracted by the possibilities for industrial action that its influence created. Reid was an intellectual and a theorist, the party's Scottish secretary. He was brought into the yard to strengthen union activism.

These Communists who dominated the unions were a remarkable breed. Gus Macdonald, now chairman of Scottish Television, who started his working life in the shipyards, recalls that they were descended from the Covenanting tradition. To the puritanism of ancestral militant Presbyterianism they added the theology of Marx.

The mix made them formidable.

Alan Ritchie, now the Scottish secretary of the construction union Ucatt, worked with Airlie as a joiner. He recalls that at that time the yards were full of sectarianism. The Orange Order was balanced by Catholic Action and the Knights of St Columba. 'Jimmy always seemed to unite them and break these barriers. He made them see the logic of combining together,' Ritchie said.

Though Airlie's own father had been a boilermaker, this elite craft was the butt of his jokes. It used to be said that if your daughter married a boilermaker it would make headlines in the Govan Press, such was the social cachet.

What distinguished Airlie as a union leader was his realism and ability to deliver a settlement to which he had put his name. He knew when to end a dispute, even if his followers did not. Christie recalled how, in two Scottish disputes of the Eighties – at Caterpillar and Timex – he employed the rough language of the shipyards to override the local leadership, or went over their heads to mass meetings where his aggressive '130-decibel' rhetoric laced with humour rarely failed him.

Charlie Whelan, Airlie's assistant at the AEU and in 1997 Gordon Brown's press secretary, said: 'When he was on the AEU executive, Terry Duffy and the right wing were horrified that he got the job, because he was the most intelligent of the Left. They thought that the way to get him off – because his election was only in Scotland – was to keep him tied up in London. So they put him on the Ford negotiating committee. But the head of Ford of America rang up Duffy and said: 'What have we got this Communist bastard for? What have we done to deserve this?' And, of course, Jimmy led the last big Ford strike in 1985, when the whole of Ford Europe closed down within two weeks.'

Airlie, said Whelan, was seen as 'the most formidable negotiator in the trade union movement, a giant. He was also prepared to say to the workforce, "You're wrong, you've got to go back to work". He was willing to take the stick.'

Perhaps his greatest disappointment came in 1987, when Ford's plan, secretly hatched with himself and Laird, to build a single-union component plant in Dundee with 1,000 jobs foundered on TGWU opposition.

There have, since 1821, been 13 shipyards on the Upper Clyde, their names now a litany for a vanished society. Yarrow still builds warships and Kvaerner clings to life on the old Fairfield yard at Govan. Few commentators think either will survive for more than a couple of years. Airlie couldn't reverse the flight of capital from his beloved river. But he had a damn good try.

In this interview with Gus Macdonald, later Lord Macdonald of Tradeston, Minister for Transport in the Blair government, Kemp looked at the intellectual journey he had made from his Trotskyist starting point. This largely mirrored the shift in the Labour movement, from the militantism of the 1970s to the pragmatism of New Labour in the 1990s.

From a Trot to a gallop.

'Political ingénue?' snorts Gus Macdonald supping his tea. 'For people to say that is daft.' It is the charge of political innocence that most irks the media mogul and former Clydeside shop steward turned Scottish Office Minister.

'I was New Labour before New Labour was invented. And although I left the Labour Party about 20 years ago. I have retained a passion for policy.' he said

It was to this West End flat that Donald Dewar, who lives round the corner, came to plan the announcement that Macdonald would take charge of key economic programmes and go to the House of Lords *[in 1998]*.

Since then the fur has been flying in Scotland's over-heated political atmosphere. The dominant charge, of 'cronyism', he dismisses. Dewar is someone he likes and respects but they are not bosom friends. Sunday's was the first visit Dewar had made to the Macdonald home. As chairman of the Glasgow Young Socialists, a mixed bag of Trots and others, the youthful Macdonald may even have debated against Dewar at the university union, his team was disqualified because it declined to give the vote of thanks on the grounds that it was 'bourgeois'.

Macdonald's career, from apprentice fitter in the shipyard of Alexander Stephen & Sons at Linthouse to chairman of SMG by way of World in Action and Granada Television, has been well chronicled. Less well known is the intellectual journey that brought him from youthful activism in the Trotskyist Left to an embrace of the free market – which, he believes, can be a shield for working people against a state hijacked or corrupted by elites. He recalls: 'I grew up in an anti-Stalinist tradition, always arguing about the incompetence and corruption of the Soviet bloc. I had a good grounding in Trotsky and our target was state capitalism.'

As a television professional he was influenced by the industries' appalling labour relations, the featherbedding and overmanning. 'It was worse than Fleet Street, he said.

He was World in Action's first reporter and later its editor. Its aim was to exploit the flexibility of new lightweight cameras and use film as 'evidence' in investigative journalism. The reality in the industry was 'dreadful'. Union demands were 'squeezing the life out of programmes'. The ultimate absurdity came in Union World, he says, when the crew demanded a 'hen wrangler', or handler, for shots involving poultry.

'It was hard to take these well-paid and privileged folks seriously,' he says of the trade unionists he had to deal with. 'They used the defensive mechanisms of the industrial working class for all sorts of petty resentments.

By the end of the seventies any commitment to Old Labour had been eroded by the failure of the Callaghan Government and the 'winter of discontent' and he left the party. 'But I was never tempted to the Conservative Party because blood ties were too strong.'

In a nursing home across the road from his house in Glasgow he would visit an old Red Clydesider, Harry McShane. McShane had broken with his old trade union mates and moved awards the 'libertarian' left. 'Harry told me: "We've got it wrong about Adam Smith," he urged me to read him.' Macdonald continues: 'Adam Smith argues that the moral force of the market would empower people. The market looks after the poor better than the central state which can be stolen and corrupted by elites.'

Out of 'intellectual curiosity' he went to the first meeting of Keith Joseph's Centre For Policy Studies, a seminal influence in the development of Thatcherism. As we spoke Macdonald fetched a book from the shelf. It is *The Spirit of Democratic Capitalism* (1982) by Michael Novak, a former Catholic priest now on the staff of the conservative American Enterprise Institute. Novak tried to reconcile Catholic teaching to capitalism and to show that it was capable of acting as a force for the general good. It could be evil, using sex to sell, but it could also make clothes and cars. Macdonald says: 'I was very influenced by it.'

7
Towards a Scottish parliament

TIMELINE: THE THATCHER YEARS

1979   The Conservatives under Margaret Thatcher win the General
       Election with 22 Scottish MPs.
1983   General Election: Conservatives win with 21 Scottish seats.
1984-5 The miners' strike is defeated, a milestone in the decline of indust-
       rial Scotland.
1987   General Election: Conservatives win with 10 Scottish seats.
1988   On a visit to Scotland, Margaret Thatcher addresses the General
       Assembly of the Church of Scotland – 'The Sermon on the Mound'.
1990   Margaret Thatcher leaves office; John Major becomes PM.
1992   General Election: Conservatives under John Major win another term
       with 11 Scottish seats.
1992   The closure of Ravenscraig steel mill.
1994   Death of Scottish leader of the Labour party John Smith.
1997   Labour wins the General Election under Tony Blair with 56 Scottish
       seats – the Conservatives win none.
1997   74% vote yes in a devolution referendum.
1998   The Scotland Act.
1999   July 1, the Queen opens the first Scottish Parliament since 1707.

The miners' strike of 1984 was a watershed in post-war British history, Kemp
looked back on this when he attended the funeral of Mick McGahey (1925-
99), Scottish miners' leader during the strike.

The mourners came like travellers from an antique land, old
Reds from the days when Communism counted, miners from the
remnants of the coalfields, comrades who lived through the apogee
of union power, old friends and, perhaps, some old enemies.

Along with Scottish Secretary Donald Dewar and a clutch of
MPs, about 800 people gathered at a crematorium on a windy slope
to the south of Edinburgh and filled the chapel to overflowing.

Mick McGahey, 73, died on 30 January and was cremated last
Thursday in an uncompromisingly secular ceremony. The organ played
Paul Robeson's 'The Riddle Song' and John Lennon's 'Imagine'.

There were tributes from Nicky Wilson, the Scottish president of the National Union of Mineworkers, and from Communists William Doolan and Jack Ashton. They recalled his kindness, his strength, his courtesy, his friendship, his leadership, his loyalty, and his foibles. His favourite poet was Shelley. He liked a dram or two and greatly relished the convivial discourse of the Gilmerton Miners' Welfare Club.

As his body was committed to the fire, they sang 'The Red Flag', not rousingly, but as a sweet, melancholy and nostalgic anthem to a hero of his people. There was a reception at the welfare club, not far from the last Scottish mining complex at Longannet.

Over the tea, sausage rolls and pints, they talked of him not just with respect but with love. He was an autodidact of the old working class. His hero was the Scottish revolutionary John Maclean. He committed the union movement to home rule 30 years ago, but did not live to see the Scottish Parliament which will be elected on 6 May.

There was iron in McGahey, too. For him the class struggle was not at all theoretical. He came from a family where the women were devout Catholics, the men devout Communists. His old party comrade Jimmy Reid recalled that McGahey's father had been jailed for his activism.

He was briefly an altar boy to please his mother, but at 14 followed his father down the pit in Lanarkshire and into the Communist Party.

He led the left-wing caucus of the NUM until Arthur Scargill supplanted him, but was vice-president until he retired in 1987. He was loyal to a fault, true to the doctrine of collective responsibility, carried his feelings about Scargill to the grave. But once he nearly punched him.

Scargill slipped in just before the service started on Thursday, bringing with him a whiff of smoke from old battlefields. Somewhere, too, borne on the scudding clouds, was surely the ghost of Joe Gormley, the fiercely anti-Communist NUM president who helped Edward Heath and the Tory press to demonise McGahey as 'Red Mick'. Gormley's machinations deprived McGahey of the succession.

Before Scargill left he paid bland tribute to McGahey. During the 1984-85 miners' strike, he said, they worked shoulder-to-shoulder. 'The only disagreement we ever had was whether to drink tea or coffee. We were against the class enemy.'

The truth is perhaps a little different. Scargill shot to prominence in the 1972-73 miners' strike in which McGahey played a decisive part. The historian Vic Allen wrote that the strike, which humiliated the Heath Government, had many leaders who improvised a complex system of flying pickets.

But, he added, McGahey had a 'steel-hard unwillingness to make concessions' which reflected the 'stubborn, uncompromising feelings' of the miners themselves. The Government should have studied it, not 'castigated' it.

By the end of the second strike of 1974, which drove Heath to the country, the NUM's unity had fractured. Gormley, who had played the anti-Communist card when he defeated McGahey for the presidency in 1971, manipulated the rules to isolate the Left. And he postponed his own retirement until, under these same rules, McGahey was too old for the job.

By then, intense rivalry had broken out between McGahey and Scargill. But when McGahey's own chance passed in 1980, he threw his weight behind Scargill, healing the rift.

Gormley hoped, reflects Reid, that Scargill would mature in office, but he called the disastrous 1984-85 strike without a ballot. In public, McGahey never broke ranks, but in private things were different.

Ian Bruce, then the *Glasgow Herald*'s industrial correspondent, last week published an account of an incident he saw at the height of the strike. Ian MacGregor, called in by Margaret Thatcher to lead the National Coal Board, flew in to make an improved 'final' offer. McGahey advised acceptance. Scargill refused, 'overruling everyone else in a fit of not uncharacteristic egotism'.

'The argument became heated and McGahey snapped, pinning the union president briefly to a wall before they were separated,' Bruce wrote. Reid believed this account to be true.

McGahey never broke his silence. An authorised biography was abandoned because of his reticence. Nor, recalled Reid, was he a stooge of the Soviet Union. He came to criticise it, believing it had betrayed communism.

He remained a member of the Democratic Left, into which the mainstream party mutated, and joined the Scottish Communist Party. He would say, recalled Reid, that the Inquisition had been bloody, but Christianity had survived. He was born a Communist and he died a Communist, loyal to the end.

Kemp's portrait of Scotland after ten years of Thatcherism, from *The Herald*, January 1989.

Public squalor and private affluence, Professor Galbraith's *[American-Canadian economist, 1908-2006]* famous phrase, implies a polity where individual wealth and consumption are encouraged and public spending restrained.

In a broadcast on Radio 4, the professor recognised that this polity was very much alive in Britain after almost 10 years of Thatcherism, and he found this recognition in the humdrum shape of bags of uncollected rubbish in London.

Residents of Glasgow's West End, where roaming dogs and feral cats root in dustbins and in the impromptu middens that suddenly appear at handy corners, will recognise the symptoms. So will those unfortunate enough to live near a fast-food shop, a taxi rank or a bus-stop. The morning harvest of fried chicken boxes, chip papers and drink cans has no resale value. This is, alas, no harvest; these are the droppings of the consumer society (the Latin root consumere means to destroy). The pessimistic conclusion must be that human careless-ness will defeat the most enlightened Government.

A visitor transported to Scotland from 30 years ago would hard-ly recognise the place. The churches are fewer and emptier, and in every high street or thoroughfare there is a profusion of video shops, bars, off-licences, travel agents.

The visitor would not know that some of these businesses are subsidised by unemployed people working for very low rates 'off the books.' He would not know that the prisons are bulging and squalid; or that there is a plague of housebreaking, shoplifting and petty thieving which has reduced the authorities to impotence; or that the life-style of the people too often undermines their health; or that vandalism adds millions to the cost of maintaining schools.

He would not know that there had been a convulsive loss of employment in manufacturing. He would not know that Scotland showed a relatively poor performance in the formation of new busi-ness. But he would undoubtedly notice the enhanced prosperity of the people, though as each jet takes off for the Mediterranean and each new yet more splendid shopping mall opens he could be excused for wondering where all the money was coming from. Sometimes, in darker moments, he might conclude that it was all being borne on a bubble of consumer credit that could easily burst.

These are practical problems. Political will and resources could moderate them. More serious, and more corroding, is the moral flaw at the heart of policies which encourage private affluence at the expense of public services, and which leave charities to fill the gaps left by public parsimony.

It is this: these policies must discriminate against the weaker, the poorer, the less able, and against those who cannot supplement at their own expense what the state provides. Such policies run the risk of producing social alienation among those standing in the cold outside Mrs Thatcher's emporium with their noses pressed against the glass (a point also made by our bulging jails). They produce that oddest of sights – a Chancellor with nothing to spend our money on.

Professor Galbraith said: 'Few things are as immutable as the addiction of political groups to the ideas by which they once won office.' It has always been a tenet of Thatcherism that prosperity is the prerequisite of effective social policy. Thatcherites are fond of quoting Abraham Lincoln's dictum that you don't help the weak by enfeebling the strong. The Government has certainly helped the strong grow stronger but the rest of the message seems to have got lost somewhere along the way to the bank. Charity helps, but it is not enough.

As the Thatcher era drew to a close, Kemp looked at the economic theories of the day.

Most of what little knowledge I have about economics has been gleaned from colleagues and contacts down the years, together with a bit of reading. The result is a strange brew in which the chief ingredient is confusion. I take comfort from the fact that I do not seem to be alone; our policy-makers often seem just as muddled.

I have lived through two distinct eras of official economic management. First, through the fifties to the seventies, there was Keynesian orthodoxy. Then there was Reaganism or its clone Thatcherism. In the first period my guru was the late JD Vassie, a leader-writer on *The Scotsman*. He was a sweet man, much given to uttering economic theorems, and he often turned the editorial conference into a seminar. He died this year. (1991).

He was a Labour man of the old school but was not easily able to express this in his leaders. Once when he had written an editorial on housing, the editor of the day (Murray Watson) had not liked it and had placed the Conservative manifesto on Jim's desk. 'This, Vassie,' he said, 'is our policy on housing.'

The result was that his leaders had a cloudy or occluded quality. Perhaps he should have chosen an academic career because his conversation, by contrast, was didactic in the best sense. The minutes to deadline would tick away unnoticed as he discoursed. To his interest in economics he added a passion for football, and his conversation would mingle both subjects in a delightful way.

He subscribed to four leading truths. The first was that the essential art of attacking football was to draw your opponent and then pass to an unmarked team-mate. The second was that Stafford Cripps should have funded the sterling balances after the war, thus making the pound less vulnerable to external pressures. The third was that the post-war expansion of world trade under the rules of Gatt had been funded by the liquidity created by Eurodollars. Fourthly, he would aver that inflation was caused when the value of money incomes exceeded the value of goods and services produced. This was the orthodoxy of the day. A central principle of Keynesianism, which after the war had helped the European nations to enjoy sustained economic growth, was that government action could avoid downturns in the business cycle (an unreversed downturn had led to the recession before the war).

A certain amount of inflation, it was accepted, would be the inevitable result of this pump-priming. But as long as prices went up faster than wages this would correct itself in the upswing. What went wrong with Keynesian economic management was that the opposite eventually occurred.

People began to anticipate or discount inflation and pay themselves increases not justified by higher production. (Down the years this has not changed much: in the year to this September wages rose by 7.9% and prices by 3.7%. An optimist might hope the difference reflected gains in efficiency and productivity. A realist in the Vassie mould would fear the worst.)

From this habit came Britain's long obsession with incomes policy (it survives in some manifestoes but is widely discredited). From it, also, flowed the Thatcherite reaction. The belief was that if public spending were cut, state enterprises dismantled and union power broken, then we could escape from stagflation: the market would allocate resources more efficiently than government and create growth. Mrs Thatcher's certitude, and her gifts of explaining everything in terms of household management, swept all objections aside. A mature judgment on the Thatcher years must await the historians. But I began to notice during her terms that JD Vassie's explanations of inflation were incomplete if still fundamentally sound. There were other varieties of the disease. If goods or services were in short supply – if there was a lack of economic capacity, for example, or a shortage of land for housing – that would cause prices to rise. (It might also suck in imports, but that's another story.)

But the chief new strain in the virus was easy credit. It was made more virulent by a housing policy which slashed the building pro-gramme in the public sector and threw every advantage in the direc-tion of private ownership. In Scotland where there was a low level of home ownership that was no bad thing. In the South of England it is not too much to say that it caused a disaster.

The scenario was simple. Banks and building societies fought to lend, often offering 100% mortgages to double-income families. In the south houses were in short supply. Because of green-belt policy new land was not released. Instead of enabling labour mobility (a classic failure of the council-house system, it was alleged), the policy produced severe imbalances in house prices which made things worse: how could someone in the north afford a house in the south? And people in the south could sell a semi and buy a castle in the north.

The system created social inequities by making some people very rich and others very poor. On one side of the coin people borrowed rashly, lumbering themselves with unsustainable commitments. On the other, just as perniciously, the rapid rise in house prices allowed people to release equity from their properties. This they spent freely on consumer durables and leisure, among other things. I remem-bered enough of my Vassie tutorials to realise that this money was not underpinned by any real increase in the value of the assets: the houses had not changed. It was therefore highly inflationary.

Now the prices have collapsed, the market stagnates. The Government is grappling with ways of alleviating the human misery that has resulted. It is obviously electorally expedient to do so; it is also right, though it is sad that the Government's compassion does not extend to other impoverished groups.

Because we have accepted the disciplines of the exchange-rate mechanism of the European monetary system, we can no longer fool ourselves. We cannot use resources that do not exist. We cannot pay ourselves more if we have not produced more. We cannot cheat our way back to international competitiveness by devaluing the currency. If JD Vassie were sitting across the table from me now, he would, I suspect, warn us that quite a hard decade was coming. He would probably be right. The Government will get the blame. For myself I blame the banks. They did the daft lending which put the economy into reverse; their competition made the building societies take leave of their normally conservative senses. Scotland didn't have the disease but it had to take the cure. And the Maxwell fiasco reminds us of the truth of Keynes's famous dictum. When you owe the bank a thousand, it owns you. When you owe it a million, you own it. Next time the bank manager gets above himself, remember that.

The poll tax was deeply unpopular in Scotland where it was introduced first. Shortly after its introduction in England – where it sparked a riot – Margaret Thatcher was forced to resign. On the brink of her departure Kemp reflected on her time in office and what she had meant to Scotland. *The Herald*, November 1990.

Like those of many people my feelings towards Mrs Thatcher are complicated, a compound of admiration and irritation. She has been such a fixed point on the Scottish political landscape that her removal will have a disorientating and confusing effect. When her time to go does come – and she said on Monday that she would stay on for a 'little bit longer' – some of the verities of Scottish politics will no longer apply.

It has been my good fortune to meet the Prime Minister about half a dozen times. On the first occasion – a visit to our offices during our bicentenary in 1983 – her populist gifts were very much in evidence. She charmed everyone from the chairman to the teaboy, and some hardened socialists were leaping around taking snaps of her as she made a progress through the departments that could only be described as royal.

Another occasion, just before the General Election of 1987, saw a group of Scottish editors and media people dining with her in Downing Street. We Scots were at our girning worst, moaning on about Ravenscraig, the health service and so on. At a time when the Scottish economy was undergoing profound changes and was being outperformed by the South-east, the grievances were perhaps not too surprising.

Mrs Thatcher spoke to her brief and painted as cheerful a picture as possible. She was clearly distressed by her apparent failure to make much impression and went to great lengths to change the atmosphere, even staying on with the company for drinks after dinner to a time well beyond the call of duty. A senior aide told me later that she had been profoundly depressed by the occasion, but the editors and others were doing no more than expressing Scotland's general sense of estrangement from her.

This feeling was apparent at the General Election, when the number of Scottish Tory MPs was more than halved to 10 and the Scots engaged in widespread tactical voting. The tendency in each constituency was for the most convincing anti-Thatcher candidate, whether Labour, Nationalist or Alliance, to be supported and some kenspeckle figures, like the late Sir Alex Fletcher, were swept away.

In her next administration, the decision was taken to 'tough it out' in Scotland in the expectation that the policies which the Scots did not like, such as the poll tax, would eventually yield a political dividend. The Secretary of State, Mr Malcolm Rifkind, went through a phase of being an abrasive Thatcherite, a persona that did not sit easily on him. He has since wisely abandoned it and adopted a more consensual attitude while 'sorting out' the truly abrasive Mr Michael Forsyth whose brief tenure as party chairman in Scotland had brought the voluntary wing and the business community to the verge of rebellion.

The strategy to force Scots to 'take their medicine' whether they liked it or not was, in retrospect, a mistake, at least in rhetorical terms, for it compounded their dislike of London Government and bespoke an underlying arrogance. We are a stiff-necked people and our anti- Thatcherism has not always been logical, a factor made all the clearer in the last year by Scotland's relatively strong economic performance.

During the second term, my few meetings with Mrs Thatcher were first social and then professional. In February last year she was the guest of honour at a luncheon of the Newspaper Press Fund and, as then chairman of the West of Scotland branch, I was able to observe her again at close quarters. My admiration of her qualities as a professional politician was increased by the very great patience and grace with which she put up with importunate demands for her to pose for pictures with various notabilities and visitors.

People observing us in conversation over lunch probably thought we were discussing matters of state, but among the things she told me was that she very much enjoyed a simple supper on a Saturday night of bacon and eggs. Anyone overexposed to rich food in the course of professional life will know exactly how she feels.

Later that year, in May, Geoffrey Parkhouse [1935-97, *political editor of* The Herald *for 22 years*], and I interviewed her for *The Herald*. She had just come back from a punishing trip to Brussels and some signs of fatigue were not surprisingly in evidence. She struggled when she spoke to her detailed Scottish brief – she had obviously not grasped the issues surrounding the future of Prestwick Airport, for example – but dealt more confidently with non-Scottish matters.

With hindsight, we now know, she gave us a fascinating foretaste of things to come when she spoke with genuine regret of the need for elder statesmen occasionally to be retired to the back benches. Some of the other newspapers interpreted this as a reference to Mr Nigel Lawson, then Chancellor of the Exchequer, and indeed he later resigned; but my own hunch remains that she had Sir Geoffrey Howe in mind. Now it is she who faces this prospect, but her love of her job, at which she works enormously hard, will make it very hard for her to accept it emotionally.

Mrs Thatcher, conscientious in all things, did her best to understand the Scots but she never really managed it. Resentment of her north of the Border was partly rational, arising out of rapid industrial decline and change and a perceived attack on social expenditures, and partly emotional. My mother, who died earlier this year, entertained a lively dislike of Mrs Thatcher, saying contemptuously 'That woman!' whenever she saw her on television. I never could quite work out the reason for my mother's dislike, for on the face of it she was not at all at odds with the Prime Minister's philosophies of thrift and hard work. It was more that she spoke down to the Scots who sensed, and they were right, that many members of Mrs Thatcher's Cabinet, if not Mrs Thatcher herself, had an impatience with Scottish feelings amounting to a contemptuous dismissal of them.

In its rejection of Mrs Thatcher Scotland has achieved a unity of which it might otherwise rarely be capable. The theory of the historian Professor Christopher Smout is that she has been a scapegoat for us, an external explanation of our failures. There is some truth in this.

Labour support has been artificially inflated and grassroots Tory workers have often confessed that her personality has been their most difficult obstacle. As long as such sentiments were confined to Scotland, Mrs Thatcher could live with them. The poll tax, which will prove to be her greatest political misjudgment, brought her similar contumely in the South where it combined with anger over interest rates, a deepening recession and congestion.

Now that so much of our trade, more than half, is with the European Community, her dubious commitment to its political and economic development also became a serious irritant for the business classes. Last week a Scottish manufacturer of quality rainwear told me emphatically that he would vote for a Conservative Party led by Mr Heseltine but not for one led by Mrs Thatcher.

In Scotland, her departure, when it comes, will throw political loyalties into a new period of volatility. The Conservatives will have some chance of a comeback. The rivalry between Labour and the Nationalists will become even more vicious. The Nationalists will lose their best totem and Labour may well find their geological dominance of Scottish politics slipping away: the true colour of Scottish opinion, so long concealed under the cloak of anti-Thatcherism, may at last become manifest, assuming that the next Tory leader does not alienate us too. The Thatcher era is not yet over, but its end is sufficiently near for us to sense the consequences of its passing.

The leadership of the Conservative government was taken over by John Major. November 1990, *The Herald*.

The Queen is dead, long live the King. As far as the Scots are concerned John Major will promise nothing but a change of style and perhaps the end of the poll tax. Scotland has barely been mentioned in the contest and none of the contenders has been ready to contemplate any change of policy. Mr Major has specifically rejected a parliament with tax-raising powers and evidently assumed that Mrs Thatcher's departure and a review of the community charge would have a sufficiently tonic effect on the party's fortunes north of the Border. He may be mistaken.

The Conservative party's long term decline and failure to reap any political dividend from policies they firmly believed to be in Scotland's interests, led to what Kemp called a 'long Scottish huff'.

Hanging over Rosyth like a cloud is Tory disillusion with Scottish political attitudes. The Prime Minister has been told, apparently, that if Rosyth is saved he should expect no political dividend. This sombre conclusion has been reached by Michael Ancram, who lost his Edinburgh South seat in 1987, and others because of their bruising experiences during the eighties in general and because of what happened at Ravenscraig in particular.

In November 1982 Ancram, then Conservative chairman in Scotland, went to an STUC conference in Motherwell and committed the party to fight for Ravenscraig's survival. Its closure, he said, would be unacceptable to any party.

When he made this statement he was going out on a limb. In retrospect, he wonders if it was the right course. It might have been better, he now reflects, to have taken the pain of closure when first threatened. Perhaps some other industry or opportunity might have arisen before the eighties dissolved into the recession of the nineties. In 1983 Ancram became a Minister in the Scottish Office. I have heard senior civil servants speak highly of his ability, to get money out of the Treasury among other things. He himself says that, quite against the national trend, he managed during his tenure to increase public spending on housing in Scotland.

He and the party got no thanks for that either, he says ruefully. Nor did the major public expenditure during this period on the revival of Glasgow produce any political rewards.

Politics is carried on by human beings and so we should not be entirely surprised that even a great political party is capable of taking the huff with a whole country.

To put it politely, this seems a flawed way in which to conduct the affairs of one of the nations in the UK. Ancram's analysis of the Ravenscraig episode is also incomplete. Fine words butter no parsnips: once British Steel had been privatised the Government effectively lost control of its decisions.

Michael Ancram and George Younger are old-fashioned Conservatives, caring toffs. It was their misfortune during the eighties that the times were unfavourable to them. It was the age of the brutish radical. But until the Tory Party comes out of its long Scottish huff and makes a more careful and sensitive analysis of recent Scottish political history, it will continue to be both baffled and infuriated by us. Incomprehension is the real name and nature of the disease which Michael Ancram classifies as ingratitude.

After the election of the Labour government under Tony Blair, a new referendum on devolution finally took place. On its eve, Kemp contributed this piece to *The Herald*, September 10, 1997.

Those of us who remember the fiasco of 1979 approach tomorrow with nervousness. In the last days of that referendum campaign the Yes majority dissolved and Scotland lost its nerve. A generation that had worked for change felt disillusioned and betrayed. The Thatcher years began and a political winter fell upon Scotland.

This time, I believe and hope, things are different. A genuine consensus for change has developed, the No camp no longer frightens us with its prophecies of doom.

In another sense, 1997 is very different from 1979: the English political establishment has largely swallowed its dislike of Scottish home rule, which it used to see as a sign of base Scottish ingratitude for the ineffable privileges of being part of Westminster governance. English commentators still may not like what they see as Scotland's preferential financial treatment but they realise that to end it would be to drive Scotland to Independence. And although a few MPs from the shires might say good riddance, there is generally no desire at the heart of the political system to see Scotland sever herself from it.

Although Tony Blair this week promised the modernisation of the monarchy, the country's parliamentary institutions are more urgently in need of treatment. The House of Commons has been discredited by sleaze and its vapid confrontationalism.

Next week the Irish peace talks resume with Sinn Fein at the table and the prospect of a new constitutional settlement in Northern Ireland. Scotland's parliament has begun, to many English eyes, to look like the trigger for constitutional reform.

A weakening of Scotland's resolution at the eleventh hour would thus be singularly damaging for our reputation within the British polity. For years – since the days of Gladstone – we have been prosing on about the need for home rule. Now we have the chance to make it happen. To bottle out now would be to invite contempt and ridicule.

In the devolutionary cycle of this century, home rule has seemed close on several occasions. Characteristically it has dissolved at the point of consummation. Home Rule schemes fell with the First World War, and with the first Ramsay MacDonald administration. The Scotland Act was the last banana skin for the Callaghan government in 1979.

After that disappointment I came to believe I should not see Home Rule in my lifetime. But the late John Smith made sure that it remained a commitment of honour for the Labour Party. Tony Blair and Donald Dewar have stood by that pledge. The sinuous legal mind of Lord Irvine has taken much of the devil out of the detail.

Now it is down to us. If we fail we shall for ever afterwards be regarded as a joke nation that toyed with Home Rule but never really meant it. Our dance of the seven veils, having promised so much, will end in pathetic detumescence.

From time to time I have thought that for Scotland Home Rule was merely a tactic, never a strategy; that we maintained a demand for the principle, without ever pushing it to a conclusion, as a means of putting leverage on the British state.

And I suppose it worked. Willie Ross used the nationalist card during the Wilson administrations to ratchet up Scotland's share of public expenditure. Scotland, unusually among stateless nations, has ever since the rise of the modern SNP had the opportunity of securing independence through the ballot box but has never chosen to exercise it.

After tomorrow it is a card that never can be played again. If, as I hope and pray, the principle is endorsed in a resounding double Yes tomorrow, our new parliamentarians will carry an enormous responsibility. They will be expected not just to legislate and scrutinise with maturity and good sense, free of the childish rhetoric that has so damaged Westminster's standing, but also to validate the general principle of diffusing power from the centre.

After Scottish Home Rule and a new settlement in Ireland must come reform of the upper chamber and the development of regional assemblies in England. The mawkish soap opera of the royal family may continue to preoccupy us. But the paradox is that the binding force of the constitutional monarchy itself is what makes it possible for us to embrace Home Rule without putting the Union at risk.

But it was Alex Salmond and the SNP who largely reaped the benefits of the new settlement and Tony Blair appeared baffled by the perverse Scots in 1998.

Scottish secretary Donald Dewar wears a hunted look. His season of political unhappiness seems without end. It may often may be measured in dollops of the absurd, but the stakes are high. At risk are Labour's long dominance in Scotland and the integrity of the Union itself.

For the moment SNP leader Alex Salmond walks on air if not on water, deftly keeping Labour on the defensive and milking the disaffection within its ranks. Old Labour lives in Scotland: its fights with the modernisers are often bitter and personal. The suppression of 'unsuitable' candidates for Holyrood is feeding resentments.

In May, a poll on voting intentions for the first Scottish parliament put the SNP ahead of Labour for the first time. Last week another blow fell: 52% of Scots, according to another survey, would vote for independence in a referendum.

Even more troubling for Blair, who hoped home rule would consign the SNP and its aims to history, is the inference from the poll that many who support independence are Labour voters.

Blair is said to be baffled, like Margaret Thatcher before him, by the apparent perversity of the Scots. In the Commons last week his attack on Salmond over Dounreay, was unusually personal.

For Labour in Scotland, like the melting of an ice age, the end of Thatcherism has revealed a changed landscape in which a Labour government stands committed not to tax and spend but to rigorous restraint.

Now, much more rapidly than in England and Wales, Labour is acquiring in Scotland the unpopularity that goes with office. And because the Tories, for all the brave talk of William Hague in Glasgow yesterday, are still a busted flush, and because the Liberal Democrats prosper only patchily, the SNP has become the chief receptacle for opposition. For the first time it may be making serious inroads in the cities and Labour's urban heartlands.

Blair may have to accept that the consequence of home rule is not to lock Scotland into the Union but to stimulate its divergence within it. If he can stop the process there, he may have to be content. Some strategists believe that by over-reacting to the SNP Dewar is inflating its importance. 'Let them stew in their success,' said a senior source last week.

The Scottish Parliament reconvened for the first time since 1707 in May 1999. From *The Observer*.

It was new and yet it seemed as if it had been there for ever, perhaps because it was meeting in the Assembly Hall where in 1948 the world rediscovered Sir David Lindsay's *Three Estates*. No Flattery or Divine Correction, no bawdy abbesses revealed in undergarments of lurird purple, just men and women dressed as if for church and Tommy Sheridan in a suit which said that Trotskyite socialism is compatible with elegance.

Like most people of my generation I could scarcely watch the opening of the Scottish Parliament, designedly low key though it was, without a twitch of emotion. I thought of the many people who had campaigned for it but did not live to see it and of the hundreds of increasingly plaintive editorials I had penned down the lean years. I thought of my father who, when we were children, would take us to Parliament Hall where the advocates walked with their clients. For him, and therefore for us, it was full of echoes of a lost sovereignty.

There was many a time, in the Eighties in particular, when I gave up hope that home rule would come in my own lifetime, so implacably hostile was Mrs Thatcher to it and so permanent seemed her grip on power. But through the Thatcher years, the flame was kept alight by Canon Kenyon Wright and his fellow campaigners, and sustained by Labour's decision to join the constitutional convention. As a result much of the theoretical work, that led to the Scotland Act, so great an improvement on its aborted predecessor, had been done by the time Tony Blair moved to complete John Smith's unfinished business.

And so we were entitled for a moment at least, to savour last week's images of a sober and unpretentious institution full of a quiet determination to win respect for itself in the larger world and avoid the petty insults of Westminster. But, of course, malice and rancour are as resilient as rats and have already boarded the parliamentary ship. When Donald Dewar, after his election as First Secretary, shook everybody's hand but that of Dennis Canavan, the independent MSP neatly rebuked him by offering him his own in a gesture of conciliation that Dewar could not refuse.

Soon, however, sweetness was in increasingly short supply. As the coalition talks came to an uneasy conclusion, Donald Gorrie, that Lib Dem of venerable service in local government, quickly broke with Westminster tradition but not in the way the more pious had expected: in an exasperated comment to journalists he denounced Labour as 'the biggest bunch of liars you could ever meet.'

Queen Elizabeth ll of England and I of Scotland officially opened the Parliament a month later. Kemp recalled the controversy over her coronation and advised her not to carry a handbag.

The Scottish Parliament will be opened by the Queen on Thursday after a good deal of muddle about protocol and symbolism. The result is a ceremony designed to preserve traditional British theories about sovereignty and to keep the new body in its place. There is a nod in the direction of historical continuity (a 'civic procession' will walk from the old parliament House to the Mound) but the central thrust will be that this is a subordinate body, a creature of statute.

Those who want to subvert this view argue that different principles of sovereignty apply in Scotland, where it rests with the people and not with the Crown in the UK Parliament. This argument seems loosely based on the Scottish democratic tradition. But the old Scottish Parliament was composed of elites. Our democratic tradition flows more from our religious history and from a national church which refused to recognise the monarch as its head.

The last time the subject came up was in the Fifties when Elizabeth succeeded to the throne. The pioneer of modern nationalism, the late John McCormick, and his young friend and follower Ian Hamilton (now QC), brought an action to contest the legality in Scotland of the title Queen Elizabeth II, on the grounds that she was the first to rule over a United Kingdom.

This brought forth the famous Cooper judgement. My recollection is that Lord Cooper did not accept the principle argument but in his ruling said that certain articles of the Treaty of Union were inalienable and could not be challenged by the UK Parliament. Under this interpretation, Westminster was a new parliament, dating from 1707, combining the sovereignty of England and Scotland, and not, as English constitutionalists argued, the English parliament in continuous session – the so-called '1,000 years of history' which the Tory right frequently invokes when attacking the euro. In short, the Treaty of Union (called merely an Act by Westminster) is for Scotland an inalienable constitutional document.

Thus, Scottish sovereignty has not passed to Edinburgh but remains at Westminster. The modernising element wanted to weaken this principle by introducing a new, informal monarchy to the world in implicit recognition of a new era of people power.

Not surprisingly, the palace did not agree. It may think it cannot win, whatever line it takes. In 1953, when the Queen came to Edinburgh to receive the Honours of Scotland, the old Scottish aristrocracy decked itself in its finery and turned up to find the Queen wearing a raincoat and carrying a handbag. Such was the fuss that the official painting of the event, which hangs in Holyrood, expunged the handbag.

Today, the Palace is criticised for clinging to the old horsedrawn pomp: then, its informality offended – because after the theatre of the coronation, it seemed like a calculated snub, denying Scotland its place in a Union it perceived as a 'partnership of equals' but which England clearly saw as an act of absorption.

In the real world, sovereignty continues to change. It is not bright and shining, like a crown but soft and malleable, like putty. The sovereignty of Westminster has been pulled by the EU in one direction, the Scottish Parliament will give it a tug in the other. Increasingly, sovereignty is shared. Indeed, elected politicians recognise the limitation on their own powers by their increasing use of the referendum to stamp decisions with the irreversible authority of the people.

Although they are consultative rather than legislative, referendums give a de facto role for the people in the constitution. Alex Salmond hopes to use them as a ladder. His tactical aim is to make the new Parliament work. The strategic objective is to secure control of it and immediately hold a referendum on independence.

Once, I would have said that Scotland would remain staunchly Unionist in almost every circumstance. But there is a new Union – in Europe, still fragile but inexorably developing – which makes the importance of the old questionable.

The court clings to its trappings but it must listen, too, to the march of the people. One final word of advice to her Majesty: don't carry a handbag on Thursday.

A defence of Holyrood from 2002.

The more that its implacable critics attack the Scottish Parliament and the more they attempt to discredit it upon whatever pretext comes to hand, the more they seem to feed the case for independence. If they calculate that Scotland will be persuaded to renounce what devolution it has and return to the full embrace of the Union Parliament, they are surely misguided. The result might be just the opposite.

As Europe agonises after the French presidential elections and the assassination of Pim Fortuyn [*A Dutch politician with extreme views on Muslim immigration*], one of the explanations emerging for the electorates' drift to the Right and for a growing alienation from the political process, is the gap between the élites and the people. The European decision-making process is too remote, too technocratic, said the German Chancellor Gerhard Schröder in an interview with the *Guardian*.

If that analysis is correct, then we need more, rather than less, devolution.

John Swinney and Alex Salmond clearly intend to use the discontent fomented by the anti-Holyrood press to agitate for independence sooner rather than later. I think their impatience is premature. Rome was not built in a day. But it would be no more than the Holyrood cavillers deserve if their sour labours produced a result precisely opposite to that which they intended.

In October 2002, Donald Dewar, Scotland's first First Minister, died.

Like many, I felt a strong sense of personal loss when I heard the news of Donald Dewar's death, although he was a valued acquaintance rather than a close friend. By a coincidence, he died in the same hospital as my father and of the same condition. By another, both had undergone serious medical intervention in the months before.

My father lingered painfully on for a few days and his death was a release. I am glad that Donald's end was swift and that he was spared a twilight of failing powers or mental incompetence. For a man who valued his own intellect so highly that would have been a cruel end indeed.

He would have scoffed at the idea of personal sainthood; and beside his unpretentiousness, sometimes, sat the peevishness of the dominie dealing with an intractable child.

In the Eighties, we both attended a Scottish Council forum at Gleneagles, an event more valued for its social encounters than its formal proceedings. In the morning, I came somewhat blearily down to breakfast and at the next table observed Donald deep in the paper which I edited at the time and to which I had contributed, I felt, a pretty sound editorial that morning.

Suddenly, Dewar scowled, threw the paper to the floor and stamped on it. A little shaken, I decided that my editorial must have touched a raw nerve. But that evening, over drinks, he told me that what had infuriated him was a quotation in a news story attributed to a senior colleague. Its disloyalty had displeased him.

The obituarists have rightly identified loyalty as one of his outstanding virtues. Donald's series of 'safe houses', in which he found some consolation for the loss of his own family life, included that of the BBC producer, Matt Spicer, and his wife, Olive, and of my old friend, Bob McLaughlin, at whose funeral Donald delivered the oration last year. There he could speak freely and openly, safe in the knowledge that they would not betray him to the press.

It must have been in the early Eighties that I met him at a dinner party given by Bob and Ann McLaughlin. He arrived late, consumed prodigious amounts of pudding and rounded fiercely on me when I suggested that Labour under Callaghan had been content to see devolution go down into the sand.

But to Bob, who had made a journey from his student days and was now a committed Thatcherite, Donald was fondly indulgent, rising only mildly to Bob's sallies. Friendship was thicker than dogma. Like Bob, Donald argued in the best Scottish way – fiercely, rationally and without personal rancour. That evening, he laid down such an awesome barrage of fact and detail that I had to beat as graceful a retreat as I could.

His success as a politician depended, at least in part, on his mastery of detail. Some years later, when he was still in opposition, I met him on the BA flight to London. At that time, passengers got a cup of tea and a Twix. From friends and crew he cadged about five more and consumed them in a flash.

His mastery of detail, as much as his waspish wit, made him feared by his opponents. But waspishness there undoubtedly was. We do not know the full story of why he fell out so badly with Dennis Canavan, or why he tried to block Sean Connery's knighthood. He never really explained himself on either question; when I phoned him one Saturday afternoon to ask him about the Connery business, he simply said: 'I just can't say anything.'

By this, he meant, I suspect, that the process of honours was confidential. And that was another quality which explained why he was so trusted by Tony Blair and senior colleagues – he had iron discretion without which politicians rarely rise.

His epitaph on Bob McLaughlin could serve for himself: 'He was someone of great character, and formidable learning but, above all, a decent man, civilised and caring.'

On Donald Dewar's funeral.

On Wednesday, I attended Donald Dewar's funeral. I relished the irony of hearing 'The Internationale' played by Aly Bain and Phil Cunningham in a cathedral presided over by that true-blue Tory, Bill Morris.

Indeed, a senior Scottish Tory remarked rather sourly as we left the cathedral that the service had been 'air-brushed' by New Labour, and I suppose that was to some extent true, although I am sure Donald would have approved. When Gordon Brown rose to deliver the eulogy, I feared that it was to be a party political broadcast. Perhaps he was speaking a little more loudly than necessary because there had been a partial microphone failure during Tony Blair's reading from Isaiah. But as Gordon went on, the power and sincerity of his words became utterly convincing.

It was as if Brown, though he invited the congregation to rededicate itself to Dewar's principles was reminding himself what they were.

In a piece published the day after the death of Princess Margaret (1930-2002), Kemp recorded why, despite arguing so strongly for Scottish home rule throughout his professional life, he remained in the end a reluctant royalist.

In fairy tales the princess lives happily ever after. Margaret did not, having renounced her prince to avert a constitutional crisis. She was perhaps the first of the modern royals whose private life became media fodder as she dwindled into addiction, ill health and a drifting hedonism. Her personal fortunes seem to reflect those of the monarchy itself.

Those old enough to remember the youthful princess, who had animation and beauty, must feel regret and sorrow over her life and her death. I cannot claim to have had more than a fleeting glimpse of her, but it was enough to make me sense that beneath her pose of languid unconcern there burned a spark of real anger. She never much enjoyed her official duties, but she did insist on the deference which she thought her due even when deference itself was dying.

In 1983 the *Glasgow Herald*, of which I was then editor, celebrated its bicentenary, which was marked by a visit from Mrs Thatcher and then from the Queen. Mrs Thatcher was exuberantly regal but the monarch's style was altogether quieter. I had an anxiety dream the night before her visit: as I escorted her round the building she turned to me and said kindly: 'Arnold, you're doing quite well, but you'll need to do something about your suits.'

In the event she of course offered no such advice. She was interested, motherly even, and as she left gave me a real smile which lit up her face. Some time later I received a reciprocal invitation to a reception at Buckingham Palace.

That afternoon I was summoned from the smoke-room of my London club by Jock, a rough-tongued servant who in the Walter Scott tradition was allowed a certain licence – he was downright rude – but who, in his ruminative moments, would talk knowledgeably of the Compromise of 1850 and the Fugitive Slave Act by which Congress sought to appease the south, or of the origin of the word doolally (after the Indian resort to which war-stressed soldiers of the Raj were sent), which he clearly thought applied to most of the members.

'Mr Kemp!' he barked in his roughest tones. 'You're wanted on the phone by Buckingham Palace!' My fellow members jerked out of their postprandial stupor and looked at me with new respect. When I got to the phone I found myself speaking to a Lady Somebody-Something, who told me that Princess Margaret was 'frightfully keen' to meet me. Would I make sure to make myself known to her?

My heart sank but I made the promise. When we arrived at the palace, we found that the reception, which stretched over several state rooms, was simply enormous. Reciprocal hospitality, it seemed, was being offered to a couple of thousand members of the British media. There was no sign of the Princess but, true to my promise, I went in search of her. The thronged rooms and galleries seemed endless and my evening began to take on the quality of a dream, but this time it was a nightmare.

After about an hour I spotted her, sitting on a yellow sofa, surrounded by courtiers. In a state of some anxiety, and in any case feeling by now that my mission was interfering with my enjoyment of the royal champagne, I rather impatiently pushed my way to the front, addressed her directly and perhaps a little brusquely, and said: 'Your Royal Highness, I believe you wanted to speak to me.'

This no doubt breached protocol in numerous ways. I should have made myself known to an acolyte, perhaps, or found some way of making a less direct, more deferential approach. Whatever the reason, there was a long and frigid silence. You could sense the ice forming around the little group.

Eventually she spoke. 'I say,' she said. 'Would you mind fetching me an ashtray?' Chastened, and by now quite angry, I obliged, and then took myself off. Later I found myself in a pleasant conversation with Prince Charles, who seemed without what used to be called 'side'.

I have, of course, dined out on this story ever since. And despite the slightly bruising experience, I find, somewhat to my own surprise, that I remain a reluctant royalist. I found the Diana Cult irrational and disturbing, though perhaps not surprising in our witch-doctor culture which seems to prefer urban myth or tabloid rumour to facts or rational debate. The Queen, of course, grievously misjudged the mood in the country. But in the case of Princess Margaret the royal family's traditional stoicism will be able to reassert itself without public objection. To my younger friends Princess Margaret is an object of pity or indifference, if not derision.

Why am I a royalist? I suppose I have always subscribed to the view that the royal family, by neutralising the formal centre of power in our odd constitution, has formed some sort of bulwark against instability. Just say President Thatcher and then think about it. Nor does the old society which the royalty headed, of country families and landed gents, seem markedly worse than our new world in which vapid celebrity rules.

That, perhaps, is the challenge the royals have failed to accept: how do you transform something that is distant and revered into something more familiar without loss of respect? Now that we have got rid of hereditary peers, where will it all stop? But then, as historian Robert Lacey has observed, logic and royalty are very distant cousins.

PART III
CULTURE

8
Literature and language

WEST END Vs EAST END: a popular take on Glasgow's poetry.

> Here's the bell that never rang,
> And here's the fish that never swam,
> Here's to the bird that never flew,
> From off the tree that never grew.
> Hurrah! Let Glasgow Flourish.

These familiar lines come from James Manson's celebratory poem about Glasgow of 1863. Manson worked on *The Glasgow Herald* but came from Kilwinning, anticipating its designation by Tom Shields as Ayrshire's burgh of culture.

It is one of more than 130 poems about the city gathered up by Hamish Whyte in an anthology, *Mungo's Tongues*.

Whyte has trawled the Mitchell Library with discrimination and has rescued some interesting material. The Kailyard's writ does not run here. There is little sentimentality but a continuous thread of sometimes baffled love mixed with anger about the dark industrial night of poverty, drunkenness and squalor, an anger than runs through to the poetry of our own time. William Watt's Saturday in Glasgow [c1825] deals with a theme ancient and modern:

> Now nicht throws east her dusky wing,-
> To rouse the thievish varlets
> And thrang frae a' the closses spring
> Great troops o' lustful harlots.

Thomas Campbell's Lines on Revisiting a Scottish River [1827] lament the pollution of the Clyde, once a pastoral and romantic stream. A student parodist, C.M.P., asks:

> Know you the city ...
> Where the dirt of the streets and the clouds of the sky
> In colour are equal, in blackness may vie,
> And often the river is purple with dye?

In a bitter little satire from 1832, Alexander Rodger, a polymath and pawnbroker, imprisoned as a radical, begs to be released from the squalid trade of pledging and taken back into employment at the Barrowfield Dyeworks:

He'll fire your furnaces, or weigh your coals,
Wheel barrows, riddle ashes, mend up holes,
Beat cloth, strip shades; in short, do anything ...

It is, however, in the modern material that the anthology's strength remains. A handful of great poets are supported by many good ones. The sardonic Hugh MacDiarmid, in Glasgow, 1960, returning to the city after long exile, sees the crowds going to the big game at Ibrox and fantasises:

I gasped. The newsboys came running along,
'Special! Turkish Poet's Abstruse New Song.
Scottish Authors' Opinions' – and, holy snakes,
I saw the edition sell like hot cakes!

MacDiarmid's sparring partner Edwin Muir is represented by the cooler, fastidious Industrial Scene *[1935]*. The elegiac You Lived in Glasgow *[1970]*, from which we got the title for the collection of pictures from the Outram archive, *Dear Happy Ghosts*, is one of two poems from Iain Crichton Smith.

You were happier than anywhere, you said.
Such fine, good neighbours helping when your child
Almost died of croup. Those pleasant Wildes
Removed with the fallen rubble have now gone
In the building programme which renews each stone.
I stand in a cleaner city, better fed,
In my diced coat, brown hat, my paler hands
Leafing a copy of the latest book.
Dear ghosts, I love you, haunting sunlit winds,
Dear happy dented ghosts, dear prodigal folk.

And of course there is the compelling voice of Edwin Morgan, answering MacDiarmid's put-downs and exploring high-rise blues in his Glasgow Sonnets, or turning 'Let Glasgow Flourish' upside down in a jeu d'esprit that arrives at the motto through 48 mutations beginning with 'Let gallows languish'.

Other personal favourites are here. Tom McGrath's account of how Charlie Tully scored directly from a corner – and then did it again after the referee chalked it off – still has the power to make me laugh. Beneath the humour of Stephen Mulrine's Wee Malkies lurks the menace of the teenage Visigoths terrorising the tower blocks.

Haw missis, whit'll ye dae when the wee Malkies come,
If they dreep doon affy the wash-hoose dyke,
An pit the hems oan the sterrheid light,
An play wee heidies oan the clean close wa',
An bloo'er yir windae in wi' the baw,
Missis, whit'll ye dae?

And Tom Leonard's unpunctuated elided verses catch perfectly the cadences of urban speech:

ahll tellyi sun
see if ah wiz Scot Symon
ahd tell him wherrty stuff their team

The later poetry is divided into two schools. The first, which I shall call the East-End school, is scornful of the City of Culture and full of anger, as in Cath Craig's Glasgow's Alive, as hard and cutting and as polished as a diamond:

Glasgow's alive and kicking,
Glasgow's alive and stabbing,
Glasgow's alive and shooting
Heroin into its veins.

Then there is the West-End school, which celebrates the raffish charms of Great Western Road. I very much warmed to Donny O'Rourke's evocation of that great thoroughfare. His experience of rising on Saturday with the virtuous intention of walking in the country and then spending a pleasurable day pottering around Great Western Road read familiarly to me.

I too enjoy the animation of Kelvinbridge. Here fish shops vie, Roots and Fruits purvey fruit and flowers, and scholars browse in

Caledonian Books. Here, in the gallery of Annie Good's fashion shop, Moon, Ian Murray with his bookshop Word of Mouth nests like Wise Owl. Here, in the delicatessen, you may queue behind one of our most attractive television personalities as she garners the makings of a dinner party.

God Glasgow it's glorious
just to gulp it down in heartfuls
feeling something quite like love.

If pushed, I would have to go with the West-End school. But Whyte has united the tendencies skilfully. Alasdair Gray's great painting, Cowcaddens 1950, adorns the cover of the book. Does it hang in any of our galleries? If not, it should.

On the centenary of Hugh MacDiarmid: allegations of neglect. The highlight of the hundredth anniversary of the birth of CM Grieve in 1992 was a BBC Radio Scotland broadcast on a Tuesday evening, mostly from the Queen Street studio in Edinburgh before an invited audience but partly from the snug in Milne's Bar.

Norman MacCaig and Adam McNaughtan read poetry, MacCaig including his famous recommendation that MacDiarmid's centenary should be marked by a minute's pandemonium.

Under the generic heading, 'The Flyting', a panel of educationalists dealt with MacDiarmid's place – or lack of it – in the curriculum. Since this was a Scottish occasion there was a great deal of girning and resentment at the educational establishment's alleged neglect of him.

The admirable Lesley Riddoch, who compered the occasion, interrogated the audience to establish if educated Scots could quote from MacDiarmid. Many there could but it was hardly a random sample. Most of the audience had some prior interest in the MacDiarmid oeuvre or were from Langholm, his home town. A recorded vox pop among school children demonstrated that few had knowledge of or interest in the poet.

There was some dark muttering, which drew a cheer, that MacDiarmid's politics explained his neglect by the establishment. To this a member of the panel indignantly replied that he had never voted Tory in his life.

I reflected on how Scottish all this was – the pessimism, the search for scapegoats, the failure to agree, the depressing distance between literary culture and popular taste, the lamentation over the erosion of the Scottish linguistic tradition. Yet often we have tunnel vision and a phenomenon which we identify as being Scottish is in fact universal.

In the western world it is a long time since the popular and literary cultures coincided. Literature is something you get at school. It is hard work. It is forbidding. Popular culture is powerful and ubiquitous and usually frowned on by the literary elite. It is not that the unlettered school children of today do not know poetry. They know the words of their songs. And if you talk to a middle-class, middle-aged Scot he or she, though unlikely to know any MacDiarmid, may be able to quote from Bob Dylan.

(A random poll in our Edinburgh office, where this is being written, does not support this theory. One claims to be able to recite The Bonnie Broukit Bairn in its entirety and make a decent stab at The Watergaw. None can quote more than a snippet from Dylan.)

In the tradition of flyting, I will not let such facts stand in the way of the argument. The failure of the literary elite to touch base with the general public is now an accepted part of the scene. Frighteningly few copies of new novels are bought unless they break through to become bestsellers. Publishers struggling to survive not only have to subsidise the book trade by supplying it on a sale-or-return basis. They now also seek to sustain sales by publishing books aimed at those who do not read but who might be tempted into buying books about golf, gardening, cooking, and so on.

The distance between literary and popular values has in London spawned a new school of critics committed to treating popular culture seriously.

Only in totalitarian regimes, it seems, do literature and popular culture coincide. In Russia the poem, the novel and the play carried the burden of dissent, often in cipher, often disguised. The reverence that the Russians have for their poets is seen in the care with which they tend their graves, perpetually adorned with flowers. It is one of the sadder consequences of glasnost and all its consequences that literature, or the purchase of books, is in rapid decline in Russia and other parts of Eastern Europe .

Here in the affluent over-amused West, and not just in Scotland, we have to accept that the serious poet will reach only a minority audience, and that each new generation will have to seek out MacDiarmid and the others for themselves. Yet my own reflection at the end of Tuesday evening was that here was much of which a Scot could feel proud. Whatever distance there is between art and the general public, our culture is far from dead.

What's in a name? A lot, but only if it's pronounced correctly.

The idea that we just let our old names and words go is too liberal for me. In all cultures the pronunciation of some names will not correspond to their spelling. When I went to work in England I came adrift on Magdelene College (Maudlin), Beaulieu (Bewley) and Cholmondley (Chumley), among others. In Scotland the examples that defeat foreigners include Milngavie, Strathaven and Alford. In these examples the 'correct' or traditional pronunciation is defended by local usage but in the case of the old Scots name 'Menzies' the battle seems largely lost.

The correct pronunciation, Mingus, has generally disappeared. The source of the confusion is the old Scots character z which had a different value from the identical English letter. It was what in phonetics is called the yod, a sound at the start of words like yet or at the end of French words like bataille. It survives in other Scots names like Dalzell and words like capercailzie, though again by the process of hypercorrection the z is often sounded here too. As a result many Scots will swear blind that the proper pronunciation is MENzies with the English z.

When the name Menzies travelled abroad its holder either accepted the change philosophically (for example, the late Sir Robert Menzies, Prime Minister of Australia) or adjusted the spelling. Charles Mingus, the great jazz musician, may have had some Scottish blood in him, or else an ancestor may have acquired the name from a Scottish slave boss.

Burns as Elvis? A rammy among scholars. (2002)

When literary scholar Dr Andrew Noble arrived the other day at Glasgow's bus station, he noticed a poster featuring Robert Burns, whose name will be celebrated this week all over the world.

What struck him was that the Burns in the poster was not the man from the rather effete standard image of the Naysmith portrait.

He bore a strong resemblance to Elvis Presley, complete with sideburns and hint of a sultry leer. The poster was even headed 'Rock
and Roll'.

Burns, who has a worldwide following, is an important asset for
the Scottish tourist industry and the poster advertised the heritage
park at his birthplace of Alloway in Ayrshire.

But by exploiting the iconic potency of Burns and the sexuality
that drove his life and work, it exemplified one of the few themes
that united scholars gathered at the University of Strathclyde for a
major symposium on the poet. They were in accord that in an age of
sexual frankness there was no longer any need to sanitise the image
of Burns, who has been described as an 'eroto-maniac'.

Behind the dispassionate scholarly inquiry at the conference
raged a bitter row about a new edition of the poet's work. *The
Canongate Burns, – [edited by Noble and Patrick Hogg]*, contains 11
poems attributed to him which, say the editors, show that he continued to produce radical but anonymous work after 1793, when he is
said to have suspended his attacks on the establishment for fear of
losing his job as an excise officer in Dumfries. He died three years
later.

The row has become increasingly bitter. There have been allegations of smear campaigns and anonymous calls to newspapers. But
behind it lies a bid to restore Burns – traduced, sentimentalised and
ghettoised – to his position as one of the greatest poets of his age and
a radical who never truly recanted.

Hogg and Noble's most persistent critic was Dr Gerard
Carruthers of Glasgow University, a former colleague.

Carruthers established from holograph evidence that two disputed poems were not by Burns but by the radical poet Alexander
Geddes, a Roman Catholic priest.

Carruthers emphasised that he had no quarrel with the political
line of the edition. 'I'm left-wing. I would want a more political
Burns than appears in some biographies and commentaries. My
heart politically would be with Noble and Hogg, all other things
being equal.'

Burns scholar Carol McGuirk, professor of English at Florida
Atlantic University, defended their inclusion. 'It's good for Burns
scholarship – otherwise successive editions will just repeat or rubber-
stamp the earlier ones,' she said.

She thought there was a convincing case for many of the poems and was sympathetic to the thrust of *The Canongate Burns*. It argues that the poet had not just written 'a few love songs' after 1793. Evidence of his continuing creative and radical drive could be found in such late poems as A Man's a Man for A' That, published anonymously in 1795.

McGuirk first noted the phenomenon of Burns as a sexual icon during her postgraduate research in Glasgow – even in Victorian images of Burns, the sideburns were beginning to emerge. She drew attention to the resemblance with the Presley cult in an essay.

Early biographers and commentators bowdlerised both Burns's life and work. In a paper to the conference, Noble said that Scotland needed to 'recover' the radical Burns. He compared the 'protean Burns' to Mozart. In the genius of both, he argued, the spirit was driven by the flesh. He believes Scotland must recover Burns and his radical generation, whose importance was suppressed after their deaths for political reasons.

A case for Laidlaw closes on a painful chapter. (1991)

I finally got round to reading William McIlvanney's latest book, *Strange Loyalties*. It is the latest and, Willie tells me, the last of the novels about Jack Laidlaw. In the book the Glasgow detective goes in search of the truth about the death of his brother. As a crime novel it seems to me considerably superior to the new Elmore Leonard, Maximum Bob, which is piled so high in all the bookshops.

There's more to it than just crime. Willie uses it to explore some of his favourite themes – Scotland, violence, working-class heroism and despair. It is a reflective and compassionate book with a great deal of charm. But what gives it real power is that it deals with one of the most persistent motifs in Scottish writing, that of the doppelganger.

'His last gift from the grave for me,' concludes the detective about his brother, 'had been perhaps a more intense vision of the blackness in myself. It gave me a proper fear of who I was.' His pursuit of his brother has been a pursuit of his own tortured conscience. As I closed the book I, for my part, reflected that here was a writer every bit as good, if not better, than many of the modern American school so widely celebrated and so much in vogue. It is a cruel business devoting your life to your art in a small land. It is that much harder to be heard in the wider world. Worse, you may be treated shabbily in your own patch.

It is not the case, of course, that Willie has been neglected. He has achieved considerable critical standing internationally. The Big Man was filmed. His books are, moreover, popular with the public. But Willie's experience with Laidlaw has been a painful one. Over a period of more than a year Willie talked to STV about a series based on Laidlaw.

Willie recalls the last meeting at STV particularly well because he left his coat there. As they parted he was told that STV were commissioning a programme called Thriller. This was the first of Taggart, the series that has since gone on to be a great money-spinner for STV.

At first Willie was not too worried, perhaps naively. But then a friend at STV, the late Clark Tait, came to him in some alarm. He had seen the rushes. He advised Willie to consult a lawyer.

In the end Willie took no action. No doubt STV's denials that Taggart is derivative of Laidlaw are sincere. To me, I hope a disinterested outsider, it seems the connection is so obvious as to make any denial disingenuous. It remains, I should have thought, something of a burden on STV's corporate conscience. It is, of course, true that Taggart, once launched, developed directions of its own. Taggart and Laidlaw are more distant cousins now. But that is not really the point.

Willie has put the disappointment behind him. Although this is the last Laidlaw book, the new novel on which he is working will feature as the first-person voice a character called Tom Docherty who flits in and out of *Strange Loyalties* as a distant and slightly oracular figure. He is the grandson of the eponymous hero of *Docherty*, the novel which brought McIlvanney serious critical appraisal in 1975.

For Laidlaw Tom is something of a mentor, but for my part I hear in him the voice of Willie himself. Here is Tom on literary criticism: 'It's nearly all about register. There's a lot of po-faced crap that gets highly praised because of its tone of voice. "I'm serious, I'm cultured," it's telling you all the time. Bollocks.'

Willie, through Tom, is touching on a very serious problem for contemporary literature and for the book trade which has put publishers, in particular, under severe financial pressure. It is that the public does not on the whole buy fiction in any great amounts. The novel is out of touch with popular taste. Those novelists who do sell well are usually sneered at.

Willie is something of an exception. His books are both popular and critically regarded. If the novel is not going to vanish into the antechamber of high art, or become, as in Europe, an intellectual crossword puzzle, the genre needs more of his kind.

The Highland Clearances and the marginalised of today. (2001)

If, as Ambrose Bierce argued, a violin is the revenge exacted by the intestines of a dead cat then history, in the hands of a skilled interpreter, may avenge vanished generations. The Highland Clearances are a good example of the phenomenon.

One view is that landowners brutally swept away the native people. Harder-nosed academics say that the Clearances were part of an inevitable change. But although we are in an age of opulence, a time when, in the words of Luiz Felipe Scolari, the Brazilian football coach, we tie dogs up with sausages, we seem to grow ever more bitter about the misfortunes of our Highland forebears who lived not in Arcadia but often in poverty.

Despite the evidence Greens, New Agers and eco-freaks continue to romanticise the days when crofters dwelt with their cattle in the black houses. Resentment still festers over post-Culloden genocide, the indifference to the plight of the native people of an anglicised lairdocracy, and the evils of a free market in estates operating under feudal law.

There is no doubt about the camp to which belongs Alistair McIntosh, academic and activist, fellow of the Centre of Human Ecology in Edinburgh. Indeed, as a founding member of the Eigg Trust, he became a leader of the movement which transformed public attitudes to Highland land. The idea of community ownership now enjoys almost universal support.

The Scottish Parliament has abolished feudal tenure; the Executive has published and consulted on a draft Land Reform Bill; and now the people of Gigha have until the end of the month to raise £3.85 million to buy their island from the laird [In 2012 Gigha celebrated ten years of community ownership].

McIntosh's book Soil and Soul is a powerful addition to the literature of Highland grievance, distinguished for its attempt to set it in a world context and for the fluent grace of the writing. Some of it, I confess, I took with a pinch of impatience. McIntosh writes beautifully about his upbringing on the Isle of Lewis but can arouse irritation when, for example, he interrupts an absorbing account of bringing a stag down from the hill with reflections on the bardic tradition.

No doubt that puts me into the band of the banal and the anal for whom McIntosh has contempt, but I'm afraid I remained sceptical about his radical liberation theology, his rediscovery of the presence of God in nature and the neglected feminity of divine wisdom. On the other hand, I found his account of the Eigg people's struggle to acquire the island from the colourful Keith Schellenberg – for whom McIntosh confesses a certain affection – gripping and often moving. So too was the story of how he mustered a theological and spiritual case against Redland Aggregates' plan for a superquarry that would have removed a mountain in the south of Harris.

He enlisted the support of both the Rev Professor John Macleod of the Free Church College and Sulian Stone Eagle Herney, paramount chief of the Canadian Mi'Kmaq Indians. Upon arrival in Scotland the chief grew irritated when McIntosh took him to the Faslane peace camp, where he was given vegetarian stew. I imagine a decent Scottish breakfast might have done more for his temper.

The reporter at the public inquiry into the superquarry, Gillian Pain, was irked by McIntosh's idealistic presentation. Whether that contributed to her decision to come out in favour of the development I cannot say. Her finding was in any case overturned by Sam Galbraith [*Labour politician, Holyrood's environment minister at the time*] on the grounds that she had erroneously defined the national interest by expressing it in terms of the south of England.

No matter what you may think of his philosophy, you cannot question McIntosh's sincerity or integrity. His campaigning damaged his career at Edinburgh University, where he was postgraduate teaching director in human ecology. He is now seeking new sources of funds to continue his work with marginalised commmunities.

There is, of course, an ample supply in that part of Scotland from which he largely averts his eyes – urban, industrialised Lowland Scotland, to which so many Highlanders migrated and which has had sufferings of its own. But it lacks the sad sweet songs of Gaeldom.

9
Food – Scotland's changing tastes

REFLECTIONS ON PHILLIPO AND THE creator of *Rumpole of the Bailey*.

Somewhere in the Italian lakes, perhaps, a tall and portly head waiter called Philippo is presiding theatrically over an elegant, fashionable, and suitably expensive restaurant. In my mind's eye I can see him clearly against a background of lake and mountain, and can hear the rolling cadences as he tells some party of diners about the day's bill of fare. What he does not know is that he almost certainly if indirectly inspired a character in the latest Rumpole by John Mortimer.

Philippo used to be head waiter at the Malmaison, Glasgow, in the last days of that famous restaurant which for so long was effortlessly the best in Scotland. It was about 10 years ago that I first made his acquaintance when I went there to dine with a party of friends.

Philippo, I was later to learn, carried the art of professional sycophancy to a point of elaboration that approached satire; but on this night he must have been in a bad mood. He did not know us and he might never see us again.

He began his ritual incantation about the fresh fish and how they were to be done, and the exquisite sauce in which the beef was to be cooked, cheerfully enough. Perhaps he felt he was being silently mocked and his manner suddenly and subtly changed. Into his discourse crept the distinct innuendo that all this magnificence was too rich and expensive for the likes of us.

Irritation grew among us. He was being patronising and offensive. In a spirit of pure revenge I asked: 'Have you got any mince?' Philippo, outraged, drew himself up to his full height and screeched in his Italian accent: 'Mince? Mince? Is there something the matter with your teeth?'

After a delay, during which the ambient temperature dropped by about five degrees, he produced a particularly unappetising plate of minced steak, which had no seasoning and had barely been cooked. He had me there: I ate it without complaint.

Later Philippo and I became friendly. He would welcome me like a long-lost brother. But slowly the restaurant began to die. The pianist no longer appeared in the evening. The à la carte stopped at lunchtime and was replaced by a businessman's menu. One day a friend and I watched a party of trade-union leaders walk out in protest at this move down-market.

Then the restaurant closed. Philippo said to me sadly: 'A town gets the restaurants it deserves.' For a while he shared the franchise in La Fourchette, the cheap and cheerful place into which the Malmaison had mutated. He worked hopefully, bustling about with all his old theatrical officiousness. But one night, driving up Hope Street, I saw him rather sadly standing on the pavement, smoking a cigarette in the cool night air, and I wondered how things were going.

A couple of days later there was a paragraph in the paper. Philippo had abruptly gone back to Italy . When last heard of, he was working for a famous restaurant at Lake Como. For me he lived on as the subject of the anecdote about the mince.

How does Rumpole come into it? A couple of years ago John Mortimer won the People's Prize, sponsored by the Scottish Libraries Association and *The Herald*, and he came up to Scotland to pick it up. He did not have time to linger at the presentation but a few months later, in Edinburgh, John Linklater and I had lunch with him in an Italian restaurant. In the course of a very pleasant conversation I told him the story about Philippo.

It was therefore with I hope not self-deluding proprietorial pleasure that I read the first story in *Rumpole à la Carte*. Rumpole is in a restaurant with his wife Hilda and her cousin. He is being patronised by the head waiter. 'Madame, messieurs. Tonight Jean-Pierre recommends, for the main course, la poesie de la poitrine du canard aux celeris et epinards crus ... '

Rumpole rebels. He asks for a 'poesie of steak and kidney pudding, not pie, with mashed potatoes and a big scoop of boiled cabbage. English mustard, if you have it.'

'Rumpole!' Hilda's whisper was menacing. 'Behave yourself!'

Now it is perfectly possible that John Mortimer has no recollection of our conversation and simply invented the incident. I will continue to believe that his head waiter is a literary metamorphosis of Philippo.

In the heyday of the Malmaison, expensive restaurants were used by relatively few – the wealthy and those on business expenses. In Scotland nowadays eating out is an almost universal pastime but the head waiters are an ordinary lot by comparison with Philippo.

Too many have the absolutely infuriating and detestable habit of interrupting you, as you are about to deliver the punchline of an anecdote, to ask: 'Is everything all right, sir?' Just about as annoying is the waiter who unceremoniously barks: 'Who's having the chips?'

Philippo would assume that everything was all right. Under his direction the waiter would know who was having the chips. Not many of our waiters in Scotland would last five minutes in a busy Parisian brasserie: earlier this year I dined in the Terminus du Nord in a party of 20; the waiters allocated each dish to the person who had ordered it without inquiry, faultlessly.

But I digress. If anyone sees Philippo, somewhere round Lake Como I should think, they should tell him about Rumpole and the Head Waiter. But they should phrase it with care to avoid some subtle reprisal.

'For a tense moment,' thought Rumpole, 'it seemed as though the looming, priestly figure of Georges was about to excommunicate me ... '

That's Philippo, to the life. Wherever he is, I wish him well.

*Postscript: When Philippo became Filippo.
Faithful readers may recall that on September 7 I wrote about Philippo of the Malmaison who, I suggested, was the model on which a character in the new Rumpole stories was based. Filippo Zoanni [I apologise for mis-spelling his name] has received a copy of the piece from a friend in Glasgow and has written me a charming note. He is maître at what he calls a 'lovely restaurant' called Tout Paris, in Menaggio on the shores of 'beautiful Lake Como'.

He writes: 'I often think about my years in Glasgow – and with a certain nostalgia. People in that city are so very friendly and have such a keen sense of humour.'

One day, I hope, we shall meet again.

In praise of the convivial lunch with a Tory grandee. (1991)

This week I returned after a long absence to a favourite restaurant. I was welcomed back with forgiveness. Tony was too kind to refer to my infidelity and soon had a delicious meal on the table. Even if he had posed the question in the indirect way of restaurateurs – Long time no see? – I would have been hard put to answer him, for I have always liked the place and used it regularly when I came to Glasgow almost 10 years ago.

The answer, I think, was that I enjoyed myself too much and too well. The lunch break became too leisurely, too pleasurable. The wine and the crusty bread, even before any courses appeared, were too much of a temptation.

In the seventies such dalliance was acceptable: I and many of my colleagues spent more time in the old Doric Tavern in Edinburgh than I care to remember. But in the thrusting Thatcherite eighties it became passé. 'Lunch is for wimps,' said the anti-hero in Oliver Stone's movie, Wall Street, and that summed up the philosophy of the age. Lunch was to be taken at the desk, out of a brown bag, or, if it were unavoidable, briefly and without alcohol, and so I joined the sandwich brigade.

Doubtless this is a very good thing both for work and for health. But sandwiches are boring and there is nothing to beat a good lunch occasionally. Nothing irritates me more than the ostentatious self-satisfaction with which companies which invite you for lunch inform you that drink on the premises is barred by company policy; and I must confess to a certain mischievous and irresponsible delight when at a recent such affair at the ScotRail HQ in Port Dundas proceedings were interrupted by a bomb scare and we had to adjourn to the nearest Italian restaurant and a bottle of something stimulating and refreshing.

There is a genuinely good reason for journalists to socialise. That is the way they pick up information and get ideas. It's their way of beating the bushes. In London journalism lunch is both a pleasure and a necessity. The political or financial journalist, in particular, must make use of this pleasant institution as a starting point for much that he may write and a source of understanding of processes that are complex and veiled.

In the clubs particularly favoured by journalists the sun comes out at lunchtime. Round the long club tables there is a jolly camaraderie that makes you think of school lunches with booze. Women are right: men never really grow up.

One day after lunch in such a club I emerged into the sunshine in the company of a very rich and senior Tory who had joined us that day. He asked me to accompany him along the street where he promised he would show me something interesting. We entered one of those very expensive shops done in the old genteel style. Grocer is too humble a word for it. Licensed victualler or provisioner might do. There were boxes and jars and barrels made of a rich wood that gleamed in the dim, polite light. A grave steward in a long apron approached us. 'Good afternoon, Sir – ,' he said.

'Can I have the key, Graves ?' asked my companion.

'Her ladyship forbids it,' said the steward with sombre dignity.

Just then there was a light step on the spiral staircase that led upstairs to further racks of barrels and jars. An elegant lady appeared. My friend introduced me and asked her for the key again. She was most charming to her unexpected and I imagine unwelcome visitors; and she authorised the steward to disgorge it.

We went downstairs to the cellar. There was a large barrel containing his private reserve of malt whisky. It was locked with a padlock and beside it sat two cheap white cups. Carefully he unlocked the tap and drew two large measures. He seated himself beside the barrel with aplomb, as if he were in his own sitting room, but I felt rather furtive. Making rather stilted conversation we drank the whisky and then bade the shop – which he owned – a polite farewell.

Pondering the incident afterwards I must assume that the wife was worried about her husband's drinking and had prohibited him the barrel; and that he had used me as a means of circumventing the ban. He gave no signs of having any drink problem at all and, like many senior politicians, appeared to have a considerable capacity that left his eye undimmed.

The public rarely appreciates the stresses inherent in the political life. For every eminent politician there are a hundred who labour in obscurity. The availability of bars at almost all hours is a considerable temptation and some are overcome by it.

But others go through their life enjoying the fruits of the earth with evident enjoyment and great appetite. Few have done this with more gusto then Denis Healey. It was once my privilege to be in his company at Lockett's, a restaurant near the Palace of Westminster where they sound the division bells. Clearly he is a man of very robust constitution. That night he dined well and enjoyed the excellent wine. But what impressed me was the clarity of his mind, his love of life, his energy and the sheer entertaining force of his discourse. It was an unforgettable evening.

Do Highlanders hate vegetables? Scotland embraces broccoli. From 1993.

They are serving broccoli again at the White House, as a side dish to taxation stew. Mrs Clinton has restored them to the menu from which they had been hounded by Mr Bush. He also banned them from the presidential jet, Air Force One.

Mr Bush made no secret of his detestation for broccoli. Many Scottish males will have sympathised with him, for broccoli seem supremely the kind of vegetable foisted on them by improving females, of whom Mrs Clinton is now the world's leading example. A childhood of being told to eat green things 'because they're good for you' must lie behind Mr Bush's prejudice.

My own old dislike of broccoli has no such justification, since my mother, an excellent cook in other respects, entertained a dislike amounting to contempt for vegetables. My youth was innocent not only of broccoli but also of parsnips, courgettes and aubergines (though no doubt the war had something to do with this too). For salad she reserved her most withering scorn. 'Rabbit food,' she would say as she served it under protest.

She had been brought up in the north-east of Scotland, in a fishing village, and she subscribed to the rather romantic notion that there was Arcadian virtue in the old Scots diet of oatmeal, herring, potatoes, and kail; and it is true that some modern historians believe it to have been much better than the additive-rich and packaged fodder of our own age.

My mother's attitude, and the superior quality of the fruit and vegetables I discovered when I went to live in England for a while, led me to believe that there was a strong cultural and historical basis for Scotland 's neglect of broccoli and other such exotica.

The industrial urban culture, with its need for the energy and gratification of starch and sugar, helps to explain why people in Scotland still underdose on fruit and vegetables, just as Scotland 's relative poverty meant that it was unable to sustain markets as highly developed as those of a more populous country. According to our Catherine Brown, in her *Scottish Cookery* Scottish consumption of vegetables continues below the UK average, and of fruit only slightly better.

But the idea that the Scots have a specific prejudice against vegetables I discover to be far from the truth. F Marian McNeill, in her classic book *The Scots Kitchen* did refer to a generalised dislike of them but ascribed it to Highlanders.

The vogue of kail was confined to the Lowlands; the Highlander preferred nettles for his broth 'and regarded the use of kail as a symptom of effeminacy'. A Gaelic poem on the battle of Killiecrankie, that supreme triumph of Highland arms, mocks the defeated soldiers as men of 'kail and brose'.

The Lowland Scots, on the other hand, were enthusiastic cultivators of vegetables. They played a leading part in the agricultural revolution. By the end of the eighteenth century abundant quantities of broccoli and other delicacies were available in our cities.

In Edinburgh the kail-wives took their stance at the Tron, with creels full of produce from Musselburgh. Meg Dodds, writing in 1826, recorded that the 'vegetable markets of most towns have ... undergone a wonderful improvement ... so that a healthful luxury is within the reach of all classes'.

Scottish gardens became famed for their beauty. The 'best houses' in England would have a French chef and a Scottish gardener. In one of the Jane Austen novels there is a reference to the appointment of a Scottish gardener and the question of whether the 'old prejudice' against the Scots could now be overcome (in the seventeenth century the Scots army sent to England in support of the Parliamentarians exacted free quarters and became deeply unpopular). PG Wodehouse's Lord Emsworth went in perpetual terror of his Scottish gardener, a tyrant of the rake.

Few prejudices can be sustained when exposed to the light of reality and reason. Broccoli have been scurvily treated by their detractors. They are a brassica, a member of the cabbage family. They originate in Italy and their name is treated as a plural noun because it is derived from *broccolo*, meaning a cabbage sprout.

A couple of years ago, at a dinner party in Dublin, I was in full flow in a diatribe against effete vegetables like broccoli, aubergines and courgettes. They were, I suggested, expressive of do-goodery and faddism. My hostess listened politely and then lifted the lids from the serving dishes. There they were; broccoli, aubergines and courgettes.

Crestfallen, I resolved never to be rude about them again. I eat them with a pleasure that is genuine if still a little dutiful. I shall be buying some broccoli this weekend. These past 10 years the quality of fruit and vegetables available here in the West End of Glasgow has improved greatly, though it is still rather below the standard to be found in England (the same applies to cheese). But we travel hopefully. Mrs Clinton's gesture is overdue: even I concede it is time broccoli came in from the cold.

My Heart Belongs to a Haddie.

Scotland's greatest gift to international cuisine is not, I submit, salmon, beef, mutton broth, haggis or oatcakes, or even the simple bacon roll, that blessed balm for over-indulgence. It is the finnan haddock, served with a poached egg on top.

The other night friends brought it to table for a late supper. I can think of nothing more delicious at the end of a long day, or anything as satisfying that sits as lightly on the stomach.

The fish that we know today differs greatly from the dish our ancestors ate. In the days before the railway the smokers in Findon, a fishing village south of Aberdeen, had to salt the fish well before consigning it south by stage-coach.

According to Sir Walter Scott, they dried it over the smoke of sea-weed, sprinkling it with salt water. This gave it a peculiar, and indeed unique, flavour. My colleague in Aberdeen, George MacDonald, tells me that according to local lore a woman in the village had hung out her haddock to dry in the sun, when a fire started underneath; she found she had created a new delicacy.

F Marian McNeill gives a method that smokes it over peat or hardwood. But all imitations produced elsewhere were found inferi-or – Sir Walter attended a blind tasting in Edinburgh from which the Aberdeenshire fish emerged triumphant.

Finnan haddie travelled so well that it wound up in a Cole Porter song (My Heart Belongs to Daddy) and it still appears in the pages of *Larousse Gastronomique*, that international bible of cuisine. Larousse, I think, is living in the past, for it recommends soaking the fish for a couple of hours in water before it is cooked (poached but not boiled, otherwise it becomes stringy).

That is a throwback to older days. Even when the railway sup-planted the stage-coach and the smoked fish became less leathery, they still had to be heavily salted to prolong their shelf life. Now, in this age of refrigerated transport, they are more lightly cured, and have lost their geographical particularity. Finnan haddies are pro-duced by most fish-houses which smoke fish and differ from ordi-nary smoked haddock in that they are smoked on the bone.

It is a general truth that fish is best left on the bone. If it is to be filleted, the skin is best left on one side (as it is sold in Ireland). In the case of finnan haddock, various writers also warn us to beware of inferior versions where dye has been added to the brine. Like kippers of lesser quality, these golden cutlets have a bright and unnatural yellow glow.

Jane Grigson, who suggested that a statue should be erected in Findon to the inventor of the finnan haddie, gave particularly strict advice, in her book *Fish Cookery* that if it wasn't finnan haddock it wasn't worth buying at all: 'so much "smoked fillet" on sale is neither haddock nor smoked.' As she rightly pointed out, dyed fish can give you indigestion and have a coarser taste. She also found a place of honour for the Glasgow pale, the Arbroath smokie and the Eyemouth cured.

Unsmoked haddock is a fish that must be eaten straight out of the sea, for its flavour deteriorates rapidly. (In a fish-and-chip shop it also is better to have it freshly fried rather than taken from the hot compartment.)

In this haddock may be contrasted with sole, which Grigson named, along with turbot, as king of the sea fish. Sole's exceptional palatability is apparently because about three days after its death its flesh develops a chemical substance which improves its flavour. It is therefore a fish that can travel long distances. This explains not only its popularity but, I imagine, why we do not have smoked sole.

But back to our haddock: the amiable Keith Floyd, in his book *Floyd on Fish*, is dismissive of it, describing it as merely useful; but for my money, taken fresh or smoked, it can rival the sole in any contest. It must be lightly cooked; in Mrs Beeton's age they overdid it and turned it into a grey travesty.

But deep-fried in batter, it was the national dish of our working class. Smoked with a poached egg on top, it was the favourite meal of the Duke of Windsor; it was the last dish brought to him before his death in Paris in 1972, an oddly homely finale to an exotic life. Not the least of its virtues is that its derivatives are also great adornments of our national cuisine. There is, of course, Cullen skink, that cottage recipe from the shores of the Moray Firth. Marian McNeill advises that the milk should be heated separately and added to the stock and flaked fish; the final touches are enough mashed potato to thicken it and a knob of butter.

A cholesterol bomb? Yes, but no matter: keep taking that medicinal glass of red wine. For my last meal on earth I might too choose a finnan haddock.

Another recipe appeared in this column on five-minute recipes for chore-dodgers called Man in an Apron in *The Scotsman* on 3 January 1970.

> One morning I had been deputed to make the lunch. There was, I had been assured, a nice piece of boiling beef left in the fridge for soup.
>
> Blearily I stumbled out of bed and to the refrigerator. There was beef. I put in in a pot together with dehydrated vegetables etc, That soup simmered all morning. it was superb. The neighbours were invited in to sample it. I bragged about it for hours. All was well until my wife emerged from the refrigerator with the boiling beef in her hand. I apparently had made the soup with fillet steak.
>
> Of course I was accused of all sorts of crimes; extravagance, carelessness, irresponsibility. When I make a decent soup nowadays there is always an unspoken assumption that I have cheated. I have used fillet steak.

Haste ye back? But No Late Breakfast.

> The ills of Scottish tourism are familiar. To the natural disadvantages of climate may be added a lack of national aptitude.
>
> It has always been my impression that the Irish take more naturally to tourism than the Scots. Proprietors of guest houses in the Republic do not, for example, tend to snarl at visitors, or send them away hungry if they are ten minutes late for breakfast, or festoon their premises with notices, about such matters as bathing, which have an implacable sternness unmatched since the renunciation of the Edict of Nantes.
>
> The Irish, too, have exploited their golf courses as a major tourist resource; the Scots, who invented the game, have signally failed to do so. The Irish have also supported their tourist authority with far greater resources.
>
> The Scottish board's chairman, Lord Gordon, has protested about the intemperance of the criticism it has encountered. And it is true that no central authority, no matter how well funded, could entirely compensate for the under-capitalisation and uncertain revenue streams which explain much of tourism's difficulties in Scotland, any more than it could wave a wand and banish from our two-star hotels those characteristic aromas of disinfectant and stale frying fat. Or outlaw the surly barman who makes clear his distaste

for all except the local drunks, and the maladroit waiter who inadvertently clips the diner's ear with the plate while serving soup.

Yet we must persist in our efforts to raise standards and to provide better training. Apart from fish farming, forestry and farming, tourism is the only hope for our remoter communities. If the Scottish Tourist Board needs top-flight management, it also needs more money and more powers to disqualify the incompetent from its seals of approval.

It also needs a strong wind of political will behind it, to resist the squeals from offended regional or commercial interests. A serious drive for higher standards will not be painless. Unfortunately our political leaders seem to lack the bottle for the task.

10
Sport

ON TOUR WITH THE TARTAN Army for an away game, September 2001.

In Brussels, after cordially booing the referee for denying Scotland a penalty, I felt cleansed of life's petty irritations.

Our expedition was what used to be called a wayzgoose, or a works outing, by some of the Scots on *The Observer*. Such expeditions sometimes meet the fate that befell Louis XVI's flight to Varennes: they can be fatally ruined by long lunches.

But by dint of iron discipline and a little luck, we made it to the ground on time and found the Tartan Army in good heart; as ever, it was full of booze, hope and humour. After the game, it responded with resigned patience to the extraordinary inefficiency of the Brussels authorities, who grotesquely over-policed the crowd and, at the end, lured the Scottish foot soldiers into an interminable march through the outer city suburbs before depositing them at a Metro station where, two hours later, the queues had barely diminished. The King Baudouin Stadium is a long way out of town but this great capital of the European is oddly short of taxis. As for the buses, they ran inscrutably to remote destinations, anywhere but to the city centre.

As we marched, some brave spirit relieved the monotony by plunging into the pool below a fountain, but in general the mood was a sad acceptance that the team simply had not been good enough.

We used to believe that though we were a small country we could, on our day, beat the best. Occasionally we did so, although we often stumbled, as if out of ennui, against lesser sides. But since the daft days of Ally McLeod, Scottish coaches, from Stein onwards, have not just managed the team but have managed the expectations of the fans, too. This has had some beneficial results. Triumphalism of the English sort is not only unattractive; it is clearly unobtainable and, therefore, ludicrous. And so the Tartan Army has made its good behaviour its calling card and dignity in defeat its motto.

But we must move on and recover some of our old cockiness. Lloyd George said: 'Don't be afraid to take big steps. You can't cross a chasm in two small jumps.' We must stop thinking small.

A Confused Duty to Support England. (2002.)

John Major once said that the Scots, the Irish and the Welsh defined their nationalism in terms of England but the English did so in terms of the French or the Germans. This, I think, explains why the English, or a good chunk of them, have tended to support the Scottish football team on the international stage and why Scots find it so hard to reciprocate – and why I received the following email from a friend holidaying in the south.

He wrote (the text is slightly expurgated): 'Have just been walking round Hereford. Pubs are full of smelly, yobby, fat, singing smug oafs. And it's not just that. Think of what it will be like if they win the cup. Imagine 50 million smug Ss wandering about with big smug smiles. (S being the name of a mutual friend who takes a less Corinthian view of Scotland than many of his countrymen.) Personally, I would rather be in Kashmir.'

This is going a bit far. And yet, despite my resolution to support England because of the kindness with which I have always been received in the south, I know what he means. It's not the English who annoy us, though some of their supporters, the bovine, beer-swilling, pot-bellied kind, are rebarbative.

No, it's the English media in general and the television commentators in particular who get our goat. The late Kenneth Wolstenholme was famously patronising about Scotland. But behind such attitudes lies an unconscious arrogance which assumes that England should win and that if they don't there's something profoundly amiss. This explains why the sporting press swings so violently between suicidal depression and unreasoning euphoria.

Yet even this old grievance of ours is fading away. The half-time analytical teams on television are liberally sprinkled with Celts. And our own football commentators can be just as guilty of bias. We must be content to feed our grievances, these days, on a few rampaging Scotophobes in the London print media (I would name them except that in this politically correct age it might be defamatory to do so).

Despite all my inner counselling, I found my own attitude somewhat confused. I sat in a deserted corner of the pub out of sight of the television, eating my lunch, with a glass of wine. The fact that I couldn't see the game worried me less than I thought it might, and I managed to miss Beckham's penalty, which found me between pub and office. I was pleased, but I found it difficult to cheer.

The Japanese have taught us a great deal, with the excellence of their stadiums and of their manners. But they haven't quite managed to suppress the old rivalry with their co-host, South Korea. Perhaps it's too much like asking a Scot to support England. And yet, as the tournament rolls on, I shall do my conscientious best.

On the return of the football fixtures between Scotland and England:

Dreaming the dream once more. (1999)

Europe has brought us much – our language and our culture for a start. Now it has revived the football fixture between Scotland and England, killed off after alcoholic excesses at Wembley but as much a part of my youthful world as 'Oor Wullie' and 'The Broons'.

Although my father took us to all the rugby internationals at Murrayfield, a visit to Wembley was out of the question. Instead we would listen to the breathless commentary on the radio in what can only be described as an agony of anxiety.

Many Scots of my generation have imprinted on their memory the condescending tones of Raymond Glendinning as England cruised to a victory, I think in the Fifties. 'I say,' he said patronisingly as Scotland attacked, 'this looks dangerous.' Reilly scored in the last minute to even the match and our satisfaction was as much over the puncturing of Glendinning as the goal itself.

Our own commentators were not perfect. This I recall: we were sitting in a cabin on one of the ships that used to ply between Leith and Aberdeen, bound for a holiday in Orkney and Shetland, when Peter Thomson's excited voice came over the airwaves: 'he's scored (delirium at sea) no, he's no' (despair). I always had a soft spot for Thomson, though, especially after he once pronounced: 'And now, over to our Carpenter, Harry Commentator.'

The fixture ended with the Home Internationals in the Eighties. But it was the match at Wembley in 1977 which spelled its end. When the crowd invaded the pitch and broke the goalposts – I was in the press box throughout, m'lud – the crowd was drunk, certainly, boisterous of course, but not vicious. The Metropolitan Police formed a circle and looked nervous: but wisely left the fans to dig up little patches of the sacred turf. Among them was a Labour MP who is now an independent-minded member of the Scottish parliament. Kenneth Wolstenholme, pompous as ever, vented his bile over the result by denouncing the Scottish fans.

So much damage was done that the authorities had to respond. The late Frank McElhone, as Sports Minister, produced a White Paper. It led to an act of Parliament which banned alcohol at sports grounds and on buses and trains to them. It produced a significant improvement in behaviour. So did stadiums with more seating.

But ahead in the long grass lay more snakes. The following year Ally MacLeod took a talented team to Argentina which celebrated too soon and was humbled by Peru. We enjoyed the premature euphoria – summed up in Alan Bold's verse: 'Poor poor Peru/If only you knew/What the boys in Blue/Are going to do to you./Too true.'

The disappointment was severe. Ever since then Scottish managers have sought to manage rather than encourage Scotland's hopes. We have learned not to expect too much. Indeed, I rather welcome the freedom from anxiety and stress that the old fixture used to bring.

Now I must attune myself once more to this peculiarly stressful passage of ephemera. So let's enjoy it. In the old days we used to believe that we could beat England, and very often did. So let's dream our dreams once more and hope that the Tartan Army can keep its cool and not be provoked.

A long on/off love affair with Hibs.

Football loyalties run deep. I became a Hibs supporter in the late forties when the Famous Five were beginning their dominance of the Scottish game. If there were any religious or ethnic undertones to the question of which club to follow in Edinburgh, then I was happily unaware of them: the sound of the crowd from Easter Road a mile or so away carried in the winter air to stir the imagination of the small boys who kicked a ball around in the local park. Most of us wanted to be Gordon Smith.

My old friend the sportswriter Ian Wood, a great fan of Gordon Smith, had a favourite tale about visiting his barber in Musselburgh and hearing Smith denounced as being selfish. 'He beat about five men, took it to the byline, but he wouldnae pass,' whined the critic as he clipped the hair.

'What happened?' asked Ian.

'Oh,' said the barber, 'he scored.'

I can remember, in what must have been one of the last games the great Billy Steel played for Dundee, seeing Smith 'selfishly' take a pass on the half-way line, head straight for goal and score with a powerful low drive from outside the penalty area.

Popular theory had it that Willie McCartney built the great Hibs team and that his successors reaped the benefit of his shrewd signings. Whatever the truth of that, Hibs won the league title four times after the war. Their fitful brilliance gave them a great appeal to Edinburgh's floating supporters, and they attracted a mixed bunch of followers – lawyers, doctors, journalists, truanting schoolboys from Fettes and the Academy, Italian restaurateurs, and of course the henpecked husbands who shouted lurid abuse at the referee every Saturday, usually wee bauchles who looked as if they'd be blown away in the next puff of wind.

They were the first Scottish team to enter the European Cup, being knocked out by Liege in the semi-final in 1956. Their raffish quality was summed up by a story told by a journalist who accompanied them. On his return he was asked by chairman Harry Swan, fishing for compliments, what he thought of them.

'Very fine team, Harry,' the journalist replied. 'But where did they learn all that bad language?'

'How the fuck should I know?' the boss is supposed to have replied.

From the great days of the Famous Five there was a slow decline, but on the road down there were many consolations and delights. There was the truly sensational Joe Baker, a centre forward who ran like a greyhound and jumped like a trout. He still holds the club's goal-scoring record, with 42 in season 1959/60. Hibs with Baker beat Barcelona in a famous European victory in 1960: the Edinburgh polis marched on to the pitch to protect the referee from the infuriated Spanish players after Kinloch had won the game with a penalty.

I missed the Willie Hamilton era – the player that Jock Stein described as the finest he had ever come across – but I was lucky enough to be in Edinburgh at the time of Pat Stanton's team, with Alan Gordon, Alex Cropley, Arthur Duncan, John Blackley and the rest. They gave much pleasure without ever winning very much, though they did beat Celtic to win the League Cup in the 1972/73 season. There was a dying fall in 1979 when the genius of George Best flickered, briefly and fitfully but with moments of magic, at Easter Road.

The benighted Hearts had their magic too. They had the 'Terrible Trio' – Conn, Bauld and Wardhaugh. I remember Jimmy Wardhaugh telling me of how even a reserve game at Tynecastle against the Rangers could attract a crowd of 20,000. Later there were Alex Young and others. I remember, too, staunch fullbacks like Bobby Parker who always gave Gordon Smith a hard time.

In those days, the Hibs-Hearts games were good-humoured. The partisanship was vigorous but blessedly free of that corroding hatred later to be emptily copied from Northern Ireland and mouthed without understanding. The greatest encounter I can remember – I am biased – was the cup-tie which ended 4-3 for Hibs. The brilliant Joe Baker rattled in some goals in the first half; Hearts struck back and only Lawrie Leslie, with a wonderfully athletic performance in goal, denied them a draw. I seem to remember even the Hearts fans enjoyed that one, or perhaps I delude myself in the rosy glow of nostalgia.

The terminal decline of Hibs started when the Edinburgh builder Tom Hart sold them. He had run them not in a disinterested way – that would be too much to expect – but with a real commitment. After that, it seemed, things went downhill.

About five years ago I went to a Hibs match in the middle of winter. It was raining. The car park was strewn with rubble. I went to the loo at halftime, passing the window of the visitors' dressing room. I could hear dimly through the glass the manager's pep talk, which seemed to be a string of expletives. Since the visitors were Dundee United and the manager was Jim McLean, I must have been mistaken.

The shabby wall that passed for a gentlemen's lavatory was awash with urine and rain. The scene was squalid. I have not been back since. I have followed the team's undistinguished fortunes from a distance, with decreasing interest.

Social mores and the sound of bat on ball.

My interest in cricket has been furtive and intermittent but in 1993 the brooding figure of Mervyn Hughes, destroyer of English wickets and morale, took hold of my imagination and I set off with a companion to Headingley to see him in the flesh.

In the end my eye was taken as much by the social mores of the event as by the match itself, though Hughes did not disappoint his followers: he took his 200th test wicket on the final day and helped to defeat a dispirited English team which, I suspect, made the

Australians look better than they are.

He is not, however, the sinister moustachioed figure of imagination. He is avuncular, with the bucolic air of the village blacksmith. Between his own overs, when fielding in the deep, he would pause between balls to sign autographs for the kids, who adore him.

But he is tough all right. The idyllic picture of cricket, of the sound of bat on ball in dreamy sunshine heard amid the drowsy hum of bees from beneath spreading trees, is of course phoney. It is a hard and unforgiving game, played with a ball that can become a lethal missile, and full of gamesmanship. Its long stalemates, its sudden flurries, the subtle shifts in fortunes – these are the qualities that can make it addictive even for a Scot.

What I had forgotten was the intensity of the class antagonisms among those who watch cricket in England, though I suspect they have become worse in the past decade or so. Perhaps these tensions convey a larger social truth.

Our arrangements had fallen down: ticketless at a sell-out, I was forced to patronise the touts. At a cost which comfortably exceeded the asking price of the best seats in the house, we found ourselves in the second row at the 'popular end' on the north terracing.

Beside us were sitting four lads from Manchester who were having a day out and had come by coach. They had supped the canned ale in their ice-box and were on to buying pints in plastic glasses. Three of them were friendly enough but one was put out by our arrival. 'I thought they didn't let members in here,' he growled in disgust and with evident hostility.

It was nothing personal, we instantly realised: we were wearing blazers and ties and had broken the dress code for this part of the ground. Everyone here was in T-shirts and jeans. Some, according to custom, had dressed up – as monks or clowns or Mickey Mouse. Exuberant and childish jokes rose in the air like vapour from the pints.

The crowd's yobbishness was good natured but volatile. There was a crassness in its behaviour, a kind of drunken innocence, that made you think you were part of some very ancient ritual, like a medieval fair. At an equivalent occasion in Scotland, the language might have been very much worse.

Our friends from Manchester had sold our tickets to the touts at face value and still seemed to think they had a moral if not a beneficial interest in them. How much had we paid? Fearing that I would set off a riot if I told them, I prevaricated. A matter of private grief, I said. They were not easily satisfied and intermittently quizzed me through the afternoon.

At Headingley you can stroll right round the field. In other parts of the ground we discovered a much different social scene. The tented village and the corporate suites in the various stands were full of suited snouts in the corporate trough. Their seats were conspicuously empty when play resumed after lunch, and when they did return it could be seen, through binoculars, that they too had drinks in hand.

Sponsors have become the major source of revenue and get the best seats. And because the team sponsors are brewers, large quantities of their product are by agreement sold to the crowd. Not surprisingly many get high and have to be ejected by the stewards.

Some Yorkshire members think the game has sold its soul. Their own dress code could not be more different from that of the yobs. Club ties and blazers, or even suits, are required. A hat of ancient lineage is preferred.

For them, watching cricket is a serious business, like going to church; it requires a knowledge of historical statistics equivalent to a mastery of scripture.

And so there is a developed and distinctive hierarchy. The sponsors and their guests live like the high priests and have excluded the members from the best seats. The members resent it and look down on both the sponsors and the yobs. As for the yobs, they hate all the toffs, sponsors or members, and express their dislike through dress, language and behaviour.

Back at the popular end, the ale was drinking well. My hostile neighbour contrived to spill his pint over my blazer. His apologies were profuse and, I think, genuine. He then fell into a slumber from which he occasionally emerged to shout for England. My companion's enthusiastic applause for the Australians did not improve the atmosphere and, as the sun went down, I felt it grow chilly.

As English batsmen came and went, an air of depression settled over the kop to which the antidote was the supping of yet more ale which inspired yet more crass jokes. A plastic sheep was thrown on to the field, arousing great merriment. The stewards threw a few people out.

At the close, as we filed out, I felt a shove in the back and a hand sent my Panama flying. The perpetrator and his friends giggled like drunken schoolboys as they ran off. My companion was incensed and gave chase but I was not much annoyed. After all, it was nothing personal: he was a yob, and proud of it, and he thought I was a member.

Golf and the Scottish mind.

Why, said a colleague, end 15 years of happiness by going back on the golf course? It was a question to which there was no sensible answer but the end of March 1993 found me, on a glorious spring day, playing a few holes with a friend at Balmore.

It is a lovely shorter course, innocent of par fives but with some holes no less intimidating. It lies in the cradle of the Campsies, this week still streaked with snow. The brilliant weather soothed even the restless spirits in the rookery overlooking the first tee. Members drive off not only under the gaze of the watching critics in the bar but also to the raucous and cynical commentary of this colony of crows.

They were silent and indulgent as we set off. Birds of the golfing variety, I am afraid, did not figure on my card. I could claim that my game had not much deterioriated since I last struck the ball in earnest all these years ago. There were still the same old squirts and sclaffs, the same old intimacy with the bunkers and the burns. And, just occasionally, there would be a glimpse of life as it should be as the ball flew straight.

Golf was a game I had always enjoyed in a sociable way with old friends in Edinburgh who were endlessly patient, forgiving, and encouraging. My mistake was to join a club. I found that people took the thing seriously, worried about their handicaps and their medal rounds. For the first time I practised. My game grew worse. The fun evaporated and I gave my clubs away.

It is no accident that the Scots invented golf and the English cricket. Golf is a game ideally designed for individuals in a sparsely populated landscape where there is no shortage of suitable ground. Cricket is the game of a populous and wealthy country with a developed system of villages. You cannot have an enjoyable game of cricket by yourself; golf permits even solitary pleasure.

Cricket reflects the structures of a complex society. England has more layers, strata, and class baggage. An accent may place its owner at a precise point on the scale or may be used as artifice to conceal origin. The spin bowler is the very personification of Perfidious

Albion, for he is never what he seems.

By contrast golf flows naturally from the Scottish mind, forged as it was in the legalistic religious attitudes of the Reformation. In the Presbyterian creed an individual is alone before God; and on the golf course if the player cheats he cheats himself.

Off the field, golf has another set of rules, about jackets, spikes, and the place of women. The noticeboard carries sets of precisely worded regulations covering such matters as slow play and local dispensations for bad lies.

Behind all this you can sense a love of order and decency but Scotland has sometimes carried its legalism too far. The gift of compromise has sometimes eluded us as a nation, and for many golfers the rules if officiously imposed are an irritant.

Balmore seems a congenial, liberal sort of place. The crows are basking in the spring air. The club kitten chases phantoms on the last green. An older member plays a cunning little pitch and run, gives himself the putt, and repairs to the bar. Here they are polishing the trophies for the annual presentation. No doubt there are rules about that, too. If only the game itself could be as precise; but its infuriating waywardness and its glimpses of perfection bring us back for more. That, and the company of friends.

Rugby's bacchanalian rites. (1991).

A Rugby international at Murrayfield ranks high in the calendar of bourgeois festivals. It finds Edinburgh at its most hospitable and convivial and it releases in the middle class a sense of national pride which it often suppresses in its professional life or political behaviour.

Edinburgh, though the intellectual centre of radical nationalist politics, has been a sore disappointment to the SNP, and there are few more bizarre sights in Scottish life than that of some Edinburgh lawyer, the very soul of unionism, getting his dander up in the cause of Scotland.

Such is the delightful innocence of Murrayfield. There is more to the occasion, of course, than a brief efflorescence of a half-forgotten patriotism. Once upon a time the internationals were simple, even naive affairs. You got on the special bus at St Andrews Square which took you almost to the ground. On the short walk that remained there were a few traders peddling souvenirs and unofficial programmes, together with the famous Edinburgh one-man band of whom it was popularly said that he had become so rich from his art that he lived in a bungalow in Ravelston Dykes.

Above all, there was less booze. Now Murrayfield is awash on a sea of drink (though of course within the terms of the Act). I do not know who the god of rugby is but an international is assuredly a celebration in honour of Bacchus. Its bacchanalian nature was brought home to me vividly last year, after the grand slam game against England, when a group of roistering English supporters stripped a comrade naked, tied him to a lamp-post in the New Town, and then wound about 100 yards of Cellophane around him.

Nowhere is the middle-class nature of rugby more evident than in its rules and the way they are interpreted. In football the rules are simple if sometimes ambiguous. Decisions by the referee are disputed by spectators and players alike, often, in the latter case, with great histrionic skill.

It is not surprising that someone like me, who has not played rugby for more than 30 years, should now find the rules so baffling, particularly those which apply to the scrum and the loose ball. As far as I can see many of the spectators share my confusion.

What is surprising, on the face of it, is that the players often seem baffled too. Some of them, indeed, have what appears to be a pretty vague grasp of the law. But they obey the referee instantly. The only dissonance is the aggression directed against opposing players which from time to time gets out of hand.

All this goes to the very heart of rugby's ethos. Remember it is a game which was developed for those being prepared to fight the battles, administer the laws and conduct the commerce of empire. Be tenacious, industrious and brave; be brilliant if you can; but never forget that authority is remote and does not have to explain itself; like God, it moves in mysterious ways.

Now, of course, the class distinctions surrounding both rugby and football are fading. Indeed there is no place for them in the meritocratic culture of Mr Major's Britain (the PM supports Chelsea). Yet the social origins of the games have left a mark not easily removed.

Yesterday I laid in the drink for my Irish friends. I have booked the table for dinner. We shall call upon various people in Edinburgh before and after the game. We shall, I hope, have a good day. I may even understand something of what happens on the field (not, you note, on the park, as in football). Perhaps, as if to prove me wrong, a player will dispute some decision by the referee and be sent sulking to an early bath. But I doubt it.

11
Places

THE PLUSES AND PENALTIES OF London from 1991.

Like a Chancellor of the Exchequer seeing a swallow and finding a summer, the clerk in the hotel tells me that the recession is ending: the businessmen are back. But the tourists are not yet to be seen en masse and there are plenty of unhired taxis in the streets. On the Piccadilly Line there is a fault on the indicator that I've noticed before.

The electronic message above the platform says the next train is for Uxbridge but when it arrives the sign on the front tells a different story: Heathrow. Last time this confusion arose I watched a party of Japanese depart in the wrong train from Acton Town where the line bifurcates. Attempts to warn them were too late, but they waved cheerfully as they went: another adventure. On my train the other day the rush-hour has not quite started and seats are to be had.

Opposite is a fellow Scot. Somehow we make mutual recognition and get talking. He too is heading back to Glasgow. He has had a miserable day, down on the 7.15, one meeting after another, and now he can't wait to get back to Newton Mearns. He looks around with distaste. London, he says, is a terrible place. It doesn't take a couple of Scots long to get into an argument and I find myself disagreeing. London is a great city, one of the world's great cities, comparable in the range of what it has to offer to New York and Paris (the only other cities in the world, perhaps, which are in its league).

That previous evening I had spent a wonderful couple of hours in Ronnie Scott's listening to Bobby Watson and his group, Horizon. They played a delightful, dizzying and extended set of variations that somehow turned, at the end, into Duke Ellington's In A Sentimental Mood. At the Hayward there is the superb Toulouse Lautrec exhibition. And that is hardly touching London's great cultural wealth. London, my new acquaintance replies, is too mixed.

He glances round at the compartment. There are people from just about every cultural grouping in the world. He can't, it seems, really handle it. Yet that cosmopolitan variety is another quality that makes London great, just as, for all its troubles, it makes New York an oddly and touchingly inspiring place in a world increasingly riven by racism and ugly nationalism, I think because the city somehow keeps on going. In our train a man reading a newspaper in Urdu glances up in irritation as the train sways and a girl, a tourist, I think, from Italy, almost falls into his lap. Living together: that will be the requisite gift of the twenty-first century.

But, for all that it is a great city, the state of London seems increasingly parlous and the conditions in which so many of its people are being asked to live often pitiable. You can see the penalties of living in London with your own eyes: the crowded trains, the struggle for a decent place to live, the severely underdeveloped road system, the wealth and comfort of some who buy and sell their houses at prices beyond the dreams of most. For most of my professional life Scottish politics has been the politics of grievance but whatever our problems, they pale beside those of London .

When we got to Heathrow my one-shot card, which allows you to book your seat by means of a computer terminal, got me quickly on to the 5.15, the last passenger to board. My friend from Newton Mearns had to buy a ticket and, I think, missed the flight. For him, perhaps, it was the last reverse of a bad day.

A certain something in the New England air. (*The Herald*, 1991)

It has turned suddenly cool and the fall is upon us. The trees, rolling away in gentle hills as far as the eye can see, are turning now, and a few flame-like reds and bronzes are glowing in the sea of green. We are two hours out from the assaulting noise of New York but we might as well be in another country.

This is quiet, civilised Connecticut. Here, within a few square miles it seems, live most of America's leading contemporary novelists. Henry Kissinger has his place somewhere near but unlike the literati is not seen in the village store picking up the *New York Times*: he is said to come and go by helicopter.

A few sheep and cattle still graze but agriculture is in decline and the creeping forest is taking over the fields again. In the night there is an embracing peace under a fat harvest moon. We are just too late for the fireflies, whose glowing mating flight so magically illuminates the evenings of late summer. But in the silence of the forest there are deafening small noises. Even the sudden fall of the spider can wake the sleeper used to the constant urban murmur.

And there is life in the woods – deer, quarrelsome wild turkey, owls, blue heron, vultures, and a skunk who sometimes pollutes the night with his stink. Our hosts sniff the air and fret that their dog has disturbed the skunk and has been drenched. If so, she will stink too. To everyone's relief, it is a false alarm. The other smell in the air is of money, serious money. The elegant, countrified wooden houses reek of it – their neat fences smartly painted white, their lawns trim but not forced into suburban rectangles, their bushes tonsorially cropped, their expensive furniture clad in Country Life chintz, the shining four-by-fours parked outside.

The resident literati and artists can pursue their living here for theirs are cottage industries; they are no different from the other working people, except that they are rich and famous. But mostly the wealth here is that of weekenders from New York, advertising men, movie and media folk, lawyers, doctors, dentists, or of those who have made so much money in the city that they will never have to work again. The local people depend on them: the economy is largely concerned with servicing their needs. They live their dreams and pursue the happiness to which the American Constitution entitles them if they can afford it.

Health fads proliferate, magic potions, food cleansed of all toxic ingredients, packages that boast of recyclability. A fashionable tennis coach teaches the game to music. To a rock accompaniment you work up your strokes. Forehand, backhand, dance around the court. You only get the ball later and even then you don't have to hit it unless it happens to come your way for you mustn't break the rhythm. Our friend Tom, shimmying round the floor to demonstrate the method, makes us laugh but such gimmicks are not unexpected in a wealthy and valetudinarian society wide open to medicine men, witch doctors and mountebanks.

In one of the prettified villages a retired lawyer presides over a bookshop which is like a Hollywood dream of Old England: exquisitely dressed in cashmere like some British film actor from the forties, he looks up over half-moon spectacles from the antiquarian volume he is perusing in an attitude of studied scholasticism. There is a complete set of Sir Walter Scott among the works for sale.

A grandfather clock ticks sleepily. The phone rings occasionally – polite calls from fellow dealers with news of a coveted volume in circulation. New York? He shudders. It is easy to laugh at all this earnest culture. Yet it is real enough and can put Europeans to shame. In an art gallery along from the bookshop there is an exhibition of drawings. The works are in a numbered series, each called Caryatid – Caryatid I, Caryatid II, and so on. They are abstracts. 'For the life of me,' says I to my friends, emerging from the gallery on to the porch, 'I can't remember what a caryatid is.' 'Excuse me, sir,' says a soft voice, and a man materialises from behind a pillar. He is dressed carefully in a long trenchcoat, a floppy country hat and smokes a scholarly pipe. 'Perhaps I can help. In architecture a caryatid is a female figure supporting an entableture.'

He takes another puff. 'It comes from the Greek Karyatis, a priestess of Artemis at Karya.' We thank him, but he is not finished. Another puff. 'In marble architecture caryatids first appeared in three small buildings, treasuries at Delphi, between 500 and 530 BC.' We thank him again and tell him we are most impressed. 'Well,' he says apologetically. 'It so happens that I am a professor of fine art.'

Along the highways the villages and towns are a litany of Old England – Kent, Cornwall, Sheffield, Preston, Litchfield. There is old money here. The opulent art gallery at Williamstown, stuffed with impressionists, is endowed with a fortune derived indirectly from the Singer sewing machine. But there is new money too.

Down the road an advertising man from Madison Avenue has created his dream. His house is exquisite, a vision of country living. It has a catering-sized kitchen, Jacuzzis upstairs and down, an outdoor swimming pool with a changing room in the form of a Grecian temple. He comes only at the weekend, and not always then, and he spends most of the time cutting the grass on the tractor-mower of which he is clearly very fond (Americans love machines). He never cooks on the magnificent, shining range and he doesn't have time to use either of the Jacuzzis.

Outside the forest sweeps all the way to the Appalachians. In the dark a fox barks. For all the cosiness of cultivated Connecticut, America remains vast and mysterious, always with a hint of wildness. Down the road an advertising man from Madison Avenue has created his dream. His house is exquisite but he comes only at the weekend. Yet he is content for he carries his dream around with him in dog-eat-dog New York .

Ireland: An ancient landscape swept by winds of change. [1991]

As day breaks the storms blow in again from the south-west. From the radio, left on overnight, come the strains of a sonata; heard faintly against the noise of the wind, it sounds like an Aeolian harp, the notes carried as if from a great and mysterious distance.

Later in the day the tourists walk stiffly but resolutely on the beach as the waves roll in from the Atlantic . Behind them the mist clings to the slopes of an elemental landscape of bog and crag.

A sense of the supernatural is strong. Rocks glimpsed obscurely in the haze take on eerie shapes; anthropomorphic belief comes naturally here. Our modern God is everywhere too. The churches are full on Sundays and round some corner you may come upon a shrine, devoutly tended. Paul Durcan wrote:

Being the sensible, superstitious old lady that she was,
My aunt Sarah knew that, while to know God was good,
To get the Ear of his Mother was a more practical step.

Into this ancient landscape the modern world is inexorably intruding. New houses sprout all over the countryside, cheerfully painted in white, their bungaloid facades broken by the ubiquitous Spanish arches much favoured by local taste and reminiscent, surely, of happy Mediterranean holidays.

The hay has been mown; some of the old-timers still laboriously cut reeds which they use to give the stacks a waterproof crown. But most people find it handier to cover them with impermeable plastic coalbags, which they secure with stones suspended on twine.

In the hard world of small farming little goes to waste. Nothing is discarded until it has yielded its full economic potential. Cars are run in to the ground. As in the Hebrides, their rotting remains crouch in the fields and provide shelter for sheep against the chill winds. A van that once sold cakes around the working-class suburbs of Dublin is a familiar site on the narrow roads. The cake company is now defunct and the van has acquired a bump or two since its more elegant days. But its sign, gaily painted in the French fashion, still advertises fresh gateau. What it sells now, in fact, are the services of a bull. Sultan, as we call him, peers out imperiously from the trailer in which the van tows him to his next assignment. Rheumy-eyed, mournful, he looks like a powdered and bewigged grandee of pre-revolutionary France. It costs £20 to send for him and his off-spring now sprinkle the landscape.

Our neighbour here has finally got in the electricity. Thomas, we suppose, lives like many others on the farmers' dole, a modest state payment that sustains rural life where it must surely otherwise die. He can keep the odds and ends he may earn on top, but his tastes are simple and his needs few.

His cottage is plain but clean. He does not smoke and rarely drinks. He gets around on a bicycle and, though well past middle age, is still as supple as a young man. In the dark of winter he sits before his turf fire. Until a few months ago he went to bed early. Now he watches television.

He is a kindly man. Last night he brought us a gift of fresh herring and this morning he let us have some turf. He no longer has to cut it in the old way, laboriously with a slane. Instead a machine comes and cuts it for a small fee. Its arrival in the district is announced in church and in a day it devours more of the bog than a man could manage in a fortnight.

As in Scotland, modern ways are not always welcomed and there is a constant tension between the conservation and development interests. Thomas has no sentimentality about having the machine cut his turf. Why should he? But the conservationists bemoan its capacity to destroy the bog created so slowly, from moss and forest, in ancient times. A frequent visitor from England writes a play which an amateur group performs in a local hall. In the drama, St Patrick descends from heaven to save the bog from the machine.

To a Scot it is again a familiar scenario. Conservationists tend to be outsiders and the locals often think them officious. But sometimes they unite.

In its own way tourism, another staple of the local economy, is also a pollutant, though in Ireland it has on the whole been well managed. John Herdman has memorably denounced its impact on Scottish life and character, and Ireland has not entirely escaped its trivialising influence. There is an Irish 'kailyard' every bit as sentimentally shallow as the Scottish equivalent.

The 'old' thatched cottage which you sometimes see being built here is likely to owe more to a judicious investment by a businessman than to a genuine respect for the old ways. The locals remember the thatch, with its holes and its vermin, with rueful nostalgia.

In a lively market town east of Galway, a court has been hearing a case involving the secretary of the local gun club. He was accused of assaulting the man acting as guide for a French shooting party. Anti-French notices had been put up in the town during the night and the secretary had told the party to 'eff off back to France'.

In disposing of the case the judge seemed less concerned about the assault, during which one man had pointed a loaded shotgun at the other, than by the effect the case might have on tourism. It might, he said, damage Ireland's reputation as the land of a hundred thousand welcomes. He fined the accused £10.

The judge's fears seem groundless. The French are here in considerable numbers and as far as we can tell are made as welcome as everybody else. But his point was right. Like it or not, countries like Scotland and Ireland have little choice but to make the most of tourism.

From Glasgow to Galway with a futon in tow.

After several days of steady rain the skies have cleared. The 12 Bens of Connemara are for once without the covering of cloud which they usually suck in from the Atlantic. A French yacht is making gingerly progress up the sound where hidden rocks await the unwary. Sitting in the sun, amid the nettles and the thistles which I have promised to eradicate tomorrow, I raise my glass in a toast to the sailors down below for I am celebrating a victory over an old enemy.

It was five years ago that without much thought we bought a futon from a shop in Candleriggs, Glasgow, as a cheap way of adding a spare bed to the cottage here. It cost little more than £150, consisting simply of a pine frame which folded into a third of its full length, and a buttoned mattress.

So far so good. Now to transport it all. Try as I might I could not fit the frame into the boot or even slantwise in the car itself. A roof rack? A couple of calls established that this would cost £250 and that the nearest one in stock was in Ayr. The cost and the journey seemed disproportionate so the futon was entrusted to a carrier. Could he get it to the west of Ireland? No problem (these are words which, as I grow older, increasingly fill me with foreboding).

In due course the futon and its frame arrived in Dublin. A customs charge of £75, something our cheerful carrier had not mentioned when accepting the business, was levied, together with the price of the cartage (£100). By now the cost of the futon had doubled and it had got as far as a depot in a fairly grim industrial suburb on the outskirts of Dublin which we found with some difficulty. Declan, the friendly and optimistic clerk in the office, was also much given to the phrase 'no problem'. He guaranteed to deliver the futon to Connemara on the Tuesday, when the van made its regular run west. Tuesday came, the day wore on, but there was no sign of the van.

A call from the phone box found Declan in chastened and apologetic mood, there was in fact a problem. The van, it turned out, went no farther than Ballinasloe, a lively and occasionally riotous market town a little west of the Shannon but about 90 miles short of the Atlantic shore where the futon was to be installed. When Declan had so cheerfully accepted the load, he now explained, he had no idea that the cottage was so remote. There was only one thing for it. Back it went to Dublin, where it remained in store for several months (without charge, I acknowledge) until our next visit. By this time I had been obliged to buy the roof rack that I should have got in the first place.

In pouring rain we wrapped the frame in plastic sheeting, loaded it on to the rack and finally brought it to its destination. By now it had become the most expensive futon in the history of the bedding trade (£150 + £100 + £75 + £250 = £575). But it had more unpleasant surprises in store. The frame had no handles and was hard to carry about. It drew blood on several occasions as I tried to get a grip between its slats. Worse, it turned out to be excruciatingly uncomfortable. A fakir's bed would have been heaven by comparison. Last week we paid a visit to a furniture store just outside Galway. The city, said to be the fastest growing in Europe, was readying itself for its race week, the highlight of the summer season in the west of Ireland, and the sales assistants could talk of little else. But they broke off long enough to sell us a pine bed for a mere £150. They tied the mattress to the roof of the car with twine. The frame, flat packed, went into the boot, though it stuck out a bit. We made a cautious journey back over the bumpy Connemara road. At home we found a packet of screws but no instructions. After much head-scratching and some false starts we managed to put it together. It is now installed and, by comparison with the futon, is the height of luxury.

A couple of days later a bonfire, injudiciously positioned, pierced the pipe that brings our clear water off the hill. Such misfortunes guarantee unpopularity, for they always happen at the worst possible moment. In this case guests were expected and baths had been planned. At the cost of a soaking I managed to spatchcock the pipe together again to give a limited supply to the house but Michael, our builder, factotum and friend, came out and fixed it properly the next day. He would not accept payment but took the futon instead.

He will use its pine planks to make shelves. As I helped him load it into his van I thought of Stevenson's Faustian short story about the seaman who accepts a black bottle from which he may drink inexhaustibly but whose ownership will consign him to hell. He finally passes it on and the reader is powerfully relieved. With similar feelings I watched Michael drive off with the futon frame. I hope its malevolent power is destroyed when he breaks it up.

Airts and pairts: a trip to St Andrews by way of Freuchie. (From 1994.)

Off to St Andrews to fulfil a speaking engagement at which, it had been promised by a private correspondent, I would be challenged among other things about *The Herald*'s reporting of the Highland Clearances. A bit much, I thought rather resentfully, and I suppose it was a reluctance to arrive at my destination and face this historical censure that made me loiter along a route through the back roads of Fife .

Our spring has arrived, better late than never, and enormous tractors were busy in the fields. Once you leave Fife's southern industrial zone, all is order and grave beauty, and they were creating furrows of impressive straightness and regularity in the rich black soil.

Could it really be, as my grandfather had once mischievously proposed, that the devil is a Fifer? Why had the great John Junor, in his *Sunday Express* column, elevated the town of Auchtermuchty to the status of national tribune?

More questions popped into my mind as I passed the village of Freuchie. In Aberdeenshire, where my mother grew up, they used to say: 'Awa tae Freuchie and fry mice.' Clearly it was a euphemism for a curse of more vulgar stamp. The best explanation the *Scottish National Dictionary* can offer is that the expression was coined by the courtiers at Falkland Palace, hunting seat of kings from the twelfth century and where a real tennis court was established by James V.

My mind fills with images of some medieval McEnroe consigning the umpire to Freuchie. But soon my delaying strategems are exhausted and from the crest of a hill I glimpse St Andrews in its sea-bound corner, dreaming in the afternoon light. From a distance it looks Northern European, like something painted by Vermeer. It is a lovely town but its modern personality is ambiguous. As I drive in, there are white-flannelled men playing cricket on a field vivid with the first green of summer; you may imagine yourself in England

It is, of course, an impression heightened by the town's two great industries – learning and golf. The university brings many a student from England and overseas; and people come from all over the world to play the Old Course. The location of St Leonard's School, where I am to speak, appears to be a closely kept secret. In the hotel to which I turn for help there's only a vague notion. Reception does not know. A passing waitress, a strikingly pretty American, cannot help either. I repair outside for harder information, to the lane that runs beside the famous old links.

The first person I ask is from Australia, and we pause for a moment to watch a golfer play his ball off the road that crosses the first and eighteenth holes. He makes a good fist of it. There is a shower of sparks and the ball lands just short of the green, rolling back into the Valley of Sin. A bit unfair, says this chatty visitor: couldn't he lift and drop? Not without penalty, I reply with the confidence of ignorance.

Indeed, I remember Harold Henning playing off the road in the centenary Open and landing it within a few feet of the pin. We discuss Greg Norman's prospects at Turnberry. Of St Leonard's, of course, he has never heard.

My next inquiry finds a student whose accent declares that he, too, is from the Antipodes. He points me vaguely in the direction of the castle. For a while I wander about this ancient corner of the town, replete with violent history. Hereabouts Cardinal Beaton was assassinated in 1546 and here is the bottle dungeon which so eloquently evokes the cruelty of the old days.

But St Andrews lives with its history at the back of its mind; it all happened an awfully long time ago and sweet daisies now grow where once there was murder. The evening sun is falling on green lawns and there is a distant sound of tennis as I finally arrive at the school, its graceful old buildings grouped round a courtyard, to have my vague apprehensions entirely laid to rest.

The headmistress and her husband are hospitable and amusing. The senior girls who join us for dinner are charming, full of their plans for university. The audience is attentive, and my putative heckler turns out to be a gentleman of kindly manner who does not mention the Clearances at all.

A former diplomat comes up at the end. He is from Glasgow but has retired here. He recommends it; it is orderly, relatively free of crime, drier than the West, and the university has a wonderful library. Some parts of Scotland, like the East Neuk, East Lothian, and the Moray Firth, miss the worst of our weather, though they must from time to time pay for their good fortune by suffering the wretchedness of haar.

Australian tourists, students from New Zealand, American barmaids, retired diplomats: where are the locals? Yet St Andrews, we agree at dinner, remains beneath its layers a distinctively Scottish town. If you listen carefully you can hear the native woodnote, that sing-song speech of the Fifer, and the English influence at the university appears to have shed the arrogance that sometimes marked it in the eighties.

There's time for a final breath of air before setting off back to Glasgow. Beside the Old Course, an old chap is leaning on the rail and smoking a pipe. Together we cogitate over the darkling scene. You can just hear the sigh of the shore somewhere beyond the fairway. It is a soothing moment. At last, a local. Fine night, say I. He takes the pipe from his mouth. 'Sehr gemütlich,' he replies courteously.

Edinburgh's Botanic Gardens, an oasis of delight in July 1993.

For a blessed half hour this week I sat on a bench at the herbaceous border in the Royal Botanic Garden, Edinburgh. Myriad plants were in bloom below the high hedge marching gracefully above them; their subtle colours soothed the mind and emptied it of care.

I have been coming here, on and off, for most of my life. We played childhood games on the daisy-strewn turf and ran about the magically mysterious rock garden, occasionally to the kindly rebukes of the keepers.

Trees which have grown tall in my lifetime now obscure the townscape, tumbled houses climbing the hill to the craggy skyline punctuated by steeples, domes and spires. From the Viewpoint, perhaps, the poet Lewis Spence wrote *The Prows of Reekie*:

O wad this braw hie-heapit toun
Sail aff like an enchanted ship
Drift owre the warld's seas up and doun,
And kiss wi' Venice lip to lip,
Or anchor into Naples' Bay
A misty island far astray
Or set her rock to Athens' wa'.
Pillar to pillar, stane to stane,
The cruikit spell o' her backbane,
Yon shadow-mile o' spire and vane,
Wad ding them a', wad ding them a'!

In adulthood I have often returned to the garden's well of peace and solace and never found it dry, even when mobbed by visitors and tourists; I have to admit that I have been immune to its high educational content and remain horticulturally illiterate, though I can still find the monkey-puzzle tree that so fascinated us as children.

The Royal Botanic Garden is a highly virtuous example of how dubious is the slavish worship of market principles. This place of beauty was created by a society that placed a high value on education, found the resources to support it and conferred its priceless benefit on the public without entrance charge.

One of the few demands, enforced by the keepers, is that people should conduct themselves with decorum. Among the blessings of the garden is the absence of that most loutish of modern solecisms, the blaring transistor of the yobbish picnicker.

As I sat on my bench I could hear a dog barking somewhere beyond the gates where dogs belong. It might well have been a hound from the Treasury for the sunny security of the garden is now troubled by falling revenue from the state.

When I first heard that the trustees, to whom stewardship of the garden was passed by the government in 1986, might have to contemplate charging for admission, I experienced a sense of loss and even of betrayal. Free access to the Botanics has been so much part of my own life that I felt it to be a universal benefit to be prized almost as much as the health service.

The garden, I have to admit, is not a park. It is a place of peace and beauty, certainly, but also of scholarship and living education. The maintenance of its standards must take precedence over all other considerations.

And yet. I do not think I am parsimonious. But if I ever have to pay for admission to this beloved place, I shall do so with a heavy heart and find in the charge a sign of a failing civilisation.

On the Forth Bridge and a fleeting appearance as a Constable Plod.

Sometimes an event, relatively insignificant in itself, can carry a symbolic value which makes it an expression of the age in which we live. Such a thought occurred to me one afternoon this week when Cyril Bleasdale, the boss of ScotRail, popped up on the television news.

The gaffer, wearing a shiny yellow jacket, a helmet, and the cheerful smile of someone bringing good news, was standing on the Forth Railway Bridge. He told a reporter that, yes, they were not going to paint the bridge this year, for the first time in 103 years.

The sadness that crept over me had a little to do with the cheerful way Cyril gave out the information. It was all too typical of that modern black art, media manipulation. But the sense of melancholy, of betrayal even, had, I suppose, more connection with the fact that the bridge is woven into my own memories.

This is not just because, as a student, I got a part as an extra in the second film of John Buchan's novel *The Thirty-Nine Steps*, appearing as one of the policemen who emerged from a train on to the bridge in pursuit of Richard Hannay, played by Kenneth More. Having pulled the communication cord, he jumped from the train, eluded us, hung elegantly from a girder and was later seen emerging safely somewhere near North Queensferry .

The film was pretty vague on the details of how he was supposed to have managed it, and I have to admit, while admiring the power of my own brief appearance (about two seconds of being vigilant in Waverley Station – it's easy to miss unless you watch very carefully), that it is not a very good movie. Indeed, none of the three versions has been able to capture on celluloid the powerful symbolism of Buchan's novel, of the lone fugitive hunted by a machine in an empty landscape.

My own chief recollection of it is that my elder brother and I each got £5 a day, sat around doing nothing for most of the time and, returning home still in police uniform, were not required by the tram conductor to pay the fare. It was fortunate, I later reflected, that no criminal outrage or public emergency required our intervention.

When we were children a visit to the bridge made for a particularly exciting day out. The bus would drop us at South Queensferry ; we would take the ferry and, and as it sailed across the firth, watch the trains that rattled over the bridge above.

It is, I think, an artefact of singular and arresting beauty. The railway bridge remains of greater interest than its parvenu companion, the road bridge, but the complexity of the first and the grace of the second make them stimulating companions.

As we stared up from the ferry, my father would tell us of its history; of how 57 men died in its construction; of how its design, influenced by the Tay Bridge disaster, and its innovative use of steel gave it exceptional strength; of how Sir John Fowler, who with his partner Sir Benjamin Baker was mainly responsible for its construction, would take a lantern after dinner and clamber about the girders in his dinner pumps personally inspecting the rivets.

And, of course, the bridge has been continuously painted ever since, with iron oxide paint supplied by Craig & Rose according to a secret formula. The company has other fish to fry and its managing director, Colin Mitchell-Rose, has accepted BR's decision to suspend painting with considerable grace; but I imagine his private feelings may be rather different.

In the old days they would just give the painters a pot and a brush and leave them to clamber about the girders. Modern health and safety regulations require them to erect scaffolding. This has made some parts of the bridge inaccessible and they have not seen a lick of paint for years. (Perhaps, as in the Louvre pyramid in Paris, they should employ Alpinists for the inaccessible bits.)

The painting crew has carried on faithfully with the rest of it. Now work in hand will continue but the rest of next year's programme is suspended. The painting 'holiday' is symbolic of the decline to which the Government has condemned the railway system. Although it boasts of record levels of investment, this is devoted entirely to work associated with the Channel Tunnel: the rest of the network is starved. It is also symbolic of an obsession with market principles which if taken too far leads to neglect of important national assets. It is very little short of an act of vandalism.

[In 2012 a ten-year project to paint the bridge with special paint expected to last 25 years, was completed].

Excerpt from a Robert Kemp 1961 column on the Forth Bridge

My earliest memory of the old bridge goes back to the 1880s, I received it not through my own eyes but through those of my father. As a child he was taken from Glasgow on holiday to Aberdour, and so his earliest recollection was of men working on the bridge at night, by the light of naphtha flares. Think of the magnificent scene of Victorian illumination that conjures up – into what wild streamers the winds of the estuary must have blown them.

Your true Forth Bridge addict always begins with the Tay Bridge Disaster (the night of which his grannie so well remembered). This provides a cue for a note on the faulty rivets cast at Wormit and the unhappy end of the designer Sir Thomas Bouch.

Why should the Tay Bridge lead to the Forth? Those who are not Bridge-minded forget if they ever knew, that Bouch was commissioned to build over Forth as well. He designed a suspension bridge and work had begun. One brick pier of his remains to this day on Inchgarvie, under the northern cantilever of the central tower (to observe sixpence-worth of ferry essential).

The blowing down of the Tay Bridge led to a vote of no confidence in Bouch's design, and work was stopped. Thus was the way made for Sir John Fowler and Sir Benjamin Baker.

South Queensferry is the perfect vantage point for lecturing one's friends (or indeed one's enemies) on the 'Holbein straddle' According to my legend, Fowler was attending an exhibition in the company of Nasmyth inventor of the steam hammer, when the news reached them from Dundee. They were standing in front of Holbein's portrait of King Henry VIII, and Nasmyth said the Tay Bridge would still be standing if it had been given the same stance as the King's, with feet planted wide apart. Fowler took the tip – but you ought to hear me explain it at South Queensferry.

A man who knew a man who had in his youth been assistant to Baker told me that one reason for the splendid workmanship in the bridge was that the chief inspected every rivet with his own eagle eye. At night, after a good dinner and with a bottle of claret under his waistcoat, he would don those old-fashioned dancing pumps with bows and walk to the end of the narrowest girder, scrutinising as he went. Result – general consternation and every boat ordered to circle underneath so that the great man could be fished out of the water. But he never made a false step.

Of the achievements of Sir William Arrol, the actual builder, I know only that they rested entirely upon that respectable Scottish dish, singed sheep's heid. When he was a blacksmith in Glasgow, people brought their sheep's heids to be singed at his smithy, and the pennies thus earned paid for his evening classes.

[In 2012, campaigners were fighting to save Sir William Arrol's former home in Ayr from demolition].

Urban rambles amid Glasgow's grand and incongruous glories.

On summer Saturdays the rusticating traffic builds up quickly on Great Western Road, fretting at the lights, tailing back right to the motorway. As you head towards Anniesland you can see the first hills rising on the horizon. It remains one of Glasgow's glories that you can get out of it so quickly into our magnificent countryside.

But at weekends the countryside now comes under such enormous pressure that its peace has become elusive. This week the National Trust for Scotland announced measures to protect Ben Lomond from erosion, and my colleague Jim Freeman has written in this newspaper of the threat to the tranquillity and amenity of Loch Lomond. The West Highland Way, glimpsed from the road beside the Beech Tree pub at the foot of Dumgoyne, looks like Princes Street on a busy Saturday morning.

It would be too much to say that the discerning walker stays in town. But the idea of the urban ramble, about which there is so extensive a literature dating from Victorian and Edwardian times, may be worth reviving. In recent months I have found myself less inclined to join the motorcade to the hills and more of a mind to explore the quiet purlieus on my doorstep in the West End where my companions are mostly dog-walkers and joggers.

The best starting point is in the Botanics. Between 1829 and 42 they were moved, in search of purer air, from the west end of Sauchiehall Street, and they were laid out by private interests anxious to increase the commercial value of the new housing in the West End. They remained in private hands until 1891 and are now administered by the city.

One of the best results of Glasgow's recent drive for self-improvement has been the restoration and renovation of the glasshouses, of which that great Victorian flourish, the Kibble Palace, remains the most original and interesting. It was originally designed as a rich man's conservatory for John Kibble's house on Loch Long, but now it sits eerily in the gardens like some fat glass mushroom. At night, when it is illuminated, it makes you think more of some flying saucer newly arrived from space.

The gardens are, in their scope and range, not to be compared with the Botanics in Edinburgh, Kew or Dublin, but in my 10 years in Glasgow they have steadily gone up in the world (the orchid collection and other achievements led to the choice of Glasgow as the venue for the 1993 World Orchid Conference). For the walker their boundaries are too constricting, and the best bet is to take one of the paths down to the Kelvin. A section of the river lies within the Botanics themselves.

But soon you must decide to head up or downstream. Up takes you towards Maryhill, the Forth and Clyde Canal and the Kelvin aqueduct, and the headwaters in the Campsies, but my steps usually turn downstream. Below the bridge at Queen Margaret Drive, there is a weir, one of the two points at which the river acquires any sort of presence, spreading out between its precipitous banks. On one side is the back of the [the former] BBC building, with its sinister chimney, and on the other are the roofs, rising like battlements, of Wilton Street and Doune Terrace.

For these many weeks past, a large cable drum has lodged firmly in the weir, and this introduces you quickly to one of the urban pleasures of walking by the Kelvin. It is a great river for detritus, old prams, supermarket trolleys, rubber tyres and the like. Once I spotted several quires of a local freesheet evidently dumped in the river by a fatigued delivery boy.

From time to time environmental volunteers get to work to clean up the river. A party was out a couple of weekends ago. The drum has lost its grip on the weir and has fallen into the water below, waiting for the next spate to carry it away. The litter of paper and plastic which grows up like a grimy crop has been much reduced. But soon it, and the curious and incongruous objects which arrive mysteriously from dislocated lives, or as if from a fourth dimension, will return and restore to the river that slightly scruffy quality that is so much part of its personality.

Scruffiness and odd glimpses of magnificence. As you walk down the river on a summer's morning the sun glows behind the crown steeple of the Kelvin Stevenson Memorial Parish Church in Belmont Street, turning its sandstone black in silhouette against the brightness (who tends its little secret garden perched on the edge of the cliff?).

At Great Western Bridge, there is a kind of beach formed by the eddies and sometimes people have picnics there on the cocoa-coloured sand. This is an act of optimism, for always down by the Kelvin a dank, stale smell clings to the nostrils. It is much cleaner than it was, of course. Some coarse fish and minnows have returned but it does not yet have the aroma of pure hill water (in its upper reaches inadequate sewage works and contaminated industrial land will continue to pollute it for years to come). Under the bridge pigeons roost and the smells grow sour beside the inevitable graffiti.

Beyond the bridge, past a winebar that has struggled to survive beneath the arches, a footpath crosses the river and now you are in the open space that lies between Great Western Road and Gibson Street. The new mown grass, the young trees and the flowering shrubs fill it with scents which drive out the river's musk. It offers one of the most interesting panoramas of the whole walk. Behind you can still see the crown steeple of Kelvin Church and James Miller's Caledonian Mansions (1895), rightly praised as an original, playful and asymmetrical combination of the Scottish tradition with the influences of the Arts and Crafts movement. On the other side of Great Western Road are the Ionic colonnades of Glasgow Academy.

To the east the spires of Lansdowne Church and St Mary's Cathedral float in the blue summer sky, as handsome a pair as you'll find anywhere. The back of Park Road shows off its recent improvements, with sensitive and successful infills in brick. On the other side of the Kelvin, the back of Otago Street offers some real curiosities, industrial buildings from the late 1880s turning facades to the river of red and yellow brick. Washing hangs in the steep garden of a tall white villa but round in Otago Street its modest, cottage-like front gives no hint of its hidden depths. After a patch of derelict open ground, an emblem on a gable end advertises the businesses in the lane, including a clock restorer and the booksellers Voltaire and Rousseau.

At Gibson Street I leave the walkway and enter Kelvingrove Park at the gate opposite another graceful church, St Silas. The steep path that heads up Woodlands Hill gives you a bit of a puff if you walk briskly. It carries you up to the statue of Field Marshal Earl Roberts, VC, of Kandahar, Pretoria, and Waterford, who died in France in

1914. His mounted figure is resonant of imperial glory but now his memorial is daubed in shocking pink with peacenik graffiti.

Here you are on the edge of Glasgow's finest piece of town planning, laid out by various architects in about three decades from 1830. It is mostly in commercial use but a few people still live in its remaining flats. John Mauceri and others have taken up residence in the converted Trinity College, whose tower, glimpsed from the motorway, is a powerful signatory image for the returning traveller. The high path along the fringe of Park Terrace and Park Gardens gives one of the most satisfying urban views in Europe. The neo-Gothic tower of Glasgow University, clad in scaffolding, contrasts with Kelvingrove's exotic Victorian tabernacles. The Sick Children's Hospital at Yorkhill catches the sun.

The cranes stand sadly over an empty river and the south side roofs stretch away to the distant hills. Below, beyond the blossom and intoxicating green of the park, magnificent at this season, beyond the spouting fountain built to commemorate the Glasgow Water Scheme and recently restored, the Kelvin finds, at another weir, its only moment of real distinction. It flows between the university and the art gallery, beside carpets of multi-coloured rhododendrons as vivid as a coral reef. Then it passes under Partick Bridge and disappears into an industrial cutting, making its last constricted and furtive journey to the Clyde .

Now the walker too can surrender himself to pavements and Dumbarton Road; but if he wants to delay that moment he can trespass on the kindness and the grounds of the university (except on Sunday when the gates are locked) by walking through to University Avenue and then back to the Botanics by a variety of routes, all of them with a story of their own to tell.

It is not, I must admit, an unsullied idyll. In the town the worm in the apple is always visible. Litter and graffiti continue to depress me, and there are some odd types about, especially in the early morning: there is a gang who buy their breakfast cans of special brew as soon as Safeways opens at 8am. These lads seem well enough behaved. One asked me one rainy morning not for money but for a loan of my umbrella.

A colleague one night came within an inch of being thrown into the river from Kelvin Bridge by two psycopathic youths who attacked him. Recently, after writing a piece about the Kelvingrove fountain, I received a letter from a reader who warned me to take care. He had

had to curtail his morning walks in the park after being mugged, robbed and seriously injured by a couple of young thugs who had marked his customary route and lain in wait for him.

Compared with New York there's nothing much to worry about; and there are worms in the country too. In a quiet road in a glen where we sometimes walk, there are now Rottweilers and Alsatians who 'wouldn't harm a fly'. Nowhere is entirely secure, and a walking stick is a good idea in town and country. But the richness of the urban scene is there for all, even if it is not always appreciated by an age which can hardly contain its impatience to get behind the wheel and head for the crowded countryside.

12
Music

ON PIANOS AND THE PAST.

My friend had bought a new baby grand piano of German manufacture. It sat, black and beautiful, in the corner of his drawing room, reflecting the soft light from the lamps. His house stands in the grounds of a ruined chateau in the Paris banlieu: outside there were bonfire smells in the autumn dusk.

It was perfect piano country. There were no neighbours. Here no fortissimo need be restrained by a sense of social obligation. In this paradise there was, of course, a worm: my friend cannot play the piano and nor can any of his family.

With stiff fingers I tried a slow blues. It was, apparently, the first time it had been played. The children looked on in wonder: I shall never again enjoy so impressionable an audience.

As I left I promised to send them some volumes of Czerny's exercises. Since childhood Czerny has haunted me. He represents guilt and duty avoided. Arnold, you must practise your scales! How many mothers have broken their hearts and tempers on that hateful phrase? *The Ballad of Sir Patrick Spens* has similar associations:

The King sat in Dunfermline Toun,
Drinking the bluid red wine ...

I could get a little further. Despite my father's offered bribe of £1, I never did manage to learn it off by heart.

Karl Czerny, 1791-1857, was an Austrian pianist and teacher. He studied with Beethoven. Liszt was among his pupils. But his fame rests on his exercises for building and improving pianistic technique. A couple of weeks after the visit to my friends in France I remembered my promise and popped into Biggars in Sauchiehall Street, where I purchased three volumes of Czerny for them – the preliminary book of exercises, the first book of velocity, and a book of 'recreations' for beginners. I sent them off to Paris with a note whose expressions of esteem could not conceal its sadistic import. Learn Czerny, I wrote, and you will all be pianists.

I bought a volume of Czerny for myself. My own copy at home was picked up second-hand in Russo and Voltaire many years ago for about 20p and is pretty dog-eared. The fingering is shown in the old style, with an X for the thumb. The cover is laid out with satisfying floridity in an antique type:

CZERNY'S
Celebrated
Etude de la Velocité

Its ceremonious appearance would lend distinction to the most modest talent; and there are two exercises in it of such simplicity and cunning (Nos 6 and 7 for strengthening the weak fingers) that, if I do them every day, I reduce my piano handicap by at least a couple of strokes.

Alas, it is too late now. Alas, it is not given to everyone to go to Corinth. If only I had heeded my mother, or my musical granny. If only I had practised my Czerny when I was young instead of fooling about incompetently with jazz. There are no short cuts to good piano playing.

The beginnings of a love of jazz.

My love of jazz had been stimulated by listening to it on the radio and reinforced during a memorable visit to Auntie Janey and Uncle Dougal at their flat in London, in Duke Street behind Selfridge's. I must have been about 12, which would put the date of the visit around 1951. It was an enormous adventure; we travelled by ourselves by train and were given a warm welcome by our uncle and aunt and our Cousin Robin. She was younger than David but older than I, and we had become quite close to her during holidays at Birse and in Aboyne where Dougal's mother lived. According to the old adage that three's a crowd, David and Robin had sometimes ganged up on me, and I always had a soft spot for Uncle Dougal because he realised what was happening and would spend time with me to make up for it.

Dougal Alcock, a tall man from Broughty Ferry, and Dad's sister Janey had been brought together by their love of music. She had gone to London to study it, and had graduated from the Guildhall School of Music. Throughout their life they played in string quartets, he on viola, she on violin; and, at one point, were members of the Singapore Symphony Orchestra.

Dougal was at the time of our visit personnel manager of Selfridge's and the flat, I think, belonged to the company. It was about three storeys up and from its windows most mornings we watched Jean Simmons going to work on the film set at Pinewood, leaving her apartment in a sports car, her hair blowing in the breeze. We also until discovered, dropped stink bombs on the pavements below. Apart from the usual pleasures of London – Madame Tussauds, the zoo, and knickerbocker glories in the Selfridge's restaurant – there was the enchantment of Uncle Dougal's record collection. He was an aficionado not just of classical music but of jazz, and was a particular admirer of the American violinist Joe Venuti and his partner on guitar, Eddie Lang. Indeed, in his endearingly dogmatic way, he would revile the work of Stephane Grappelli and Django Reinhardt as being much inferior in comparison, though critical opinion since has rather gone the other way. The record which stimulated my own life-long love of jazz was the Venuti-Lang piece called A Mug of Ale. It made me tingle with pleasure.

Uncle Dougal was a glamorous figure in other ways. He had served in the forces and had been bitten by a cobra in India and whenever we walked on the Scottish hills together would terrify us with baleful warnings about the adders lurking in the heather which, in my imagination, grew as big as the cobra that had sunk its fangs into him. One night he produced his old service revolver and, with many a dramatic warning of its dangers, demonstrated how to load it and make it safe.

Uncle Dougal eventually left Selfridge's and worked abroad in Africa and Singapore in administrative posts. During this time he and Janey prepared for retirement and acquired a flat in Rome. Their visits home resembled a royal progress and he irritated us somewhat by asserting that Britain in general and Scotland in particular had gone to the dogs; that Mercedes cars were infinitely superior to anything produced by us; that Chinese cuisine was inexpressibly better than anything in the West; and that Fangio was far superior a racing driver to the Scottish hero Jim Clark.

We had our quiet revenges. He arranged a Chinese banquet in Scotland's first Chinese restaurant, in Chambers Street, Edinburgh, of such amplitude that it killed our appetites. Stunned, we could only look at it, drinking large quantities of cola. The chef was upset and had to be placated with a big tip. On another occasion Uncle Dougal took us to an Italian restaurant and addressed the waiter in that language: to our infinite gratification the waiter was unable to understand a word. (What I now realise, after a life time of going to restaurants, is that the waiter was probably a laddie from Leith who had assumed a fractured Italian accent to impress the customers.)

When Jim Clark surpassed Fangio – he broke his world record of 25 grand prix wins – Dad and Uncle Dougal happened to be watching television together; Uncle Dougal fell strangely silent.

When Uncle Dougal and Auntie Janey retired to Rome, they remained extremely welcoming and hospitable. He continued to harangue us about our national failings, blithely ignoring all the corruption and inefficiency in the Italian way of life and government. There he found a second career. At a party he was spotted by a film director, who cast him in a series of movies as British butlers or ambassadors. With his commanding figure, speaking Italian with a strong Broughty Ferry accent, he filled the parts splendidly. He died on the film set one day.

When Auntie Janey visited us in Scotland after his death, I got out my Venuti/Lang LP (EMI/Parlophone PMC 7091) and played her A Mug of Ale, recorded in New York City on September 13, 1927. Apart from Venuti and Lang, Arthur Schutt was on piano and Adrian Rollini on bass saxophone, hot fountain pen and goofus. The music stands up well, foreshadowing the small-group jazz of Benny Goodman and even carrying intimations of the later Bop revolution. Auntie Janey, I think, was pleased that I had remembered a fragment of the past which she had forgotten.

Festival music old and new and a virtuoso finale from 1992. Incidentally, this concert marked an important moment for composer James MacMillan who was then beginning to achieve international recognition.

Memory plays tricks. It can be strangely deceptive on points of fact yet vividly accurate on the essential nature of human transactions. You remember what you felt though you may forget, with frightening ease, the circumstantial details.

The Edinburgh Festival of 1992 closed with a concert of twentieth-century Scottish music. Despite the sniffiness of London critics about all things Scottish, it was a great popular success.

The works were of uneven quality. The two most substantial

pieces were Musgrave's Horn Concerto, and MacMillan's concerto for percussion with Evelyn Glennie presiding over a veritable battery of instruments.

Both works had strongly theatrical aspects. The Musgrave was abstract, in the sense that it had no programme or formal structure. But it had a clear sense of dialogue that often seemed sardonic and satirical as Tuckwell, with some of the other brass and wind, conversed with the rest of the orchestra.

The composer requires horns to be positioned throughout the auditorium to give a circumabulatory resonance and a sense almost of a public meeting, and one or two in the audience who had not noticed the musicians' unobtrusive movement upstairs got a bit of a fright when they opened up from stances in the dress circle and upper gallery.

The MacMillan I found a scintillating composition and no great sense of formality was possible because of the requirements imposed on the percussionist. Ms Glennie had to hasten from instrument to instrument, finally climbing the rear side stairway to sound a haunting coda on tubular bells. This gave the proceedings an air of cabaret which I enjoyed. A serious-minded friend disapproved but I have never gone along with the view that the concert hall is a temple.

Other evocations were more domestic. I once saw the great vibes player Red Norvo at the Third Eye Centre in Glasgow. Despite the dexterity and delicacy of his playing his stance and movements reminded me of a butcher happily standing at a board boning meat. Similarly Ms Glennie as she tripped lightly from vibes to drums made me think of a woman in a kitchen, preparing a meal of some complexity while dressed in finery for the imminent guests.

The concert closed with the finale, for Highland bagpipes and orchestra, from Ian Whyte's ballet Donald of the Burthens, performed at Covent Garden in 1951. This was what set my memory running, in particular the programme note which said that the great violinist Max Rostal had liked Whyte's violin concerto.

Whyte, 1901-60, was active during the Scottish literary renaissance. While writers were attempting to establish new native voices in poetry and theatre, he was trying to do the same for music. He was a prolific composer, drawing heavily on the Scottish vernacular tradition. He was a moving spirit behind the creation of the BBC Scottish Orchestra in 1935, and in 1946 became its second conductor.

He was a friend and colleague of my father and he often came round to the house in Edinburgh to work out on our Boesendorfer. (My father was inordinately proud of this lovely old piano and was somewhat dashed when Whyte told him its action was a little slow.) One day in the early fifties, no doubt to keep me out of mischief, my father took me along to the BBC studio, I think in Glasgow, where he was producing a programme involving Whyte and Rostal.

I sat in a corner as, for reasons which I now forget, the adults listened to some recordings of Orcadian folk music, featuring fiddle and double bass. At the end of each measure the bass-player's penultimate note, before he returned to the tonic, was consistently flat.

This began to interest Whyte and Rostal more than other aspects of the music. Having by that time become keen on jazz, I thought I recognised the flat note as something comparable to the blue notes. These lie off the conventional scale around the third and seventh intervals.

I was about to offer this thought, and had begun to form the sentence, when I caught my father's eye. He looked clearly horrified that an unlettered teenager should even contemplate entering a dialogue with two distinguished musicians. Crestfallen, I dutifully subsided back into respectful silence as Whyte and Rostal concluded that the Orcadian musician was simply in error.

There was a subtext here, which I understood later when I thought about the incident in the light of other remarks. Whyte and Rostal, like most serious musicians of their generation, had a contempt for jazz and popular music. They regarded them as pollutants produced by the industrial culture. Whyte, on that occasion, referred to the song Red Sails in the Sunset as 'gutter music'. Jazz's admission to Grove is of recent origin.

With great clarity I remember both the intense teenage embarrassment and the feeling that I had been frustrated in contributing something useful to the discussion. These details return to me as if they were events of yesterday but in my mind I had constructed circumstantial elements capable of being checked. These did not stand up to examination and proved comprehensively faulty.

I had the idea that Rostal had come to Scotland to perform the Whyte violin concerto with the Scottish Orchestra in a broadcast performance. In fact it was a concerto by another Scottish composer, Erik Chisholm, that he played with the orchestra, though not necessarily on that occasion.

Indeed, the reference our library found to Rostal around that time was to his recital at the Freemason's Hall during the Edinburgh Festival of 1953. *The Herald* critic admired Rostal's technique but found his playing often 'on the edge of vulgarity'.

By that time Rostal, who had been born in Austria, had settled in London, where he became the leading violin teacher of his generation. Among his pupils was Leonard Friedman. Rostal died in 1991 at the age of 85.

According to John Purser's *Scotland's Music [Mainstream Publishing, 1992]*, the Whyte violin concerto has been performed at an Edinburgh Festival and was well received. *The Herald*'s obituary in 1960, while recognising his contribution as a conductor and animateur, was a little dismissive of Whyte as a composer.

The verdict was polite but icy: 'The large number of his compositions was by no means reflected in their limited success: the sincerity that prompted all he wrote rarely found sufficient musical logic and reasoning in its formal expression.'

Given the public's enjoyment of last Saturday's concert, the SSO might think of giving the violin concerto another airing, perhaps with Leonard Friedman as soloist. Thus would my imagined circle be complete.

What does music tell us about our society? From 1990.

What does music tell us about our society? This question occurred to me during an odyssey through the Glasgow Jazz Festival. The spectrum was both historical and emotional; and it is the emotional content of the music, at any particular point in its history, that tells us something about its social context.

These moods can be sweet or dry but it is a mistake to think that joyful music must imply social harmony. The most obvious examples are the blues, very seldom the mournful dirges of myth but more often a defiant celebration of life amid poverty or the confrontation of loss; the exuberance of early New Orleans jazz which grew like flowers in a dunghill, out of brothels and low society; or the bittersweet songs of the thirties born of a depression and presaging war. All these forms, at their best, can produce great music, but only when shorn of sentimentality. Nothing kills good jazz faster than sugar.

Conversely, difficult music does not always express social anger, though it can. The musicians around Charlie Parker, including Miles

Davis whose Glasgow concert took place last night, developed an idiom requiring qualities so demanding that many less gifted players were excluded from it. Although white musicians were involved in bop more or less from the start, exclusion was at least part of its intention, arising from a black nationalism that resented the exploitation of its own music by white mercenaries.

In Eastern Europe avant-garde jazz has been an expression of political dissent and a rejection of received values. Punk rock was a rejection of the crass commercialism of Tin Pan Alley and, implicitly, materialism itself, though I have to say that I could never find anything interesting in punk rock.

Sometimes, however, abrasive music can express something quite different. This thought occurred to me at the end of a long night on Tuesday, in the Harlequin Jazz Club in Renfrew Street, where Tommy Smith was playing with his group

No-one could accuse the very gifted Tommy Smith of sentimentality. On Tuesday night his saxophone was rebarbative – big, bold, lapidescent, challenging, even unwelcoming. No hint here of melody or lyricism. It is a personality that he has presumably adopted in the light of musical fashion for I once heard him, as a very young man, give Joe Temperley a terrible fright when, warm and fluent and matching Joe every inch of the way, he stepped up to play at a gig in Edinburgh; and from other evidence we know of his considerable range.

It wasn't so much the music that caught my ear but the audience that caught my eye. Listening respectfully at their tables to this quite difficult music, despite their peer-group clothes that ape poverty, they were, well, comfortable. This, it dawned on me, was the music not of anger or alienation but of affluence, enjoyed by a society that was sated of sweetness and plenty. When Tommy Smith plays accessible music, the recession will have begun.

This was one of the last pieces Kemp wrote, a month before his sudden death from a heart attack, while on holiday in Galway. A defence of the Edinburgh Festival in *The Observer*, August 2002.

It's that time of year again. The prosecution has renewed its case against the Edinburgh Festival fringe. The newspapers are full of assertions that it is out of control. This year 15,000 performers will come to town along with 2,000 journalists and 500 talent scouts. There will be more than 20,000 performances, a record.

The programme runs the gamut from Shakespeare to Carl Ruggles and contains the usual collection of oddities, some of them in the worst possible taste. That other hardy annual, the outraged councillor, has emerged to denounce Stephen Fry's play Latin!, about a homosexual affair between a public school master and his pupil, which was first performed in Edinburgh in 1980 and is being revived this year. A more substantial controversy may surround Steven Berkoff's one-man show about the terrorist attacks of 11 September.

The case for the prosecution is led by the distinguished critic Michael Billington, for my money one of the best in the business. He wrote last month that 'the overweening, grotesquely outsized and highly commercialised fringe' threatened to swamp the festival. We have been hearing such Jeremiahs for the last decade, but somehow disaster is averted. Let me attempt a case for the defence.

The fringe had small beginnings in 1947 when eight theatre groups – mostly local amateur companies – added their contribution to the first festival. The word 'fringe' was applied a year later, in an article in the Edinburgh Evening News by my father, Robert Kemp.

By the end of the Fifties the fringe's appeal was established, although Beyond the Fringe, the review which launched the careers of Peter Cook, Dudley Moore, Alan Bennett and Jonathan Miller, was an official production. By 1962 the perpetual counterpoint of artistic experimentation and civic disapproval was also emerging: there was outrage when a nude artist's model was wheeled across the stage during John Calder and Sonia Orwell's writers' conference.

Outside newsagents' shops the following day the Daily Express bill proclaimed, with that mixture of delighted prurience and high moral dudgeon so typical of our popular press: 'Filth on the fringe!' The fringe has not only grown luxuriantly; each year it seems to start earlier. More than 30 shows had opened by the end of last month. And then there's the penumbra of the book and television festivals. Not too much will go amiss as long as the official festival remains in good standing. Its quality is essential to the fringe for it is the presence of major critics which draws the hopefuls to Edinburgh and makes them endure the extremes of public indifference and squalid accommodation. In its director, Brian McMaster, the festival has been fortunate: under his leadership it has grown in strength.

But the reason for the festival's enduring appeal, apart from the quality of the official programme, is the stage on which it takes place, the city itself, to which the fringe adds immeasurably in colour and variety. Of course some of my Edinburgh friends disagree. They head out of town, preferring the company of the Great Highland Midge. In an extreme case of festival-phobia, a friend went trout-fishing to Lumsden on the South Island of New Zealand.

The genteel Edinburgh middle-class has been the butt of some scorn. The poet Robert Garioch lampooned its pretensions in his poem 'Embro to the ploy'.

One of my father's favourite anecdotes was of a colleague who, when asked his opinion of a Goldoni play performed at an early festival, replied in best pan-loaf: 'Very Italian, Robert, very Italian.' Many years ago, I attended a performance of Ibsen's Ghosts at the Lyceum in Edinburgh. The first act, I think, ends with the burning of a barn and the disclosure that it was not insured. In front of us sat two Edinburgh lawyers or accountants, clearly perturbed. As the curtain fell one turned to the other in shocked tones: 'You know, Willie, I can't believe that they wouldn't have had the barn insured.'

But it is often forgotten that the genteel Edinburgh middle class is the backbone of the audience.

The other complaint against the festival used to be that it was élitist. But the fringe has done much to blow that away. Everybody can enjoy the parades, the street music and the street theatre.

I have found always Edinburgh a place of friendship, surprise and enchantment at festival time. Not to speak of the stunning visual delights of the cityscape itself. I introduce my chief witness for the defence, the critic Michael Coveney. He wrote this year: 'Festivals are as much about people, discoveries, landscapes and atmosphere as artistic programmes – and there is simply no city as well equipped for the party as Edinburgh.' The case rests, m'lud.

The haly kirk's Assembly-haa
nou fairly coups the creel
wi Lindsay's Three Estaitis, braw
devices of the Deil.
About our heids the satire stots
like hailstanes till we reel;
the bawrs are in auld-farrant Scots,
it's maybe jist as weill,
imphm,
in Embro to the ploy.

Whan day's anomalies are cled
in decent shades of nicht,
the Castle is transmogrified
by braw electric licht.
The toure that bields the Bruce's croun
presents an unco sicht
mair sib to Wardour Street nor Scone
wae's me for Scotland's micht,
says I
in Embro to the ploy.

A happening, incident, or splore
affrontit them that saw
a thing they'd never seen afore –
in the McEwan Haa:
a lassie in a wheelie-chair
wi naething on at aa;
jist like my luck! I wasna there,
it's no the thing ava,
tut-tut,
in Embro to the ploy.

The Café Royal and Abbotsford
are filled wi orra folk
whaes stock-in-trade's the screivit word,
or twicet-screivit joke.
Brains, weak or strang, in heavy beer,
or ordinary, soak.
Quo yin: this yill is aafie dear,
I hae nae clinks in poke
nor fauldan-money,
in Embro to the ploy.

The auld Assembly-rooms, whaur Scott
foregethert wi his fiers,
nou see a gey kenspeckle lot
ablow the chandeliers.
Til Embro drouths the Festival Club
a richt godsend appears;
it's something new to find a pub

that gaes on serving beers
eftir hours
in Embro to the ploy.

They toddle hame doun lit-up streets
filled wi synthetic joy;
aweill, the year brings few sic treats
and muckle to annoy.
There's monie hartsom braw high-jinks
mixed up in this alloy
in simmer, whan aa sorts foregether
in Embro to the ploy.

Afterword

ALTERNATIVE COMEDIAN ALEXEI SAYLE USED to tell a joke about a man in a restaurant. 'Everything all right, sir?' asks the waiter. 'Not really,' the man replies. 'I'm frightfully worried about Afghanistan.' The man in that joke was Arnold to the life.

He rarely talked about himself; he was always more interested in the wider world. He loved to argue about ideas, which he did fiercely and rationally. He was known sometimes to thump tables – but it was often at those times that he was most worth listening to as it was while engaged in passionate argument that he thought most clearly.

That disputatious spirit – in Scots the 'flyte'; along with a sense of perspective and an interest in what is happening in the wider world are key elements of his legacy.

In the second decade of the 21st century, Scotland appears to be on a road of increasing divergence from England.

There is widespread economic uncertainty and these are testing times for the European Union Arnold so passionately supported.

Meanwhile, the newspaper industry is gripped by uncertainty over its future. The digital age is upon us: how the fourth estate will find a way to survive and thrive in it is not yet clear.

At this point it may be helpful to check the map; to take stock; to glance backwards at some of the landmarks in the road we have recently travelled and to consider what it may be useful to take with us on the journey ahead.

Jackie Kemp